Destruction and Sorrow beneath the Heavens

THE HUNGARIAN LIST

László Krasznahorkai

Destruction and Sorrow beneath the Heavens:
Reportage

TRANSLATED BY OTTILIE MULZET

LONDON NEW YORK CALCUTTA

The translator acknowledges the kind support of the Translators' House in Balaton-füred, Hungary, where this translation was partially completed, as well as the invaluable assistance of Ondřej Srba in reviewing the English translations of Chinese terms.

Seagull Books, 2016

Originally published in Hungarian as *Rombolás és bánat az Ég alatt* in 2004 by Magvető, Budapest. Copyright © 2004 by László Krasznahorkai

First published in English translation by Seagull Books, 2016

English translation © Ottilie Mulzet, 2015

ISBN   978 0 8574 2 311 5

British Library Cataloguing-in-Publication Data
A catalogue record for this book is available from the British Library

Typeset and designed by Sunandini Banerjee, Seagull Books, Calcutta, India
Printed and bound by Maple Press, York, Pennsylvania, USA

CONTENTS

In Suzhou, Not At All in Suzhou

INTRODUCTION INTO AN OBSCURITY

There is nothing more hopeless in this world than the so-called South-western Regional Bus Station in Nanjing on 5 May 2002, shortly before seven o'clock in the drizzling rain and the unappeasable icy wind, as, in the vast chaos of the buses departing from the bays of this station, a regional bus, starting from the No. 5 bus stop, slowly ploughs onward—among the other buses and the puddles and the bewildered crowd of wretched, stinking, grimy people—up to the vortex of the street, then sets off into the wretched, stinking, grimy streets; there is nothing more hopeless than these streets, than these interminable barracks on either side, numbed into their own provisional eternity, because there is no word for this hopeless colour, for this slowly murderous variation of brown and grey, as it spreads over the city this morning, there is no word for the assault of this hopeless din, if the bus pauses briefly at a larger intersection or a bus stop, and the female conductor with her worn features opens the door, leans out and, hoping for a new passenger, shouts out the destination like a hoarse falcon; because there is no word which in its essence could convey whether the direction in which he now travels with his companion, his interpreter, exists in relation to the world; they are headed outwards, moving away from it, the world is ever farther and farther away, ever more behind them; they are shaken, jolted in advance in the disconsolate brown and yellow of this ever-thicker, indescribable fog; headed to where it can hardly be believed that there could be anything beyond the brown and the grey of this frighteningly dreary mixture; they sit at the back of the ramshackle bus, they are dressed for May but for a different May, so they are chilled and they shiver and they try to look out of the window but they can hardly see through the grimy glass, so they just keep repeating to themselves: Fine, good, it's all right, they can somehow put up with this situation, not to be eaten up from without and within by this grimy and hopeless fog is their only hope; and that where they are going exists, that where this bus is supposedly taking them—one of the most sacred Buddhist mountains, Jiuhuashan[1]—exists.

The woman at the ticket counter said that the trip would be roughly four hours, and then, just to be helpful, she added—tilting her head a little by way of explanation—that, well, what she meant was four or four and a half, from which it could already be suspected just what kind of bus they would be boarding; it has, however, just now, after the first hour, become obvious that no one really knows how long, because there is no way of knowing how much time it will take to get to Jiuhuashan, because the journey is slowed down by so many unforeseeable obstacles and chance occurrences—and everything, particularly the weather, is completely unpredictable—unforeseeable obstacles and chance occurrences which, as a matter of fact, are unforeseeable only to them as, for the most part, the personnel—the driver and the conductor—are to be thanked for all these unforeseeable obstacles and chance occurrences, the driver and the conductor, who—as it becomes clear soon after leaving the city—regard the task before them as their own private business venture, and so come to a halt not only at the prescribed stops but almost everywhere, trying to pick up more and more passengers from among the people walking along the side of the highway, from one kilometre to the next it is practically a hunt for yet more passengers, passengers with whom—following a negotiation which is opaque to them, because hardly a word is spoken—some kind of agreement is settled upon in a moment, money flashes in one hand, then disappears in another, on this ever-more congested route, therefore, black-market transport is taking place, that is, the *front* of the bus is packed, as is the middle, because hardly anyone is sitting at the back, to where they have been squeezed, no, they haven't gone mad, it is much colder here, because the warmth of what is no doubt the sole operational heating device near the driver's seat doesn't reach this far, so that, in the battle for seats, only the weak and the less exceptional end up here—what rotten bad luck, the two Europeans shivering in the artificial-leather seats keep repeating to themselves, that they're in Nanjing and it's May and yet it's almost like February. As for speaking, there really isn't anyone to speak to, because their Chinese travelling companions, otherwise always inclined to acquaintance and conversation—including the four people who have also ended up at the back—do not breathe a word, neither to one another nor to them, everyone sits as far away as they can from everyone else, cocooned in their coats, scarves and hats, after they have arranged their packages near their feet and on the seat next to them, they just stare wordlessly through the grimy glass out into the brown-grey fog in which no one has any idea at all where they are, because, although it is already certain that they have disappeared into the endless terrain lying to the south-west of Nanjing, it is simply impossible to determine how far they have come and how far they have yet to go; Stein observes the passing of time on his watch, and he can feel that this is going to last for a very long time, for so long that it will no longer matter how long, really, if it will be four or four and a half hours, because none of this means anything in terms of time—the bus makes a huge thud in the thick traffic on the pothole-blotched road, and the entire metal contraption shakes and rattles and throws them here and there in the ice-cold seats, but they doggedly move onward, in blind faith; and beside them on the side of the highway, piled high with their huge bundles, plastic bags, really, all those innumerable people: they are headed somewhere too, they are also going onward, walking in a row, leaning into the icy drizzling wind, into the rain, and only some of them motion yes to the shouting conductor leaning out of the bus, and they get on and it's as if the rest of them don't even hear the shouting, they just simply pull back a little from the road until the bus rumbles off from alongside this ghostly procession, then they step back onto the asphalt and continue trudging beneath the weight of the bundles and the bags, clearly with that same blind faith, just like the travellers up there in the bus—as the bus pulls away, splashing them with mud—as if there were some common reason for this faith, as if in the absurdity of this balefully obscure scene, in which there really is nothing at all, it would be enough just to believe that, today, everyone will reach their goal.

The watch on Stein's wrist shows nine minutes past eight when, in a bend hardly a hundred metres from the intersection of three main highways, the driver suddenly brakes, and picks up, from the mud on the side of the road, a middle-aged woman, clearly waiting for this bus: from this point on, that part of the journey begins in which they can no longer hide from each other the thought that perhaps they did not thoroughly consider all the difficulties inherent in their plan of going to Jiuhuashan—that is, is the risk worth it when the goal of travel is so uncertain?—because surely, says Stein to his sleepy companion, still shivering in the cold, both of them, the two white Europeans, cannot understand anything of this at all, they cannot even understand how a bus route like this operates: how could this woman know that she had to wait here, and how could the bus driver know that this woman would be waiting exactly here, in this bend in the road, and at exactly this time, let's say, at around eight o'clock, because you can't speak about schedules at all, that's how it is, it's impossible to understand anything here, the interpreter nods in agreement a little anxiously, and so this, says Stein, is just one of the many functioning rules, unknown to them, just a mere fragment of the entire system upon which they are relying, and which somehow still continues to exist, so that this route and all the others here in China can continue to operate, namely, that of these routes, every day and every morning and evening and afternoon and morning, there are a few million, and there is transportation—just one among the many, he looks at the woman as she climbs up through the open door and joins the other passengers crammed together, then without a word presses a few yuan into the conductor's hand, then squeezes among the passengers, starts off immediately to the back, to the same side where the foreigners are sitting, one row in front of them, sets down her huge bundles and, finally, sits down next to the window— she's wearing a thick quilted jacket, a peaked felt cap, a thin scarf and heavy boots, and the entire creature is soaked from head to toe, so much so that for several minutes the water keeps dripping off her, and the poor thing creates the miserable impression of a bedraggled, beaten dog, a being, moreover, entirely indistinguishable from the others: in vain does he look at that face, as much as he can see from his seat at the back, a completely interchangeable face, almost the complete average of a face, impossible to form the basis any of obser- vation, he looks in vain, he is incapable of distinguishing it from the others, because it is not possible, because it is exactly the same as thousands and thousands and millions and millions of other faces in this inconceivable mass which is China, and where can this 'China' be other than in this immeasurable and inexpressible mass of people unparalleled in world history, this is what determines it in every respect, what renders it so frighteningly massive, so frighteningly unknowable, and where the face of this woman, her entire presence, as she sits one row in front of them, on the other side, creates the feeling that they don't know, because it is impossible to say who sat down there, as anyone could have sat down there, this woman could be anyone, this woman, and this is the most pitiless of all the pitiless truths: it doesn't matter who she is—there she sits, water dripping off her, she too looks out of the grimy window—and then this interchangeable, this possibly most average of the average, this featureless being, without anything having changed in her interchangeable, average, featureless nature, does something completely unexpected, something which could not have been predicted: she opens the window—she grabs its handle, wrenches it to one side, pulls it at least halfway open, at which of course the icy cold rain and the icy cold air blow in, it is really so unexpected that in the first moments no one can really comprehend it, neither them nor the other passengers, the four passengers who with the Caucasians are squeezed in the back here; so contradictory it is to all common sense that someone who is so drenched and has spent who knows how much time out there in the cold drizzling rain, who clearly was half frozen to death when she boarded the bus, finally sits down and then opens the window onto herself and onto them—neither they nor the others can speak a single word for a while, they just look at the woman as the wind half sweeps the soaked hat off her head, they stare dumbfounded as she adjusts her hat and closes her eyes and, with her head slightly thrown back, leans on the arm rest, and she doesn't move, the wind blows in, they just stare at her and don't understand what she is doing, no one says anything for a long time—and so the bus goes on, into the fog, into the dense approaching traffic, forward, supposedly towards Jiuhuashan.

TWO PILGRIMS

They have been travelling for more than four hours when suddenly the asphalt comes to an end. The bus proceeds along a bumpy dirt road, then half an hour later passes below a Communist-era triumphal arch made out of concrete, in the centre of which they can glimpse for a moment the red star high above, and on either side a few slogans, washed away by the rain, about the glory of work, until finally, teetering among the huge potholes, they turn into a larger bus yard situated between a few unspeakably wretched huts; the driver steps on the brake, the conductor opens the door and the vehicle, with a huge groaning sound, comes to a stop.

Stein and his companion don't move, but when they see that the other travellers are lethargically beginning to gather up their things and, one after the other, getting off the bus, nothing remains for them to do but the same. They look over here, they look over there, but there is nothing remotely resembling a mountain anywhere in sight, all around them are flat cornfields, and across from them a grimy concrete building; the driver and the conductor wordlessly pack up their things and leave the bus so quickly that they can barely catch up.

'This still isn't Jiuhuashan, is it?'—they ask. 'When will the bus be leaving again?'

Neither the conductor nor the driver utters a single word, they don't even slow down; like people with some kind of urgent business, in one moment, they have already disappeared into the building. Jiuhuashan—they try again, here with one traveller, there with another, but no one answers. Jiuhuashan, they say to a few young men standing beneath the eaves of the building, but they too just look at them, then, sniggering, turn away in confusion. Then they notice a small group: there is something unusual about them, because suddenly they pick up their belongings and set off for the rear corner of the muddy yard where it seems there are a few battered minivans waiting. Nothing indicates that they might be utilized for any purpose whatsoever, nonetheless there are one or two people sitting in each, and if they are not doing anything, if they are not giving any kind of sign of waiting for passengers, it's still as if the people surging towards them somehow know better—so it seems to the two Europeans that it would be best if they too joined the back of the small group, in other respects not too reassuring looking, straining towards the minivans, and to try yet again:

'Jiuhuashan?'

A woman of about 60 looks back at them with a cheerful, friendly gaze, nods and points at a battered vehicle.

'Jiuhuashan!'

The group immediately begins to talk to a man sitting behind the steering wheel of one minivan but he just gazes indifferently ahead, as if he were completely alone in the universe. The people in the group, however, don't give up, they just keep talking and talking and talking until the man slowly turns his head, looks them up and down, then climbs out with difficulty and, as if he wasn't really in the mood for this, with a surly expression, fiddles for a long time with the lock and finally opens the door and the usual battle for seats begins, and although this time they encounter considerably more difficulty, everyone behaving as if everything were perfectly normal, and already gazing ahead readily and confidently, the man looks them up and down one by one, or in the best-case scenario as if he were counting them, then mutters something to the person sitting next to him and starts up the motor.

Inside the van are two rows of seats, and there are eight seats altogether, but, as it turns out, there are 15 people in the bus, so that, compared to the large bus in which they had travelled up to this point, an even more impossible situation is now presented: 15 people and their packages for nine places, but no one raises the question of what if, for example, another minivan from among at least the three would undertake the task of transporting the passengers, there is no grumbling, not one ill-intentioned word is spoken, on the contrary, a kind of satisfaction can be felt in the air, they press up against one another just as much as they can and, if it seemed inconceivable at the beginning, within a minute everyone is in their place, piled on top of one another, tightly squeezed against one another, but everyone is in— Stein and his companion are of course once again at the very back, although directly in front of them is the woman with the cheerful, friendly gaze as well as someone else who is clearly travelling with her, she too looks to be about 60, they are, in the strictest sense of the word, their neighbours, and the proximity of these two among the invariably none-too-reassuring faces is immediately comforting because, beyond the obvious reassurance of their presence, on the one hand, they provide a kind of guarantee that the direction in which the two foreigners wish to go is the correct one; on the other hand, they shore up the belief that there will be something which they too will be able to understand in this country, operating amid opaque rules and regulations, as, for example, what is going on here, and what is the explanation here; because this is obviously a long-distance bus terminal, but in Nanjing no one said anything about how the Nanjing buses come only this far, and then you have to get onto a smaller vehicle if you wish to go further, as they wish to, and very much so; they sit silently, pressed up against the back seat, and they look ahead towards the driver to see if they are starting off yet, and in the meantime they feel more and more relieved, really, both of them, both Stein and his interpreter: look, they weren't lost after all, they weren't going in the wrong direction, and the sacred mountain they are seeking, the hoped-for goal of their journey, Jiuhuashan, cannot be so far away now.

The road onto which they soon turn runs along a flat hillside and is much worse than any other road upon which they have travelled so far. Actually, it isn't even a road, merely two kinds of travel-worn tracks in the mud, but the passengers don't seem to be the least bit worried, on the contrary, when they are jolted around by an unavoidable pothole and the bus throws them all up against the roof, the response is loud laughter, or, when along one of these indescribable tiny roads the conditions become worse, and nothing remains except for a breathtakingly thin, serpentine strip from which the wheels on the right side practically hang off, the people do not grow anxious, saying oh my God, what will happen, we're going to slip, we're going to plummet into the abyss hardly visible in the ever-thickening fog, no, instead, a kind of liveliness spreads from the front to the back, and from the back to the front, and a conversation starts up, and even Stein immediately realizes that he is not preoccupied with the indisputable dangers and uncertainties but with the two women pressed up and squatting in front of them, because after about 10 minutes, as the passengers breathe into the bus and it begins to warm up, both of them push back their hoods onto their broadcloth coats, and their shaven heads become visible—and it can be seen that both have the same yellow travel bag, sewn from the same material, and nothing else—oh, Stein suddenly realizes, so, well, they are pilgrims, and he looks at them, particularly at the one with the more cheerful gaze who was so friendly and helpful at the bus terminus, he examines her features, and joyfully determines that the gaze is not only friendly and cheerful but also that within it is a kind of simple grace, a naive, innocent serenity, perpetually radiant, that is how she looks out of the window, that is how she observes the outburst of laughter at one huge jolt or another, that is how she looks back at him at times, at the

Caucasian with that large nose—clearly amusing to her—that gaunt white man who is just now scrutinizing where and among whom he is travelling, and just who are these people in front of him, in these identical, long coats of broadcloth, with those identical yellow bags in their laps. Her companion is very different, Stein realizes: she has a serious, intelligent, thoughtful expression, as if she were examining the road to see if they are really going in the right direction in the now drizzling rain, and, despite her identical clothing and shaven skull, it is suddenly clear that she is a completely different kind of person. He observes her delicate glasses, her elegant, cared-for hands, the evident pride and resolution in her posture, and he thinks that, unlike the other one, she is most probably wealthy and educated, and it's as if she were a little colder, or more stern, more peremptory, more worldly, one thing is certain, he establishes within himself, this woman comes from New China, the China that he, Stein, is trying to escape, so that, well, if they too are pilgrims, they are completely different from each other, and his attention keeps returning involuntarily to the more friendly of the two, as it were, betraying which one is more sympathetic to him, which of course is not so difficult: it isn't difficult to choose, as in that naive, serene, friendly creature there is something disarmingly worthy of love—he sits at the very back of the bus, he too looks at what can be seen on the road and through the chasm among the shoulders and heads bouncing up and down, then he looks again at this serenity, at this forbearance, at this innocence, and he thinks, well, she represents someone—even here, even in China, where a traveller such as him can never be careful enough, according to prudent advice—to whom one would entrust everything.

He tries to make out the landscape they are travelling through, as much as he can in a situation as difficult as this, because he can feel that they are headed upward, but for a while he sees more of the two dear female pilgrims than of the life-threatening, winding, serpentine road, plunged into ever-thicker fog, he hears the engine straining, as the driver struggles with the gearbox, because he keeps trying to force it into third gear but it can only go into second, the road is too steep and the bends are too sharp, he brakes, second, third, and quickly back into second, they tilt this way, they tilt that way; the people in front of him press down on him with such force that at times Stein feels as if it is he who is holding up the entire load, but he doesn't bother with this, he isn't interested in the difficulties because now the lively cheerfulness has infected him, and what if this is already Jiuhuashan, he thinks after a bend in the road, oh, he says loudly to the interpreter, maybe we are already in Jiuhuashan, maybe we are heading upward on Jiuhuashan—he sees that the passengers are taking out money and passing it on forward to the driver, so they ask the friendly pilgrim how much, 5 yuan per person she says, the interpreter counts out 10 for both of them, puts it in the pilgrim's hand and gestures for her to pass it forward, the high spirits are general, clearly the two foreigners are not the only ones who have made a long journey up to this point, and it can be tangibly felt that they are now in the last kilometres, it is almost certain now that they will arrive shortly, everyone will be up there very soon, and if they have no specific idea of who this everyone is—and it would be difficult, because it is hard to determine from the dark, wretched faces why they have come, if they are tourists, or if they have come here to work, or if they live up here—still, it occurs to Stein that the two women who look like pilgrims are not pilgrims but nuns from one of the nunneries up there, my God, he tries to lower his head so he can see something out of the tiny window, so here he is in Jiuhuashan, and now, on the last part of the journey going upward: he thinks back to how they set off in Nanjing and the journey from Nanjing up to this point, he recalls how at the terminus they found the bus coming here completely by chance, and it suddenly comes to mind how hopeless it was, indeed, the journey here ever- and ever- and ever-more hopeless, as in a fairytale, but at once he feels certain that he did the right thing, yes, the right thing in designating Jiuhuashan as the first goal of his journey, his planned quest for the detritus of Chinese classical culture, yes, precisely this abandoned Buddhist mountain: everyone tried to talk him out of coming here, just what are you thinking, what will you find there, his Chinese friends asked him, there's nothing there any more, nothing that you would hope for, no kind of hope at all, not least in Jiuhuashan, they noted disap-provingly and shook their heads; he however—precisely now in the perspective of this desolation—sees clearly that he *is on the right path*, that he had to come here, exactly here, on these muddy roads and these life-threatening serpentine bends, when some kind of movement starts up towards the front of the seats and his ear is struck by a fragment of an angrier conversation, it is the driver, he can tell with his companion, it is the driver repeating something in a rage, pointing at them, of course they don't understand, it emerges only slowly, in the regional dialect, what he wants: it's the money, they should pass it over to him, he says, the 10 yuan, he throws back threateningly, and the others explain and try to tell them that they, the two Caucasians, still haven't paid, the driver is ever-more enraged but now they are too, because of course they paid, the interpreter answers, they sent the money forward earlier, the interpreter looks at the serene-faced pilgrim: she does not confirm anything but, to their greatest surprise, turns her head away, she does not intervene in the conversation which, because of the 10 yuan, is growing ever-more ominous, they keep repeating that they gave it to the female pilgrim, and the driver yells that their 10 yuan never made it over to him, and he steps on the brake, this is the last straw, everyone else has paid, the female pilgrim just sits there silently and stares out of the window with her unchanging serene gaze, this is impossible, the interpreter bursts out in rage, beginning to argue with the pilgrim that they certainly handed over—right into her hand—the 10 yuan, at which point the female pilgrim says to the driver that she has no idea what money these foreigners are talking about, and at this they are struck dumb, Stein, horrified, tries to catch her gaze, the interpreter tries ever-more vehemently to force her to hand over the money, and it goes on like this for a while when suddenly two things happen: on the one hand, the companion of the female pilgrim, the more serious one, the less sympathetic one, says something softly to the other, at which point the other takes out the 10 yuan and passes it forward without a word; and on the other, Stein comprehends that this pure naivety—this innocent serenity, this sudden object of his confidence and affection— is a thief, she wanted to steal the 10 yuan, he realizes, but only with difficulty, because he simply doesn't want to believe it, but it did happen; the bus starts off again and in the ensuing silence—with the successful resolution of this affair, the people sitting in front of them become quiet—he must grasp, he must recognize, he must reconcile himself to the fact that this Buddhist pilgrim or nun cheated him, and how!—for there she sits in the same serene tranquillity, her back turned towards him, and looking out of the window with the same innocent gaze as if nothing at all had happened, as if she hadn't stolen the money; she did, however, steal it, and that hurts the most, that she is a pilgrim, a nun, in this broadcloth coat, with a pilgrim's bag, en route towards the Buddha, and that she tried to cheat a defenceless foreigner—but they are very close to the goal when, as if at the touch of a magic wand, the bus suddenly emerges from the fog, they can glimpse the peak of the mountain, and the sun is shining everywhere, it shines through the grimy windows of the minivan, every colour is sharp, deep, warm, and everything is floating in the green, it's Jiuhuashan, says the interpreter reassuringly and, to get him out of this state, places a hand on his shoulder, Jiuhuashan, he nods, but it's not so easy for him, he is still not able to recover from what just happened; out there, however, the sun is shining, they rattle alongside monks in yellow robes, yes, here they are, Stein grimly answers the interpreter, and then requests for something to be translated to the female pilgrim, because he has something to say to her—leave it, the interpreter tries to talk him out of it—no, he insists, please translate this:

'So, how are you going to settle this with the Buddha? That lousy 10 yuan? ARE YOU GOING TO SPLIT IT?'

Shush, the interpreter tries to quiet him down, and points towards the buildings amassed on one side of the mountain, and on the other side the breathtaking chasm, stop it, really, the interpreter nods at something in front of them; and already the first monastery buildings are visible, clearly this is the main street, teeming with monks, shops selling devotional objects and even lodgings—and they stop exactly here, they get out of the bus exactly here, the sun shines into their eyes and, completely blinded, they try to make out where they are, but there is just this sudden illumination and the sense that some-where over there on the left there could be the mountain's steep slope and the famous peak, about half a minute goes by until, as their eyes grow used to the light, suddenly they see the entire thing as one whole, and everywhere there are countless monasteries, they just stare at the buildings thickly woven across the side of the mountain, the wondrous yellow monastery walls and the green and the green everywhere, they gaze at the monks flocking around them curiously, further on are the paths leading up from the main street towards the monasteries—and everything is forgotten, he will try to figure out later, Stein decides, what was intended by this insignificant petty theft, how to explain it, and in general: what did it mean, what was its import, had he really misunderstood, when suddenly the female pilgrim or nun with the serious face comes over to him and, in the friendliest possible manner, explains to the interpreter—when she sees that only he understands Chinese—that the entrance in front of which they are waiting is that of some lodgings, it is quite adequate, they can go inside, she shows them, this is not the case for all the lodgings in Jiuhuashan, she warns them good-naturedly, not every one is . . . good, she tilts her head, but this one is, you can stay in this one, and so, smiling, she waves farewell with a delicate movement and as if a little in excuse for the unpleasantness which they had to suffer because of her companion, she sets off on one of the paths with quick tiny steps, up into the heights, towards a monastery, in order to reach her companion, the guilty one who, with a freshness belying her age, is already running, and for a while they can still see that naive, lovable, dear face which just shines and shines in this sharp pure sunlight, as she turns to look at them now and again as if she wanted to show them, until she is finally swallowed up by the green of the path, that nothing, but nothing will ever wipe away that admired, illusory innocence from that face—ever.

AS IF THEY WERE ANXIOUS

It took no longer than 10 to 15 minutes to settle upon the room, place their baggage on the first floor, decide what they would leave and what they would take, 10 to 15 minutes, and they stand completely astonished in front of the hotel, they hadn't been inside any longer than that, and now they look around, and they can't believe their eyes, because that pure piercing illumination, that dazzling green and green and the yellow monastery walls on the side of the mountain—has all disappeared, the fog came up from the valley, the interpreter remarks uncertainly, yes, that's obvious, both of them nod, that's what happened, but it happened so quickly, the whole thing occurred while they were reaching an agreement with the innkeeper, they settled everything as quickly as they could, so that rushing out onto the main street they could see Jiuhuashan again in the light, well, there is something completely unexpected in this incredible speed, indeed, but more precisely: something unbelievable, Stein is inclined to believe this is some decision *immediately concerning them*, it is not merely a case of someone thinking in an agitated state—as, however, he is in now—that a so-called otherworldly force is operating behind the scenes; no, Stein directly suspects an arrangement, an apparently playful illusion, but in reality unmistakeably intended personally, as if by design they were meant to see everything at first in the light and then to never see it again, to see something completely different: Jiuhuashan in the fog—and if the shock is great, and if undeniably there is disappointment as well—for, certainly, it is difficult to get away from the fact that a moment ago they saw *everything* but can now see *nothing*—this disappointment, from one moment to another, begins to yield its strength to something completely different, namely, to a slowly unfolding wonder and, as they stand there paralysed by the sight, they begin to grasp that if now the fog and the drizzling rain have become the lord of the mountain, then this fog conceals Jiuhuashan in the most wondrous conceivable form.

So what happens is that they stand on the street and see themselves very distinctly, see their immediate surroundings as well, the earth beneath their feet, and everything within a distance of 8 to 10 metres, but if they take one step forward, then with every such step, indeed with every movement, yet another piece of the earth, the buildings on the main street, the mountain, the paths, the monks, the trees, the monastery walls begin to loom obscurely before them—so that, from this point on, it is not really possible to speak of sight in Jiuhuashan—they do not see but sense things, in this place where everything that is the world and everything that is Jiuhuashan changes from one moment to another, because in the ever-thickening fog whatever is momentarily uncovered in its own uncertain form, after this or that step, immediately vanishes in the very next, different details emerge as they move around and try to find a starting point from which they may begin to discover Jiuhuashan, but that is the most difficult, to be able to know exactly where they are on the main street: the hotel vanished from sight a long time ago, and they have no idea if they have gone to the right, upward, to the left, or downward, it doesn't matter, they stand motionless, staring into this enchantingly unexpected and unusually heavy, impenetrable fog, Stein crumples the map in his hand and puts it into his pocket, because it doesn't help, because nothing helps, he flings the remark out to his companion, why the hell would anyone walk around here with a map in their hands!—because, obviously, *this is about something else*, about something, something entirely else, and as they get to the head of the first path, and head upward without a thought—because it doesn't matter what direction they go in, it won't be them who will find Jiuhuashan, Stein calls back over his shoulder, but . . . but?—his companion climbs up behind him with a certain serene forbearance—the interpreter doesn't wish to destroy his companion's wonder at the sight of this transformation and with his own usual cast of mind soothes himself by noting that, well, nightmarish, yes, this sudden change was really pretty nightmarish, but it also means, he says, that in addition to an indisputably justifiable rapture, they must, from this point on, face an unpleasantly drizzling cold rain and a fog that is totally closing in upon them, and these are circumstances, he adds soberly, which certainly call for some kind of raincoat and warm clothing . . . But he notes this in vain, for Stein is thoroughly captivated by what he sees, which immediately disappears with the next step, so that as he looks at the first row of the tall pine trees nearest to him, the trees behind them fade into the most enigmatic space until, finally, the last row of trees dissolves into nothingness—as if they had strayed into the mirage of a painting by Huang Shen[2] or Ying Yujian[3]: at times they find themselves facing a protruding cliff peak, at other times a chasm, unsuspected a moment ago, suddenly opens up beneath their feet, in a word, they proceed upward metre by metre on the steps of the path, and even the interpreter would be affected by this particular bewitchment of divine nature plunged into obscurity if he wasn't stopping from time to time to remark that the aforementioned raincoat and warm clothes would certainly be more than necessary if things continued like this. But it is obvious that nothing will change for a while, the fog doesn't move, the rain drizzles, and Jiuhuashan continuously fades away and dissolves right before their eyes; they, however, keep on walking carefully upward, on the slippery steps, holding on to the slippery railing, and they persevere up into the heights; they have no idea where they are going, although there is no doubt that this path leads somewhere, certainly in a good direction—they are convinced of that—because they don't believe that all this, this unforeseen change in the weather up here can be explained by some accident, just as it cannot be an accident that they are here on exactly this path in Jiuhuashan, between the slippery steps and the wet railings.

The first monastery which they reach could be any of the renowned temples they identified on the map earlier, but it isn't, it seems to be one of the buildings of lesser importance, even if in terms of its beauty it is certainly the equal of the others, hence they would like to know its name, as soon as they walk in they address a dozing young monk but they don't understand his reply, he is speaking in a regional dialect which the interpreter cannot translate, so they just smile at one another and have a look around the temple which is clearly under reconstruction, everywhere there is scaffolding and tools and carpenters' benches, and ladders and beams and shavings, but no work is going on, and they cannot see any workers, so perhaps no work takes place in the fog?—Stein tries to joke with the monk but he doesn't understand what the interpreter says, just as the foreigners don't understand him when he replies, so that there remains only the wordless looking around in this extremely rare interior space among Buddhist shrines; the interior of the shrine is extraordinarily elevated and, what is even more surprising, the structural supports of the ceiling are not the usual densely placed thick cedar columns and complex system of brackets but a system of vaults below the roof, in a distinctly European style which causes the space to be open, nearly monumental, and what is most important and most unusual is that in this way the ceiling *can be seen*, and the gaze drawn as much upward as towards the altar—where there is now an empty lotus throne, visibly under restoration, the Buddha is nowhere, so that, as they courteously extend their business cards to the young monk, they make an attempt, despite the difficulties, at a new question, and to their great surprise the young monk seems to understand what they want: all his previous confusion suddenly turns into the most sincere cordiality and helpfulness, he motions for them to follow, and holding the cards

delicately between his fingers as he walks, he slips them into a concealed pocket in his yellow robes, leading them with agile steps to one
of the far corners of the shrine, indiscernible before in the nearly
complete darkness looming within, he points to a colossal thing covered by cheap canvas, he points to it, he explains something and, as
if they had rebuked him, suddenly conducts himself with inexplicable
respect, he bows to Stein, then he lifts up one of the corners of the
canvas—the guests help so as to be able to see what lies beneath—
and beneath the canvas, the boy shows them, almost glowing with
pride, is a completely new statue of the Buddha, they gesture to him,
could he remove the canvas entirely, and from this point on it's as if
he understands everything, already he is fulfilling their request, the
canvas comes off, and there sits a huge, brand-new Buddha, a Buddha
next to which every other Buddha they have seen until now seems
merely new-made, exasperatingly soulless, primitive, shoddy—it is
beautiful, sublime, exactly the kind of Buddha in which a believer can
truly find the Buddha, and this beauty strikes them so unexpectedly,
they are really seeing Shakyamuni Buddha,[4] that they can't speak, the
boy is radiant, and the interpreter tries to encourage Stein and looks
at him and waits for him to indicate what should be translated.

Stein doesn't really know what to say, indeed, because of the
strength radiating from the Buddha, as yet unpainted, unvarnished,
ungilded and, judging by the fragrance, prepared from sandalwood,
even later it is hard for him to speak, so the interpreter tries to initiate
some kind of conversation, from which—as is explained a few minutes later—it turns out that the statue was made here, in Jiuhuashan,
because there is a workshop here, and in this workshop is an expert
woodcarver who makes Buddhas, well, he made their statue, the
boy, his face radiant from joy that the statue is so pleasing to the two

foreigners, points to somewhere outside, clearly to where the workshop is, with its Buddha-carving master, but they are already returning
to the table near the entrance where the boy had been dozing before,
and they spread out a piece of paper so that he can sketch for them
where this workshop is, of course they can't understand the drawing,
they don't know where they are, or what is where, generally speaking;
they look at the clumsy but basic sketch, upon which the name of the
place is also written, so that if necessary they can show the drawing
to someone, they nod as the boy, his finger following the lines he has
drawn, explains again and again where they need to go, how they can
find the workshop, then, bowing, they thank him warmly for his help
and make their way outside, but then he indicates that they should
wait, and he runs off somewhere, returning a minute later with a tiny
little bundle of gifts, two books from the Chinese translation of the
Lotus Sutra,[5] a small tourist publication about Jiuhuashan, two tiny
statues of the Buddha carved out of soapstone and tapes of Buddhist
prayers in decorated boxes, one for the interpreter and one for
Stein—presumably this is everything that the boy has, and now by all
means he wants to give this everything to them, as they stand there
in the doorway they are at a loss, because they see the kind monk finds
even this to be too little, he would like to give them something . . . or
tell them something, he tries to find the right words, he tries, in his
dialect, to speak the language of Beijing so that the interpreter can
understand, but it doesn't work, it could be some important advice,
or reassurance, or warning, but it is impossible to make out the
essence, the interpreter just shakes his head, and now Stein tries
with all his strength to help the interpreter by *how* he is listening and
looking, because the whole thing is as if the monk were trying to warn
them about something—but of course this is just guesswork, they

don't understand anything, they bow to one another with ritually folded hands, they bid farewell to one another, and finally they step out through the gate of the temple into the eddying nothingness, the touching gifts in their bags, and that colossal, unvarnished, unfinished Buddha beneath the canvas with his own unforgettable sublimity in their memories—the boy is at the gate, he bows and waves until he finally disappears in the fog, but until the end it was as if somehow, just somehow, he wanted to tell them something very important.

They are to the south of the Yangtze, and, really, they dressed for the weather in this region as it should be in May, that is, sandals, one in a light linen shirt and the other in a T-shirt, so that they froze on their journey, and now, when they step out again into the cold rain, only a few hundred metres along the water-slick steps is enough for Stein to see that the interpreter, the student from Shanghai who self-lessly, out of sheer benevolence and enthusiasm for this topic, joined Stein on this trip, is shivering from head to toe. We really need that raincoat, says Stein reassuringly, and the warm things too, he consoles him, so let's go back: they decide to somehow find the path leading down to the main street, so that they can buy something. Logically, they decide upon the row of steps at the first crossing leading down-wards, but it soon emerges that there is no sense in making decisions like this, as the stairs really do head downward for a while, but then, as if having thought things over, after a bend head upward once more. And that's how it goes from this point on, the path heads down, the path heads up, then down again and up again, they wander here and there, they come to newer and newer crossings where they have to make a decision, and they continually make bad decisions, or now for them there is no such thing as a good decision, because even the advice which they ask for and they get from the people on the path doesn't help, these people who—tourists like them, or pilgrims—smile and gesture: just keep going, they wave and nod that it's good, perfect, they could not possibly be going in a better direction, just keep going, they chirrup gaily, but Stein and the interpreter don't even know if they understand where they are trying to go, because they tried to explain through gesticulations that—even now!—they are not looking for this or that monastery but the village, where they would like to return, at which the warmest reassurance is always given, that, yes, this is exactly the right path, they should just keep going, just keep going, just keep pressing on ahead, and they will be there in no time at all, no cause for any concern—and after a few steps the passers-by cheerfully disappear once again into the fog.

So of course they do not find any path leading downward, on the contrary, they become ever-more entangled in the labyrinth of Jiuhuashan; however, on another elevation, next to a lookout pavilion, understandably deserted, they suddenly come upon vendors' tents, which jump out of the fog so unexpectedly that they nearly recoil. There are rain ponchos and plastic tea flasks but also pilgrimage tote bags, the Amida Sutra[6] printed on artificial silk, Guanyin[7] emblems, rosaries, incense, red wax-paper parasols, books, soya slices, pirated CDs and DVDs, and what is most important: hot tea, so they are saved, they breathe a sigh of relief, they buy two raincoats, two portable, lidded, plastic tea flasks which they immediately have filled with tea, then they stand beneath the tents so that the rain hardly touches them, and they both take a cup of hot steaming tea; they sip the tea, burning their mouths and their throats, and it is an unspeak- ably good feeling as it warms them up within a few minutes, as they stand there shivering, the cold finally leaving their bodies, such a good feeling that they don't even notice each other for a while, and they're not even bothered that they had to pay twice the going price, they're in China after all, they brush it off, and they just look at the vendors standing around reluctantly, and clearly sullen because of the bad business, they just look at them, are they earthly beings, or did they suddenly come here from somewhere else . . .

They come upon the workshop exactly at that moment when, wandering through the fog at a certain point, they decide to entrust themselves to fate: they will not search for the monasteries they had decided upon, that is hopeless, they will, rather, be content with whatever turns up in their path, and exactly when they are resting underneath the roof of another empty pavilion it's as if Stein hears something, some kind of hammering, in the distance, he holds up his finger, indicating to his companion to be quiet for a moment, and so they listen to the silence, and then it can be clearly heard, just not continuously, that certain hammering, and they start off immediately, because they can find it! The workshop! Stein enthusiastically shakes the frozen interpreter, it would be so fantastic, just imagine, he tries to breathe some life into the interpreter, the workshop of a Buddha-carver! And here, in Jiuhuashan! Where a workshop like that is exactly the same as it was hundreds and hundreds of years ago, because this is not a place where anything can change, he says, thank God, every-thing here is so far away from the world, it has remained intact and unspoilt; in a word, he tries to distract the interpreter's attention from the cold for, really, he is filled with enthusiasm at the thought that this hammering means that they can find the place where that wondrous Shakyamuni was made, so they go on, along the steps, like two drenched chimeras in their rain ponchos, they take a few steps in the direction of the sounds, then they come to a halt because the sound stops, then it starts again, then they hear it again, Stein says it's from this direction, the interpreter says it's from the other direction, so that they keep orienting each other among the sounds until, after about half an hour of this ghostly searching, the interpreter, frozen to the bone, runs out of patience, and says, this is exactly the point from where we started off before, and he hears the hammering sound from the same distance as before, and so there is no point to this, he can't go on, although he is not able to say exactly what his plan would be if he wouldn't go on, in any event, they sit down beneath the first pavilion they come across a few metres away, they drink some hot tea from the portable tea flasks, they gaze into that great, wondrous, dazzling nothingness all around them, and as they stare into the fog fixedly, well, they see—at a distance still visible from the pavilion, namely, no more than 10 metres to the left, on the side—the entrance of a gate looming in the fog: a gate, says Stein; and that's it, the entrance to the workshop, the place they had been searching for so much until now in vain, the hammering sound was coming from here, the hammering sound breaking off with those little pauses—the workshop in which someone created that wondrous Buddha underneath the canvas.

To their greatest surprise, the master is a very young and diminutive person, he cannot be more than 30 or 32, and when the interpreter relates who they are and why they have come, and they exchange business cards, he immediately and warmly invites them into his office which is, in reality, more like a little hut attached to the workshop, and he sits each of them down in an ornate armchair clearly kept there only for significant visitors, more precisely, he invites Stein to sit in one while he sits in the other one and the interpreter finds a place on a low kitchen stool next to the mouldy wall, and he offers them tea, and they have to relate in great detail where they have come from, what they want, how much it costs to live in Hungary, the name of which the master is decisively familiar with, indeed, he is already saying that the lifework of Sándor Petőfi[8] is known to every older Chinese, because the great figure of modern Chinese culture, Lu Xun,[9] translated the poem 'Freedom, Love', after which others, and with more frequency, tried their luck, so that the result was an apparently complete edition of Petőfi's works from which every Chinese above the age of 30 can, even today, recite Lu Xun's translation of 'Freedom, Love'; as he himself, the master, can too; after which they go on, and they have to say what the population is in Hungary, and they have to disregard the fact that neither he, nor any other Chinese, can believe that altogether it has a population of 10 million, as 10 million is nothing, let alone a people, and no kind of tiny 10 million could have ever produced such a great figure as Sándor Petőfi—or Stein, our host adds appreciatively, Stein, who honours Jiuhuashan with his visit from such a distance, of which, however, the master does have a very vague idea, he says and then he interrogates the interpreter, what is his profession, and after a while he suddenly starts to hem and haw when he hears that László Stein is a poet, and he eyes this László Stein with ever-more respect but also with a kind of searching gaze, he squints, he scratches his beard, then suddenly he is possessed by a kind of cloudless gaiety, like someone overcome by impishness, that all the same—what do centuries and geographical distance mean to him—not only is it the colleague of Petőfi but also Petőfi *himself*, or as he pronounces it, 'Peiduofei', who has popped out of the fog—so that, like a kind of Taoist God, it is Petőfi himself that he greets in the modest person of Stein, who no longer tries to attempt to explain that not only is he not Petőfi but he is also not even a poet—for it is clear from the master's beautiful, intelligent gaze that he wouldn't believe him, he would merely attribute it to obligatory modesty and obligatory courtesy, as well as to the high level of secret protection of the visit, mandated from above, so that no more is said about this topic but, rather, to the greatest joy of the guests, the conversation turns to what takes place in this workshop, how long has it been here, whom did the master learn from, and whether he was the creator of that colossal Buddha which the guests now enthusiastically describe. In the meantime, they are thoroughly warmed up by the tea and the lightly heated office, so that it is not too difficult for the interpreter to leave it and go into the workshop, where however it is exactly as cold as it is outside, because there is no heating there, and they don't even close the door, because the workers are constantly coming and going, so obviously there is no point, yet they have to go into the workshop right away and stay there for a while, because when the master hears their words of praise for his magnificent Buddha, he immediately wants to show his guests, so they can be persuaded with their own eyes that what has pleased them so much was definitely created in this workshop and by his own hands, at which point Stein says to him that it's not just only the statue pleases them but also that there is a kind of extraordinary strength within it, a kind of radiant power which can only come from the Buddha; the master's beautiful eyes become veiled, he embraces Stein around the shoulders, he leads him to his own table among the workers and has Stein sit down next to him on a three-legged chair.

This part of the atelier is like a kind of diamond-polisher's workshop, where young boys sit in a row behind small tables, each bent over a piece of wood in the pale light pouring in through the tiny windows, and with the small chisel and small light hammers in their hands they try to complete—from the piece that has been given to them—a certain phase of the work until, relates the master, they can do it perfectly; but the workshop does not only consist of this room, he says, there are also huge hangars, but there's no hurry for that, now they should watch him, he motions for Stein to come closer, and from the table he pulls onto his lap, from a huge disorderly pile, a Guanyin statue, roughly half a metre in height, seemingly nearly ready, and with a colour, more than anything else, reminiscent of the light of the full moon—he pulls it onto his lap, and with a hammer and a fine-pointed chisel in his hand, he bends over it, and from this point on does not talk, does not utter a single word, does not explain, but begins, with the chisel and hammer to form the countenance of the statue, for the most part otherwise largely finished, and for a while the guest has the feeling that he wants to show him that he's doing it for him, that he wants to initiate him into the secrets of the creation of a Guanyin head, but as time passes this feeling fades away, and finally vanishes, because after about half an hour, during which the master is completely bent above the face of the Guanyin, Stein edges up to him from one side, so that he can watch even the smallest movements, he observes as one eye comes to life, then the other, as these two eyes now see, as the living forehead of the Guanyin slowly emerges from the bare wood, its nose, lips, chin, gaze, by that time it is completely obvious that the master has ceased doing this for him, to be completely accurate: Stein has stopped existing as far as the master is concerned, *he has forgotten him*, he looks up at Stein, surprised, and Stein is certain that this is the case, because when, after about an hour's worth of work, he leans back for the first time, holding the statue away from himself and looking at it, examining it, turning it a little to the right and a little to the left, in order to determine, to measure in the incidentally falling light what the countenance of the statue now shows, he sees that the master needs time to apprehend that Stein is there beside him, for his consciousness to awaken to the fact that someone—Petőfi himself!—has been watching him the whole time, he needs just as much time as he needed an hour ago for all this to leave his head, to become immersed in his work of meticulous, breath-fine chiselling, the results of which he now displays proudly, a beautiful, otherworldly, godly gaze; it is not possible to know how he did it even though Stein was standing next him the whole time, he did not stop observing the point of the chisel, the edge of the hammer or the surface of the fragrant wood sanded down in advance, even for a moment, but he does not know how that sacrosanct, mournful beauty was conjured out of that wood, and he almost starts to cry because he *does not know*—until he observes, in the meantime, another reality, that of the interpreter who is suffering greatly, who in no way has spent this short hour in feverish immersion but paced up and down among the young workers of the workshop, because he has really begun to freeze again in the penetrating cold, as he now reveals, he must get out of this murderous, this bone-penetrating cold—endured until now so as not to be a disturbance—but right now, immediately, he is shivering desperately, he must get out, he cannot stand it any more, he looks at Stein in torment, so that, with the master at their side—who seems to be teasing them—they go back into the office, he seems to find it amusing that the interpreter is so cold, certainly, he nods roguishly, it is fairly cold considering that

it's May, as if the whole thing were just a good little joke, then everything is solved, because from somewhere in one of the little rooms
behind the office a real huo tong—a local variation of the renowned
bath heated with embers—turns up, and you can sit in it, then you
can wrap yourself up while you sit in it, it's as if the interpreter has
ended up in the redeeming vaults of heaven, with indescribable happiness on his face, he allows himself to be sat down in the warm cauldron, to be wrapped in blankets up to the waist, and then a woman
and two tiny waifs bring fresh tea, and everyone is filled with great
cheerfulness: the interpreter is sitting in the huo tong, and nearly
fainting from the beneficial effects of the heat, he closes his eyes, so
the matter of the interpreter has had a happy end; as for Stein, however, who perhaps due to the spirit of the place is this time better able
to withstand the difficulties, the master once again motions for him
to follow, and then leads him across into two gigantic workrooms
adjacent to the workshop, partially dug into the earth and connected
to each other: because standing here are enormous blocks of wood,
arranged next to one another according to the various phases of
work: here looking like wood sawed down for sale, piled up, there
already joined into one piece; or freed from the most important sur-
pluses, so that from the rough contours showing the enormous form of
a Buddha or bodhisattva[10] the workers, who seem to be older and more
experienced than the ones in the workshop, peel away, with astound-
ingly skilful and confident blows of their hatchets, any unnecessary
remaining material; the wood shavings fly in the wake of their movements, the master is very pleased that his guest is able to delight in
their work with such passion, he stands behind him proudly, at times
patting him on the shoulder and motioning for him to observe how
things operate in his workshop, to study as much as he wishes what is

going on with these amazing materials—then he tries to ask him, does he understand that the workers here are joining and pressing together and planing these huge blocks of wood, then they'll saw them down, and finally they'll carve off whatever is not necessary, all right, fine, Stein tries to convey his words with vigorous gesticulations, but *how does a Buddha emerge from this?*—at which point the master, as if he has deduced this time what Stein wants to know, stands in front of the framework of a gigantic statue, he doesn't even reach up to its knee, and with his tiny hands this tiny person points at the roughly carved head up there in the heights and, as if it were a question of some impish trick, winks at the guest and, with an indescribably expressive movement, signifies that, well, it's like this, if everything is ready, then he comes along, he climbs up there and he just carves nicely with his chisel until, well . . . there is a Buddha.

In the office, when they return, the atmosphere is good, and while the interpreter enjoys the benefits of the huo tong, Stein and the master look at a photograph album, bound in coloured fake leather, of his earlier works, which the master brings out like a treasure from one of the rooms in the back, then Stein begins to examine the statues scattered around the office, and asks if he could buy one like that one day, when he is rich—he points at a smaller Guanyin, the master suddenly looks very serious, he sits down in the armchair and points, next to himself, for his guest to sit down as well and he speaks to the interpreter, asking him to please be so kind as to translate what he is about to say, and he begins to speak animatedly, the interpreter is clearly concentrating very strongly in the tub, noting everything, but in the end he summarizes the master's address in a single short sentence which goes like this: he, the master, has become very attached to comrade Petőfi, and he would like them to be friends.

Stein, with the greatest joy, says yes, the master arises from his armchair and they embrace, then they bring out a camera and as everyone poses for a picture—the interpreter in the tub in the middle, of course, and Stein and the master and the woman with the two children around him—the master of the workshop, to his very best and his only foreign friend, solemnly promises to carve for him a Guanyin of extraordinary beauty, and let there be no worry about the cost, because he will calculate the most advantageous price for him, but still, how much, Stein asks, and the master begins to laugh confusedly, like someone who is counting within, and then he asks what size the guest was thinking of, the guest shows the size, well, he reflects, still smiling confusedly, he could prepare one, but this will be the most beautiful one that he has ever, ever prepared—he raises his index finger—well, then, he could prepare one for . . . 800 yuan—that's fine, answers Stein, let the price be 800 yuan, and it will be the most beautiful Guanyin he has ever made. They take the photographs, and in high spirits they disperse, the children and the woman behind the door, and the guests slowly prepare to leave: they write their home address on a piece of paper, where, according to the prediction of the master, a Guanyin, more beautiful than any other, will certainly arrive, they pay him the 800 yuan, and they add 2 yuan for the postage, and they are leaving, but the master, clearly overcome, stands in his office, and does not want them by any means to set off: first, he suggests they have lunch together, from this point on let them be his guests for the day, then when they tell him that so little time do they have in Jiuhuashan that if they want to see anything at all before it grows dark, even with an aching heart, they must refuse his invitation, and he becomes so sad that they can hardly console him, they must drink at least one more tea, and then another and another, and then they are finally outside in the courtyard, and they are walking towards the gate, and there he stands in the doorway of his office and he waves, and he calls after them that the Guanyin will really be the most beautiful and they can see him wracking his brain to find a reason to call them back, like someone who doesn't want them to leave, like someone who doesn't want them to be submerged—leaving the protection that he can offer to them—yet again in the unknown fog of Jiuhuashan.

The stairs are as much of an essential element of the sacred elevations in Jiuhuashan as the monasteries; they enmesh the mountain from one end to the other, they announce the presence of the resting spots, the pavilions, the connecting paths, the detours, the paths, the magnificent lookouts as well, they indicate a kind of safe passage in this particularly untraversable, precipitous slope, a decided connection between the numerous monasteries; the system, however, is so complicated, especially to figures such as the two of them in the middle of this thick fog, that even marching along continuously for hours is not enough for them to get their bearings; indeed, as far as that goes, now that they are climbing outside in this complicated and essential stairway-network, they are forced to admit that they are no closer to having any idea as to what kind of consideration brought this system into being, who built it, the knowledge of which all the same would be indispensable to traffic on the mountain—and not only are they compelled to admit this, they admit it with the greatest bitterness, for somehow, again, the long minutes—10 minutes, 20 minutes—are passing and they are not coming across even one of the monasteries they long so much to see, they just keep going, always just hoping that in the next, but in the next, moment something will certainly leap out at them, a gate leading into the Baisui Gong[11] or the Huatian Si;

but no, in the fog they find neither the Baisui Gong nor the Huatian Si while the interpreter notes with resignation that, in his opinion, it is also starting to get dark—that's not possible, Stein protests, obviously it's just the thick fog blocking the light, but no, the interpreter shakes his head listlessly, according to him this is not a mistaken impression—and here is the most tangible of reasons, that is to say, the watch on his wrist is now pointing to four o'clock, quite simply, evening has begun to fall.

If it is really four o'clock—they once again withdraw beneath the roof of the pavilion, away from the seemingly never-ending eaves— if it is already getting onto four, says Stein, that means then that the monasteries will be closed very shortly. And so nothing would be more sensible, says his companion, than to put off everything else till tomorrow, go home to the hotel, have a good bath and rest, well wrapped up, from this day of not-inconsiderable ordeals. He looks at Stein hopefully, and it is clear that he is prepared for the most vehement of debates, anything to convince the other to give up— well, that's a good idea, the other bows his head, he drinks the last sip of tea from the plastic tea flagon, and they head off towards home. It's strange, but now they suddenly find the staircase which leads downward, the one which later on does not suddenly begin heading upward again, as has happened so many times on this extraordinary day, they trudge downward, holding on to the railing, because the staircase is very slippery, when suddenly, due to the fog, once again, fairly unexpectedly, a person appears before them. Judging from his bouncy gait, it is a young man and it seems that with his rubber boots, and a plastic bag in his hand, he too is steadily heading downward, so that so far everything would be fine, it's just *how* he is going down the stairs in front of them that strikes the eye immediately, that is, on the one hand, there is an uncommon resolve in his movements, on the other, however . . . he is not walking like them, holding on to the railing, moving in a straight line; instead, he is waddling, as one used to call it in childhood, waddling here and there but all the while systematically descending; he goes from one side, let's say, from the railing on the right to the railing on the left, but, in the meantime, taking three or four steps down, so that he progresses—and this is truly the correct expression—systematically, and really, like someone who still has a few kilometres in front of him so that he does all this seriously, so it isn't possible to think that this person in front of them here—who nonetheless is certain that no one sees him—is feigning anything, no, the two visitors look at each other incredulously, he is not pretending, there is something wrong with him; moreover, when they get closer to him, and he looks back, frightened, realizing that someone is behind him, it immediately becomes obvious that he is not crazy. So what then? What is going on here? Stein looks the interpreter questioningly, but he just shakes his head and watches how, from that point on, the man in front of them does not begin to walk with a regular gait, now that he knows that they are watching him, but progresses in the same way, waddling here and there between the left and right sides of the staircase.

Stein motions to his companion to follow and, quickening his steps, catches up to the man in front of them, but since he is obliged to take up his style, he too begins to walk *in the same way*, zigzagging downward, from one side to the other, mimicking him as much as he can, so that he can speak to him, for he has not changed anything about his peculiar gait even though there is someone right beside him.

'You wouldn't happen to know where the hotel is?'

'Are you looking for the Huacheng Si?'[12]

'No, the monastery is probably closed already. The hotel.'

'The Huacheng Si is that way.'

He looks very frightened. Stein, to reassure him, gazes at him in as friendly a way as possible, as does the interpreter who translates from behind.

'Are you from here?'

'No. Just working here.'

'Is it always like this during the month of May here? The rain doesn't really want to stop.'

'Sometimes it is.'

'What's it usually like here? Is it going to rain tomorrow too?'

'Rain tomorrow. Then no more rain.'

'How do you know?'

'I watched the weather report yesterday on TV.'

They waddle on, following his zigzags, and for a while nothing comes to Stein's mind. The man speaks first.

'It's good to walk like this.'

Stein doesn't really know how to respond. Should he approve? Refute? He changes the subject.

'You said before that you work here. What kind of work is there here?'

'I make deliveries to the mountain.'

'To the mountain? Where?'

'Up. Sometimes building materials, sometimes vegetables. Whatever is needed. Everything has to be carried.'

'But this is a really long trip.'

'Twice a day. This was the second time. Going home. Don't live here.'

Once again muteness settles upon them. It's reassuring that he no longer seems so frightened, that he has regained his earlier impassiveness, but somehow Stein cannot find a way to address why they cannot speak of the most important thing: why he walks that way. They follow him as precisely as they can, but sometimes they miss a step and are obliged to cheat by taking two. He, however, never steps the wrong way, he moves in faultless tempo, quickly, briskly, in that unshakeable impassiveness now regained once and for all, he goes down the stairs from one edge to the other and back again, and then again. The stairs are winding, they see only each other: they descend in that quick pace in vain, the fog does not grow any thinner.

Once again he breaks the silence.

'Twenty yuan.'

'Twenty yuan for what? The ticket home?'

'Sometimes a little more than 20. But less than 30.'

'Oh, that's what you get for your work?'

'For one day.'

'Have to go up twice. I carry it with chinga wood.'

That's bamboo rod, the interpreter explains. The porters carry the goods with it. The bundles are hung from the two ends of the bamboo, the bamboo is flexible and, as it sways with every step, there is a tiny pause, smaller than an intake of breath, but of vital importance, when the weight is not pressed down upon the shoulders. That is when he takes a step.

So he's a porter, Stein looks at the interpreter. Yes, the interpreter confirms, and he believes that they are called mountain coolies.

My God, on these steps, with heavy packages, twice a day! For 20 yuan!

'Have you had dinner yet?'

'I don't live here.'

'But it's really time for dinner already.'

'First I'll go home. Then I'll have dinner.'

It's as if the stairs would never end. They have been going downward for at least 10 or 15 minutes. The visitors are ill at ease, because they are afraid that this person will be insulted at how they are walking exactly like him. They don't want him to think that they are mocking him.

Stein looks back at the interpreter, like someone trying to indicate that he has something important to say, and he waves at him to not walk behind their backs but beside the man, on the other side.

'It's good to go like this.'

'Yes, I understand.'

'Four steps here, four steps there.'

'So that by the fourth step you have to reach one side of the stairs, and then by the fourth step reach the other side?'

'It's good to go like this.'

'Why? Is it easier this way? You don't get as tired?'

The porter does not answer for a long time. It seems like he isn't going to when he looks at the interpreter again. Then he stops. Now he doesn't seem impassive at all. He looks with unmistakable concern at the two foreigners. Then he points to Stein, and motions to the interpreter to translate what he is saying.

'It's good to go like this.'

And he motions for them to wait. Much more slowly, he goes with four steps to one railing, he looks at Stein, then he takes four steps to the other, and he looks at Stein again. He doesn't move; the two of them slowly go down to where he is, and stand by his side. He no longer breathes a word, just looks at Stein, nodding, this is important. Stein nods too, he understands. Then he sets off again, the two following him. Suddenly a temple emerges from the fog. It stands in utter muteness, without a single trace of life, clearly long since closed. The carrier leads them up to the gate, points at it, and says: 'Huacheng Si.'

And in the next moment he is lost in the fog.

THE END, BUT OF WHAT? TANG XIAODU

Zeng Laide, the calligrapher from Sichuan Province, lives in his own glass-palace museum in a northern district of Beijing. He is wealthy, influential and celebrated; all day long, assistants and students hand him whatever he needs, and, having won the unconditional respect of some of the most prominent members of the literary and artistic circles of the capital, now, on the occasion of his 47th birthday, they—

these eminent literati—sit around the table next to relatives and friends from Sichuan. Undefined women standing close by serve magnificent, special, as-yet-untasted dishes from Sichuan, and the company, after a certain self-consciousness, quickly recovers; gay and ever-higher spirits dominate the gathering in which Zeng Laide himself—this pot-bellied, energetic person with serious, elegant eye-glasses (not really suitable for his round face) perched on his nose—is the most elated of all: he takes up the thread of conversation ever-more frequently, and tells stories and anecdotes in a loud voice, spouting the punchline to his audience who listen in grateful silence, until finally, when the dinner comes to an end, most of the guests respectfully take their leave and only a few remain.

Zeng Laide leads this small group into a large atelier where he uses one empty wall to put up—as one of his friends now explains to Stein in subdued tones—his calligraphic works, painted on finely grained, thick, snow-white paper: he puts them up here as soon as they are finished, so that he can examine them from an appropriate distance, but, really, all of them, both the large ones and the small ones, he completes them on a large table in the middle of the room, he keeps his brushes here too, it is said—Stein hears the account, he keeps the inks here, the jars, the basins, the cleaning tools, smaller pieces of paper, the plastic buckets containing prepared ink, the table is also big enough to hold quite a few books and the daily post's most urgent missives along its edge. During the short introductory talk the guests become silent, the master himself speaks to no one, he picks up things and puts them down, walks around the table, choosing between the various pieces of paper, looking into the biggest pails like someone who must ascertain that the ink is sufficient and adequately thickened; indeed, even his countenance, which only minutes ago was so full of amusement, is serious now, concentrated, almost morose, as if something were disturbing him, the two guests are thinking that maybe it is they, the European visitors, László Stein and the interpreter from Shanghai, who, having turned up so unexpectedly, are disturbing him, although it soon emerges that exactly the opposite is the case: it is for them, the two Hungarians come from afar, that the master of the house, warmed up by the hot plum wine, is preparing to do something.

The silence is now complete, but the master still walks up and down and to and fro in the atelier, placing something a little closer here, a little further away there, scraping into a jar on the table, moodily pursing his lips, like someone displeased with what he has found, then he suddenly whirls round and runs to a corner of the workshop and, with one movement, pulls out an enormous roll of white paper, dashes with it to the table and spreads it out with lightning speed, then runs back and takes a giant brush from one of the plates at the same time as he picks up from the floor a red pail half filled with ink and jumps back to where the paper is, then—continuously stirring the ink in the pail with the brush—steps back, eyes the paper, pushes his funny glasses further up his nose, bends his head forward, looks up, steps closer, steps back again, mixes the ink and eyes the paper—in short, there is something in him which makes it hard to take him completely seriously, something which makes it seem as if the entire scene is a joke, just another roguish Sichuan prank, and that the laughter will break out again in a moment, just as it has until now, over there by the dinner table, because these preparations, as he takes the slow measure of this enormous piece of paper on the

table, as he vehemently scratches away at the ink in the pail, are somehow exaggerated and theatrical: it is too amusing for anyone to think
that this master, now, with all this aromatic plum wine in that notable
belly, and with that huge pail and that huge brush in his hand, is going
to paint something amazing for his illustrious company.

It isn't possible to take in what's going on, everything happens
with such lightning speed, so that Stein can bring to mind later only
the quick movements as he painted, the violent emotions clearly inundating him, and that passion, difficult to put into words, which manifestly possessed him as he worked, because now only that can be
seen, after the earlier mixings of the ink and the walking around,
the hesitations and the somewhat humorous concentration, suddenly
there is on the piece of paper a startling, an enchanting, a genial
painting, a monumental calligraphic work, composed of two hiero-
glyphics, daubed onto the snow-white paper with black ink, the
interpreter reads it out softly from behind Stein: xie huai, 'out of
breath', yes, a poet among them, Xi Chuan, who speaks excellent
English, confirms it, but it emerges quickly that he is mistaken, out
of breath, and the master motions to one of his apprentices, and the
two quickly place it onto the wall with the magnets, and he stands
back from it, assuming the same pose, shifting his weight from one
leg to the other, now before the completed work, standing as he did
before, looking at it in the same way, eyeing it, examining it, studying
it, just as he did a short while ago with the blank paper, that is, everything is almost the same, because there is already something sober
within him, the fact of this slow distancing can be felt in his being,
the beginning of calm, he is beyond it now, even while he is still
somewhat within it, he stands, moving his head from side to side, then

he steps back again, as if he were cautiously emerging *from out of this*, he lowers the brush blindly into the pail, then puts it next to the table, and he has returned, he is among the others: he is smiling, laughing gaily, with grateful laughter he receives the exclamations of rapture from the company, as one after the other, every one of the guests, with the greatest enthusiasm, praises the creation that has suddenly taken place here; and Stein as well, who, among those present, knows the least about calligraphy, although he is capable of understanding it, after a while, with the help of another guest who is introduced to him by a Chinese living in Europe, and whom he has met here for the first time, is able to say: that what he has seen here, the speed of the contours, the plangent rhythm of the two signs, the black ink burning on the white paper, the pure natural impulse of the brush's movement, the exact harmony of the proportions, that all this together is truly amazing!

The master nods, bowing his head a little in thanks for the praise, then turns away and begins to explain something to his assistant. In a fervently broken rendition of the English language, Stein, with his helper of a moment ago, begins a conversation with Tang Xiaodu, of whom he knows only the name, but a particular mannerism of his immediately strikes his attention.

After half an hour in his presence, Stein establishes that no one else smokes in the same way, not a single being anywhere puffs away at his cigarettes in such an engaging way—no one on this entire earth—as Tang Xiaodu.

At the beginning of the birthday evening, when they met at the entrance of the building at the agreed-upon time, while they and the interpreter were pressing the buzzer, and waiting for Zeng to arrive at the entrance from some far corner of his palace of concrete columns and glass, which took a few minutes to happen, Tang Xiaodu, who had just arrived, stamped out his previous cigarette and, in the fashion of a true smoker, pulled out the box of cigarettes from his pocket and took out three, so that, in accordance with Chinese custom, he could offer one to Stein, another to the interpreter as a token of friendship and smoke the third himself, but since they weren't smokers he remained alone with his cigarette and, with the hungry movement characteristic of a passionate nicotine addict, he lit up, then turned the cigarette towards his palm, between his thumb and his index finger, holding it inward, keeping it concealed, and he smoked like that, slowly and deeply, and blew out just as slowly and deeply, cordially turning his head away so that the smoke would not be blown onto the guests, and then—as he turned his head— there came that accompanying movement: he struck the pose without being aware of it, sweeping the two Europeans off their feet at the same time and betraying everything about himself in one single instant, namely: he *held out* his right hand in which the cigarette was concealed completely distant from his body, so that the rising smoke would not disturb Stein or the interpreter, in short, so it would not disturb the people he was speaking to and who, in contrast, were not smoking . . . but to be more precise, this was just one element of his pose; the other was the angle at which he held out his arm with the smoking stub turned inward towards his palm, and held it out again so that when the breeze, despite every precaution, still swept the smoke towards someone, in this case Stein, with his left hand he would try to wave it away quickly, well, all this put together was so touching, and so revealing, that it disclosed so profoundly the nature of the owner of these gestures, this carriage of the head, the movements of the hand, of this kind of secret smoking, that Stein, standing in the entrance of the Zeng house, felt a very deep sympathy for Tang Xiaodu, although he could not suspect that the reason he felt so close to him—as this only became clear later on, and gradually, one could say as the result of a double step—that is, not too long afterward he realized that Tang Xiaodu *always* keeps his hand holding the cigarette well away, and Tang Xiaodu *always* turns his head away when he exhales, even if he is conversing with people who are smoking just like him, so that after all this, but still before dinner, when they were just standing around the dinner table and talking, during the second encounter, Stein at once perceives that in these movements, so characteristic of a dear, tactful, cordial, elegant and modest person, that what is really most moving in this deportment is that Tang Xiaodu smokes in exactly the same fashion *even when there is no one next to him.*

At the back of the atelier, sectioned off by shelves, Tang Xiaodu has his new friend sit down in a comfortable armchair, he sits down next to him, pours him a cup of tea, and it can be seen that he feels at home at Zeng's place, and Stein is happy that at last he has a chance to talk to him, and after he listens, as Tang Xiaodu slightly rectifies the explanation of a moment ago concerning the two Chinese characters, that is, the two signs conceal a release of the soul's tension as well as an inundation of the spirit, nearly bursting-out— the visitor from far away starts to say something, how he feels himself to be in such a difficult situation, for that which he admires so much, which at the beginning of this journey to China he thought still lived in the depths, unbroken, which he thought still nourished the China of today from these depths—well, he is happy that he can complain about this now to Tang Xiaodu: because he, Stein, sees this last ancient civilization, this exquisite manifestation of the creative spirit of mankind, as dead, and he is afraid that apart from Tang Xiaodu there is no one to really talk to about this, and he is afraid that there won't be anyone to talk to about this, because his experience is that people consider the opposite to be true, and celebrate the renewal of Chinese traditions in cultural monuments restored in the most dreadful and coarse ignorance, or their attention is engaged exclusively by modern life, and are altogether unconcerned with that which was, even if it has passed, their own spiritual tradition.

Tang Xiaodu begins to speak, brokenly, very softly and with long pauses:

TANG. I grew up in a world, after Mao, in which nothing was important. We had no clear goals. My generation's way of thinking really oversimplified things. We were indifferent to everything. And we did not confront the real problems.

What was essential in the ancient world was that everything we call culture was somehow applicable to everyday life: How can poetry, philosophy, music, painting, calligraphy be made personal, transmuted into the essence of everyday life, that is, how can all this become life itself—will it become my life, in the final analysis, and am I capable of leading my life according to the concepts of a highly refined tradition? In ancient tradition, art, philosophy and life were not sharply differentiated. In today's world, the connection between tradition and everyday life has been shattered.

He is silent for a long time, like someone wondering whether he has expressed himself precisely and modestly enough. It can be seen, however, that in the silence nothing remains with which he might continue his train of thought, so Stein asks: If things are like this, then what can be done?

TANG. Not much. It is possible for us to suppose that we can attempt to modify, transform, change, elevate and make ourselves, as well as the direct reality around us, more valuable. For example, a few of us intellectuals have founded a society on the basis of the old shuyua, where from time to time we conduct dialogues around the possibilities of regenerating the old culture. Here of course there are extraordinary difficulties: on the one hand, the ancient culture is deeply connected to the classical Chinese language. And on the other, particular problems are caused when we use our language of today, even when speaking of the renewal of ancient culture based upon the ancient language.

Stein knows a little about the shuyua: informal, unaffiliated academies where every now and then the illustrious literati gathered and debated questions judged to be of eternal merit. Every attempt to renew this tradition is fantastic, he says, but can it be said that this, or similar attempts, are characteristic of the intelligentsia of today?

TANG. The intelligentsia is divided. The ones known in the West as the technical intelligentsia have forged ahead here in China to an extraordinary extent, and they do not have much of a connection with intellectuals in the humanities. Neither with tradition, nor even our own classical tradition. But I have to say that this isn't such a new development. The situation of classical scholars was always dramatic in China. Things were always just as difficult for truly original thinkers and artists, as they are today—they lived solitary and oppressed in their own times, just as they are solitary and oppressed today.

They drink the tea and look at each other wordlessly. Then Tang Xiaodu bows his head, puts out a cigarette and immediately lights a new one. His shoulders are bent, his fatigue and sadness are evident. He excuses himself for being able to say so little on this topic. Later, when he comes back from the great journey, Stein will have to talk to Ouyang, Xi Chuan and Miss Wang. They know much more about this. They are all here, and introductions are made, but the conversations, as Tang Xiaodu predicts, occur only weeks later.

Because weeks are coming, weeks among the ruins of this long, nightmarish, last remaining ancient civilization.

THE GREAT JOURNEY

1. The First Steps

Not only on 5 May 2002 is Nanjing hopeless; Nanjing is *always* hopeless, because there is nothing, really nothing that is more hopeless than Nanjing: the endless millions of people, the dark, shabby streets, the pitiless, coarse, crazed traffic, the merciless minibuses with the exhaust streaming out onto the passengers—who can only find a place to sit at the back which, for some mysterious reason, is raised—the exhaust streaming out with such strength that only the most hardened can bear it, or the very exhausted who assume this sacrifice so they may sit down; the whole thing is hell, and the chilly metallic atmosphere on these buses is hellish too, the grimy face of the bus drivers and their filthy white gloves, their immovable, merciless, unshakeable indifference, just hell and hell and grime everywhere, on the walls of the barracks-like houses, on the tables in the restaurants, on the flag-stones, on a doorknob, on the side of a teacup, the litter and sticky filth in the back kitchens of the restaurants and the small canteens, the back kitchens that a customer or foreigner is never allowed to enter because they would never believe their eyes if they saw where the meat and the vegetables were being chopped, and they would never eat again; and horrifying as well is the spirit of the so-called new China: as one of its most characteristic signs—in the form of the world's most dispiriting glittering department stores—stands here on the main street, disgorging the most aggressively nauseating Chinese pop music, it relentlessly attacks from the loudspeakers, and as if every single street and corner in the city has been shot up, really, as if every single nook has been amplified with this sticky, infectious, loath-some phonic monstrosity, and this is only the earth, which is below— because this has not been mentioned yet: the sky, not a word has been said about the sky, that grey block-like heaven above them, heavier than lead, through which the sun never, but never, breaks through, and, even if it does, so much the worse because then it just makes so much more visible what is here on these streets and in the millions and millions of buildings on these streets, in the millions and millions of wretched flats inside, and what is inside this world of innumerable multitudes of writhing, rushing, hurrying, impassive faces—always ready to sell something—and for what are these countless men and women living, indeed, so unfortunate are they—who now, in this era of slackening political pressure, in the indescribable construction-fever of China striving to become a world power—can now be blinded, with the greatest delight, into mistakenly believing that, after the decades of misery, the liberation of selling and buying can bring happy redemption to them—that even if the sun would break through that heaven above, heavier than lead, it would simply bring into the light just what kind of life the people of Nanjing are living, hence the hour of arrival becomes as well the hour when the visitor immediately begins to plan where, but where to go to get out of here; he sits down on the bed in one of the 'Biedermeier' rooms in the prohibitively expensive, many-starred hotel, intended as elegant but in every respect counterfeit, he looks out of the window, he sees what is moving down there, and he has already taken out the map, he is already trying to figure out how to get the nearest taxi to the train station, because nothing helps, in vain does he suppress within himself the instinctual desire to escape created by the first impression, deciding to inspect that which according to his knowledge still 'remains' of the city after the destruction following the Taiping Uprising[13]—comparable for Europeans only with images of Berlin in 1945—what remains of this city, nearly 2,000 years old; and he finds nothing, in the entire God-given world, nothing, because everything that can be inspected on the basis of its having been restored— from the famous city walls including the Beiji Tower,[14] miserably rebuilt, and the Jiming monastery,[15] in an even more pathetic state, to the renowned Mochou Lake[16] hailing from the Song[17] and Ming[18] dynasties, as well as that copy, built as part of a miniature empire in times past to protect the grave of Zhu Yuanzhang,[19] the most famous emperor of Nanjing—all this causes Stein to fall into the deepest of apathies, for everything is so sad: sad that the monstrous devastation proved, after the Taipings, to be so irreparable; and sad, what the Chinese, murdering one another in the course of civil war, and, chiefly, the unprecedentedly bloodthirsty Japanese[20] did here; but what the man of today had made of this heap of ruins is sad as well, because the countless lies and deceptions and counterfeits are sad, the countless imitations, the ceaseless attempts by the spirit of the present age, in the name of reconstruction, to dredge something up from the illustrious past, to which then the unsuspecting visitor, coming to the city as to a great spectacle, can be led by the unscrupulous and peremptory tourist trade, so it can say to him: So, have a look, here is Nanjing with its 2,000-year-old history—so fatal, and disastrous, because no one can stop this course of development any longer, and no amount of strength can turn it back any more, because what is going on here cannot be remedied, what is happening right here and now cannot be remedied, and it doesn't help when someone, thanks to unmistakable happenstance—just because, sitting slumped on the bed, he absent-mindedly poked at the Linggu Si monastery[21] on the map in that Biedermeier hotel room—picks himself up and goes there, just as the Linggu Si, destroyed and rebuilt many times over, can be grateful to exactly that same happenstance, for the fact that one part of it, a few hundred metres behind the Wuliang Dian,[22] still exists, just as happenstance earlier led the finger of that person to this exactly distant point in the city; and if possible, it renders—let's refer to this as the Nanjing experience—even more oppressive, even more dispiriting, for this tiny fragment of the Linggu Si stands there, in the middle of this fraudulent and crumbling modernity built upon a heap of ruins, like a tiny child on the battlefield at twilight, where everyone around him lies dead—they too just stand there, László Stein and the interpreter, they stand in the cold torrential rain, immersed in the undisturbed peace of the inner enclosed courtyards of the monastery, they look at the dainty arches of the pavilion trussing, the ancient, dried-out cypress trees with their peeling trunks, they listen to the quiet steps of the monks appearing now and then on the flagstones, and how, in the centre of the courtyard, even the steady cold rain cannot completely extinguish the tiny arches and smoke of the short incense sticks placed in the enormous sacrificial bronze cauldron, then they return to the city, they pay the bill at the hotel, they head out to the station and, without even thinking about it, they get a ticket for the next train, a train which will take them away from here but which will never erase from their memories that place where, on this occasion, exactly 2,000 years came to an end.

The next train goes to Yangzhou, but this is still not completely coincidental, because the choice is swayed not merely by the plaintive haste of 'away from here!' but also by an idea born of despair that if here in Nanjing this early May eternity is so dreadful, then they should not proceed with exaggerated and preliminary caution but immediately try their luck with the opposite extreme, so they try the city of salt merchants, in the one-time economic and cultural centre of South China, at the meeting place of the Yangtze and the Grand Canal,[23] in the memorable flower garden of the Sui,[24] the Tang[25] and the Song dynasties, they try to uncover something that is alive, a few tiny intact fragments will be enough, a few tiny fragments where the light of the spirit of classical culture might have shone across the centuries, where scholars, painters, poets, calligraphers, gardeners and architects, where the 'Yangzhou pinghua',[26] the popular storytellers of the street, where the most exquisitely refined figures of Chinese erudition, its bulwarks, supporters and beneficiaries, Ouyang Xiu,[27] Su Dongpo[28] or the saint of Buddhists and the Japanese, Jianzhen,[29] came upon a place and found a home in such a memorable fashion. And it cannot be said that they don't find anything, not even considering that here everything is also in ruins and the wretchedness is the same as in Nanjing, no, exactly the opposite is the case, in Yangzhou, in the city of canals and bridges, the first thing that strikes them is that unmistakable scent of the wealth of New China, of recent wealth, where they have to hunt out the places of memory of former times but where they are also confused, although at first they think of it as a kind of beneficial relief, as the conspicuously huge mass of places of former renown practically topples onto them, because in the first hours, as in a friend's car—made available to them with the inconspicuous assistance of Tang Xiaodu—they traverse the city from one end to the other, the feeling arises that surely here everything still remains from the sought-after past: even if cordoned off, in a sense, into a ghetto by the new, modern world, the Wenfeng Ta,[30] its original form a thousand years old, and rebuilt towards the end of the Ming dynasty, still remains; the seven-storey brick pagoda, now covered with graffiti, and maybe a little too far to the south from today's city centre but formally serving as an emblem of the city, still remains; the Shisong Si[31]—once the memorial shrine for Shi Kefa,[32] the heroic commander who fought against the Manchus—now the City Museum and maintained with uncommon beauty, still remains; and the famous gardens too: the He Yuan, the Ge Yuan and the Xi Yuan[33] all remain, and they rush from the Daming Si temple,[34] from the beloved Jianzhen monastery to the recently excavated graves dating back to the Han era,[35] they dash from the Shou Xihu, the smaller West Lake[36] to the Tang-era city wall-remains, from the Guanyin temple to the Ouyang memorial temple,[37] so that the first hours—right until mid-afternoon—are filled with this running around, with this unexpected joy; it's still here, says Stein to the interpreter, this is still here, and this, and this, they take themselves all over, here and there, in the car arranged from Beijing, so that, after twilight has set in, it begins to be obvious: in the back seat of the car, they are becoming quieter and quieter, that is, they begin to go back again, in order to thoroughly examine the places of these renowned monuments, and they begin everything anew, and they go everywhere now, and Stein feels that there is some problem, there is some problem with these well-preserved gardens, with these neatly ordered temple buildings, there is some problem with the Daming Si, something is not right with the Ouyang temple, with the bank of the Xihu glimpsed only from afar, with the so-called White Stupa,[38] with the Tang-city walls, with the Guanyin temple, there is some kind of problem with *all of old* Yangzhou, Stein finally is able to state that evening in the hotel room, from which, by the middle of the night merely one bare sentence rattles around in his brain: *there is a problem with Yangzhou*, by the middle of the night this is what remains from the unclouded happiness of arrival; because of the anxiety—why can't he figure out what has to be figured out here?—he can't fall asleep. It still hasn't been determined, and they say nothing, but in the morning, when he and the interpreter look at each other over breakfast, both are thinking the same thing: that what is to come will not simply be the following day, nor even the next, in Yangzhou but perhaps the last, thinks Stein, and they begin everything again, but differently, not running here and there and all over the place but going to what is considered the most captivating garden in Yangzhou, they go to the He Yuan, and they stay there for hours, they stroll along the garden paths, they admire again the dazzlingly refined beauty of the pavilions, as the light glints on the tiny panes of glass of the glittering windows set like gems in the deep burgundy wooden structures, curved and polished with the sensitivity of lace-work, and they gaze at the lake in the garden, they observe the whole of it, and they try to understand *what is missing here*, because something is missing, this is glaring, but neither Stein, nor the interpreter, can figure out what it is, so it doesn't even occur to them to return to the Daming Si, then to the Guanyin temple and finally to the garden of the City Museum, the beautiful pavilions of the former Shisong Si—because they now are determined to avoid everything which they discovered last night to be false, fraudulent, fake, not original, rubbish, just a bad copy—it doesn't even occur to them to go back again to the Daming Si, to the Ouyang temple, to the Jianzhen Memorial or to the Xihu, it doesn't even occur to them to go back to the White Stupa, to the remains of the Tang-city walls or the so-called recreational park in Wenchang Street,[39] built where a Taoist temple used to stand, no, they decisively avoid drawing con-clusions from the tourist spectacles, newly built in the spirit of the coarsest enterprise, out of crude mercantile interests and camouflaged as authentic: they only seek out again the places that seem real, but the puzzlement, particularly within Stein, increases, and in the end, by early afternoon, they do not move away from the red facade of the City Museum, the amiable driver of the friend's car doesn't understand what's going on, so they send him off with a thank you, remaining by themselves in front of the museum, on the banks of the canal, and they begin to stroll along the banks of the canal, because they decide that this is the most beautiful, as this little narrow-bedded canal winding here and there just flows towards the west, it begins to rain, soon there are no people around them, on the two sides of the banks, beneath the swaying grasses and the plum trees and the linden trees and the wild chestnuts, they encounter not a living soul on the narrow walkway, just a dead dog, as the rainwater slowly washes, soaks through the carcass, they walk for about 400 or 500 metres, then they turn back, and walk those 400 or 500 metres again—stepping over the sodden dog cadaver again—to the museum, and it is clear by then that the interpreter would like to get out of the rain which is now falling more steadily, and of course it's getting chillier again, but Stein still cannot bear to do so, because he would like to find out what is missing here, to finally discover, well, what is the problem with Yangzhou—and he is certain that it can only happen here, here on the narrow banks of the canal, but he is mistaken, because nothing comes to him, well, then, later on the bus, he thinks to himself, then they take the taxi to the bus station, later on, when they are leaving, and they look back, and they see Yangzhou, then, in that moment of farewell, it will occur, he thinks—but no, nothing like that happens at all, no kind of clarity comes to Stein, evening arrives, they poke at the map again, and they say: Let the next stop be the unknown Zhenjiang, and they get onto a bus, and they set off, and Stein looks back, but nothing—there is Yangzhou behind him, the famous city of salt merchants, the centuries-old centre of art, but nothing is happening in his head, because he has to wait for something to happen in this inert idiotic head of his, he has to wait until Yangzhou has disappeared completely from sight, because all this— as to when and where—was prescribed in advance, because it was all prescribed that as he sits there in the rearmost seat, and gazes out of the bus' grimy window onto the dark highway, and thinks back upon Yangzhou, it has all been prescribed, he must wait for this precise moment of thinking back, because then he thinks back, and he understands that Yangzhou, well, *that wasn't even it*, that Yangzhou doesn't exist any more, *we were not in Yangzhou*, he realizes, and he takes out his little notebook, which he bought in Beijing for 8 maos,[40] in order to note down more the important events to come, and on that page where Yangzhou is written he crosses out the word with his pen and, after thinking a little, crosses out the date above that, he crosses it out with force, so that it cannot be seen, so that it will never again be possible to decipher from the contours of the pen strokes that Yangzhou had been written there nor 2002, and 7 May and 8 May.

It's evening again, and the goal of the journey is Zhenjiang, and now, by all appearances, they can really attribute their having come to Zhenjiang to coincidence, if coincidence exists, and if it has been the one to guide their fingers along the map, but it doesn't exist, says László Stein to himself, and it is not coincidence that has led his fingers, as will be completely clear in a moment, because after a good hour, cutting across the Yangtze, they head into Zhenjiang, and in the dark they see the first streets and the first people, and they no longer believe in any kind of coincidence, only in an unbending, malicious, brutally just and—to them—inordinately unfriendly spirit which, in fleeing from Yangzhou, led them to this place, so they could see, after the wretchedness of Nanjing, after the disappearance without a trace of Yangzhou, that there was still farther, farther to go, that is: farther to go downward, to sink ever lower in the experience of disillusion which this time bears the name of Zhenjiang, the trading city with a population of 2 million, at the crossroads of the Grand Canal and the Yangtze, which this time is known as the place where Wang Anshi[41] was born, and where Mi Fei[42] died, and about which it is bruited that here stands the Wenzong Ge pavilion[43] where the people of bygone times, guarding their treasures with such care, kept watch over the famous collection of volumes, the Siku Quanshu.[44] An evil spirit is following them and guiding them, and, no matter what they try to do against it, the struggle is futile, Stein perceives this towards the end of the first hour, futile, he sums up—and in subdued tones!—

his feelings to the interpreter: not only are they in the wrong place with their useless interest but also, since their first steps here, nothing but evident ill fortune could be their companion, and behold, they wave down an indescribably filthy taxi, and begin to hunt for a hotel, picked out earlier from some travel guide and the only one in that district designated as 'acceptable', an adventure in which the problem is not that the taxi driver cannot locate the hotel but, rather, that he does locate it, as the hotel—which now, in 2002, as the travel guide emphasizes, is the only acceptable choice—is unequivocally closed, and it is *how* it is closed that is so horrifying, standing there mutely and darkly in its assigned place, in wholly infernal abandonment: above, on the facade, the name can still be deciphered, according to which this is the Dahuangjia Jiudian, or the 'King Hotel', but the windows are crudely boarded up, the entrance barricaded with sheets of iron, wooden boards, plastic sheeting, as visible as the clearly hope-less attempts to break in again and again, because this barricade is already half smashed apart, and, even though you can neither see nor go in, it's as certain as death that there is nothing inside any more, absolutely nothing which could be stolen: the building's fate of being broken into again and again—perhaps to the point of its complete destruction—is completely senseless, yet these break-ins will occur, continuously and indefatigably; they stand there, silent, as behind their backs the taxi's ailing engine, like the breath of a dying man, falters for short periods, they cast a glance at the infinitely indifferent face of the taxi driver and it is clear he knew that there was nothing here, that the best they could do right now would be to make them-selves scarce, to leave this place today, to go back to where they came from, but if they want to, they can pester him some more, he's in no hurry and he will take them wherever they tell him to go, and he does, to the closest hotel which is open, and they pay him two-thirds of the amount they had bargained for—which, however, was doubled in the end—so they lose out, and they gain, as here in New China most often occurs with foreigners, then they take a mangy room, which cannot be bargained down to less than 150 yuan, on the second floor of the Fenghuang Ling hotel, originally vainly conceived as glittering but where everything is penetrated with misery, and from this point on they don't speak a word to each other, they just make an attempt at washing in the water stained with brown rust, then they give up and eat the remains of their food purchased at the bus station in Yangzhou, then they lie down on the beds, like people who have been knocked down by sheer physical exhaustion, and they sleep until next morning. The Wenzong Ge pavilion no longer exists, nor does the renowned Siku Quanshu; the house where Wang Anshi was born is completely gone, just as on Beigu Mountain,[45] not a single genuine component of the monastery remains, but this isn't as horrifying, as they began their baneful foray into Zhenjiang, as the fact that *there is no longer any sun*, it's around nine o'clock in the morning and it's as if the sun never even rose, nine o'clock and there is darkness in Zhenjiang and in the taxi which, after the first dismaying appraisals, they take to the city's most renowned site, to Jinshan[46] (because they would like to see for themselves if those temples—or at least some part of them— still stand on Jinshan Hill, temples which in former times almost completely covered this spot), they just stretch their necks out and they cannot believe their eyes, save that the whole thing is as if they were the ones exaggerating in their outburst of grief, because it is simply unbelievable, absurd and fairly frightening, as if there were an eclipse of the sun, a nearly total eclipse of the sun, for as the taxi writhes forward in the crushed-together mass of tiny streets, as it honks and brakes and turns and honks again and again, and it turns, and it brakes, and it goes on like this for a long time, even for an entire hour, and nothing can be seen, as they move forward at a snail's pace in the near night-like obscurity in which however there is plenty of time for them to seek an explanation as to what this nightmare is, and of course there is an explanation, and of course, after a bit of time it becomes clear what is happening: that on the one hand—as a kind of Zhenjiang specialty—above the narrow streets, the thick foliage of trees on either side has grown into each other so densely, forming a single perfect dense roof, and in a completely unprecedented way, not allowing even the smallest of fissures and so completely closing off the view of the sky; on the other hand, this sky hardly permits any light to descend this morning; heavy, thick, threatening, storm-grey, motionless clouds loom above them and yield no clarity, they proceed through Daxi Lun and the surrounding streets, reminiscent of a thronged, chaotic rag market, perpetually open for business, they turn, they honk, they brake, they swerve around the people wandering into view . . . and maybe the people are the most frightening of all, as seen from here, from the interior of the crawling taxi, as now and then a suspicious glance is cast at them from outside; this darkness at nine o'clock in the morning is completely natural to them, it means nothing, come on, what is so strange about it, what is so out of the ordinary?—these staring indifferent gazes are discharged onto them, and for that matter: Why? What's the difference?—they read this in the people's eyes: for it to be evening in the morning, or to see nothing, doesn't bother them—while in this partial withdrawal of the light it is nonetheless perfectly clear: not only is this unnatural fact incapable of throwing them off but also that nothing, but nothing, in this entire godforsaken world ever could; the grimy, distrustful, morose and immovable faces convey this in their own communicative way, they are going about their business, for surely they have some kind of business to attend to, if they are going somewhere, but whether it is nine in the morning or twelve at noon, whether there is darkness or light, whether the sun has come up or not, for them, for these 2 million people here in Zhenjiang, Stein and the interpreter determine as they gaze out of the car window, there is no significance at all. Jinshan and the entire area in the north-western corner of Zhenjiang is actually an island connected to the shore by a thin strip of earth, with the Yangtze flowing around it; on the island itself are the innumerable temples from the time when the Jiangtian monastery[47] flourished, their enormous significance and widespread popularity commemorated in a proverb that can be heard even today. And yet they are not surprised when it turns out that this is no longer true, and they are not surprised by only being able to reach the entrance to Jinshan by ploughing through an enormous ocean of mud, today, on this morning bereft of sunlight—what they experience once they are inside, however, causes not surprise but something which never figured in their most bewilderingly nightmarish apparitions. Before all else, after paying the arrogantly high entrance fee, immediately to the left they stumble onto an extensive playground. Dumbfounded, they stare: yes, the first thing you see at the Jinshan monastery is a playground, a playground in which everything is made of plastic, from Snow White to Donald Duck, the entire Euro-American fairytale world is present, if one can add that never on this earth has human effort ever created such a degenerate Snow White or such a vicious Donald Duck. So, here is a playground, they establish, and they quickly cut across it, then try to make their way to Zhongleng quan, 'First Spring under Heaven'[48] which they suspect could have the greatest chance of at least partial survival: because after having been brain-stunned by the brutal idiocy of the playground, they lose their sense of direction and contemplate whether something may have remained, and what the water from this well, considered by the one-time imperial guards to be of the most excellent qualities, could be like, and they even find, with great difficulty, the route that leads there, where the last 150 metres have to be made by boat across an artificial lake, but there is no one there, just a dilapidated rowboat tied to a plastic buoy in the shape of a lantern; but the person who would take this boat across the lake to where the spring is supposed to be is nowhere in sight; they yell, they make a racket, they try and call atten-tion to themselves, until after a while a sullen old man emerges from somewhere out of the dim uncertainty, and, although they greet him politely, he does not return their greeting, he doesn't speak a single word but gestures, as if he were dealing with idiots upon whom words are wasted, he gestures irritably for them to get into the boat, then he rows them across to a perfectly forlorn island; here, everything has been built to the tastes of tourists, a lifeless, repugnant garden and a few recently-slapped-together repugnant pavilions, but everything is closed, they wander around in puzzlement until they unexpectedly come upon Zhongleng quan, that is, they come upon what has become of it, because what disillusions is not even how it is sur-rounded by an unwieldy enclosure carved out of fake marble, or that the original quadrant has been diverged from, or that the dimen-sions—20 by 20—have been changed, but that the water disillusions, as it dribbles there in the basin, it is so filthy that it wouldn't be good even for watering grass, let alone as water for making tea, for which purpose it was employed with great esteem for centuries, as the very finest water which could exist; there are air bubbles on the surface, clearly this could have been the water of the source in bygone times—but already they are turning away, they return to the banks of the island, again they begin to shout, the old man comes, again they try to greet him, at least for this second meeting, but it's hopeless, he doesn't reply, he just rows them back to the far shore and is visibly relieved when they disappear from view; they return—across the inexplicable playground—to the main street of the monastery grounds, and set off onto the slopes of the Jinshan. At one time, according to the descriptions, the accounts and the drawings, the temples here were magnificent, and although only a fragment of the buildings still stand, looked at from afar, they appear to be in the best of all possible conditions; as Stein and the interpreter draw closer, however, once again they are confronted with the infinite damage done by the system of reconstruction in New China, the monstrosity of crudely vulgar taste, the implacable lack of understanding and the plethora of ignoble results, so radically at odds with the refined sensibilities of the authentic Chinese spirit; more and more they fall into a kind of enraged despair which then is transformed into the deepest repugnance; as they pass through one pavilion and then another, it rapidly becomes obvious that they are not viewing a monastery, and in particular they are not viewing Jiangtian but, rather, that they have been dropped into a safari park where nothing is real, where everything has to be paid for, because here every building is new and fake, every luohan,[49] every Buddha and every bodhisattva is new and fake, and every wood join in every column and every centimetre of golden paint is new and fake, in short, the whole thing is fraudulent, so that wherever a person goes he will encounter a vendor dressed up as some kind of Buddhist priest and who in every corner of the temple buildings will try to get him to buy—aggressively and expensively—some kind of dreadful religious junk, a pearl rosary and a Buddha necklace and a paper Guanyin, buy incense, they chant in place of sutras, buy a postcard, buy a pilgrimage bag, buy a certificate stating that you were here, a big stamp on it costs 5 yuan, the little stamp costs 2 yuan, but if you don't buy anything, that's OK, the monks corrupted into merchants snarl at the visitor, even then please pay, pay for everything, pay for stepping over here, for stepping over there, pay because you're looking at this or that 'sacred' relic, pay at the entrance, pay at the pavilions, pay and we'll ring the gong for you once, and buy something if you're hungry, and buy something if you're thirsty, of course at three times the price, the main thing is that while your yuans are decreasing, ours are increasing, so that, in the end, when it is really time to escape, and they hurry towards the entrance, it occurs to them that perhaps the evil monk Fahai,[50] who lived in this monastery more than a thousand years ago, did not bring such memorable harm only to the famous married couple in the legend but that he is also doing harm today, for it is as if he had left his spirit here and ruined this place for all eternity: for a mockery is made precisely of those who make a pilgrimage here to see the Buddha and to pray to him. In vain do they again get into a taxi, in vain do they drive across the rag market, inert in the silence of the wretched alleyways, back to the north-eastern periphery of the city, and in vain do they cross with a small ferry to the island of Jiaoshan[51]—overshadowed by the presence of the virulent tourist industry—to try to find something there among the trashy amusement parks and the trashy lookout towers, to find at least one monument which might safeguard the classical past, and there they realize: this is even more painful—in the crude modernity of an entire city, the ruinous 'preservation of tradition' dominated by the thirst for profit, the general clearance sale, the annihilating fraudulence, the mindless commerce mired in a counterfeit eternity, in short, in the extreme moral deterioration of the Armageddon of New China, a monument which has remained intact, here on the island of Jiaoshan, is much more painful than its absence would have been; for to walk into the entrance gate of the one-time Beilin,[52] moreover with the knowledge that this too can only bring fresh disappointment, to walk in and to look around the gardens and to begin to stroll, seeking the inscriptions of the stone tablets built into the walls, to walk in here and to comprehend just what kind of treasure they have happened upon immediately gives rise to the greatest anxiety within them—because how long can this last, the interpreter asks, how long until the absolute commercialization, the absolute debasement in this treacherous storm, he looks, plunged into anxiety, at the immortal inscriptions on the simple, well-maintained, whitewashed limestone walls, to which of course what else can Stein do except remain silent, silent in agreement, because what is going through his head is this: it cannot last even for a moment, this is the last day, the last hour, because the spirit of the age will immediately appear at the entrance gate, and will immediately begin the ruinous process of making this place earn its keep, and it is really much more grievous to see that it has remained, this monumental ensemble of gardens, this magnificent museum of classical calligraphy carved into stone, than to resign oneself to its absence, or to its renovation according to the criteria of the spirit of New China, and it is hard to explain why they should rejoice and not grieve that it is here, they say to each other, and just what kind of absurd figures are we in this entire escapade, for days now, for the entire week we have been searching for what might have survived from what is, to us, the only living precious order of Chinese classical culture, we set off in the entirely unfounded belief towards the traditional centres of high culture, south of the Yangtze, because we believed the original spirit of China to be alive *somewhere, in the depths,* as our European friend, Yang Lian, formulated it, and when we happen to find a piece of it—as we have right now—we weep for the fact that it is here, we weep for its defencelessness, its endangeredness, but, well, that's how it is, they share the same anxiety, and in this common anxiety they sidle up to the walls, and they stare at the magnificent creations in Beilin, the Stele Forest, or, more elegantly phrased, the Grove of Stone Tablets. The entire complex is made up of many courtyards placed symmetrically around a central axis; the individual courtyards, however, are separated by fences, into which moon gates[53] have been placed to make them accessible to one another. The individual courtyards themselves are clearly ordered according to the same principle: that everything—the walls, the gates through which one passes from one courtyard to the next, the lawn and moss gardens, the bamboo and dwarf trees decoratively arranged, the pavilions and the columns of the corridors protecting the walls, the ridge-tiles on the roofs of the corridors—everything, including the plaster on the walls and how it is applied, everything must be regularly repeated as well as subordinated to a single goal according to which every element in Beilin must emphasize the reason for which it was created, that is, the 400 stone tablets—as they immediately find out from the director of the garden, a lanky, sympathetic youth with protruding eyes—400 stone tablets, protected with sheets of glass, enclosed in brown wooden frames and placed onto the white walls, that is, as the young man explains, one's gaze—that of the esteemed guests—should be directed so that, wherever they happen to look, their gaze will rest unobstructedly on the inscriptions engraved on the steles, and they do rest there, that is what they experience, they say to the young man with recognition, then they sidle along the corridors of the square courtyards covered with tile, and happily discover—thanks to a certain knowledge of classical Chinese on the part of the interpreter—that here is the introduction Mi Fu wrote to the *Orchid Pavilion*,[54] as well as the inscription of Zhao Mengfu[55] and that of Su Shi,[56] and the words of Wei, the famous Taoist master, there are many renowned inscriptions here from all these authors, as the young man, coming again and again into view, reminds them, but then he mentions just one, and he takes them over to the stele, dating back 1,500 years, of Yi He Ming,[57] for which a special pavilion has been built, he shows them only this one—the garden, however, is filled with the masterpieces of classical Chinese calligraphy, built into the white walls outside along the corridors, and inside, within the vitrines of the various smaller pavilions, and they just wander from one courtyard and one pavilion into the other until they suddenly realize that they've been there for three hours, and for that entire time not one other person has set foot there, of course the weather is bad, they say consolingly to the young man, of course it's about to rain, they finally bid him farewell by the exit where he has accompanied them: yes, he says, tianqibuhao, bad weather, yes, he waves goodbye with a single brief movement at the gate, with a wry expression, and says as they leave: jiuyao xiayu le, yes, it really looks as if it's going start raining any moment now.

He's wearing a shabby, cheap, dark-blue suit, and because he is so tall he has to stoop a little and bow his head when he stands underneath the entrance of the moon gates, and he just stands there, sometimes looking up at the sky, to see if the first drops have fallen yet, sometimes casting a glance after them, as they depart, glancing as they depart, so that they will never, ever forget.

2. Yao, Why Are You Lying?

In Shanghai, the metropolis of indeterminate dimensions, the pride of New China, the Land of Dreams of Great Possibilities, its proprietors of wealth as was earlier unimaginable in this country, one thing is important: here, in perhaps China's most significant residential area, there is nothing for them to seek—for there is no past here which would have to be made rotten with sweaty labour, there is no monument in need of protection: this is a modern and young city in the strictest sense of the word, where the past is represented by the former French district created in the nineteenth century and a few European buildings scattered here and there, and the Yu Yuan,[58] this particularly splendid, gigantic private garden from the time of the Ming dynasty—the future doesn't exist here, which also means that not only does Shanghai not have a past but also that it doesn't have a present;

blinded by its future, it has no time for the present—so that altogether they have no expectations, indeed, they even feel a kind of relief when on one of the first evenings they stroll onto the famous boulevard, swaggering with its hundred-year-old European facades, onto the Bund[59] where, above River Huangpu,[60] they can glimpse, on the far bank, the skyscrapers of the ultra-modern district of Pudong,[61] an exhilarating sight for so many millions of New Chinese, yes, they feel relief, as they stand there by the railing on its bank, amid the mass of cheerful, thronging young people, and as they look at this Pudong they even feel a mild satisfaction, because it is good to see, Stein remarks to the interpreter, that this time it is not the illustrious past but the illustrious future that has been closed into a ghetto: for Pudong is a ghetto, an enclosed district where New China can prove to itself that it has succeeded, it has succeeded in constructing the first kilometres of the symbolic Super Expressway, clearly an object of ideology for New China and which can only lead back to the compulsively long awaited 'Middle Kingdom',[62] comprehensible only to the Chinese.

They are trying to make their way to a meeting, so that after the embittering experiences of Shanghai—acquired in the course of numerous dialogues with well-known intellectuals leading only to bad memories, the daily combat between an ostentatiously prosperous few and the decisive predominance of the struggling downtrodden, as well as a long sought-after kunqu[63] performance in Yifu Theatre[64]— so that after all this, they can share their thoughts with someone about the situation of traditional culture: they are on their way to a dinner with Yao Luren, a young, well-dressed and well-to-do university instructor who teachers literary history somewhere in a college in greater Shanghai. The meeting place is in front of the Peace Hotel; from there he leads them into a horrifically clamorous and thronged

multistorey modern restaurant. They make their way with great difficulty to the reserved table, they sit down and, after introductions
through the interpreter, László Stein reveals that he is devastated, and
that in this conversation he has prepared for something he usually
never presumes to do: to speak of his agitation frankly, disregarding
the usual courtesies, without dissimulation and, if necessary, to con-
tradict his partner, to dispute and to try and enlarge upon his thoughts
until he has felt that the other has understood. Stein does not even
wait for the hors d'oeuvres, he has already begun to talk to Yao with
particular frankness, as if he were sitting with a good friend.

Stein could not have committed a more grievous error.

As an introduction, he begins to relate to Yao: since he has been
travelling here, in this province of China most renowned for its precious traditions, he has acquired only bitter experiences. He sees the
new life of New China—the locus of a monstrously vehement desire
for money and things that can be gained with money, he sees the
masses of tourists inundating the so-called cultural monuments, but
he also sees that these people have no connection with their own
classical culture, for their cultural monuments no longer exist—in the
name of restoration, their essence has been annihilated, annihilated
by the most common of tastes and the cheapest of investments as
well as by the terrorizing principle of the greatest gain. Stein asks if
this impression coincides with Yao's. He asks if he sees things at all
correctly in thinking that the position of classical culture in China
has been completely laid to waste.

YAO. That is certainly not the case. Indeed, in my opinion, classical
culture is in a much better position than it has ever been. I mean
to say that, in a historical sense, when at the beginning of the last

century the process of modernization began in China, it never condemned classical culture to annihilation. Moreover, this wasn't necessary because a very important aspect of classical culture is that it is very adaptable, very open towards other cultures, it creates connections very easily and does not reject other cultures when confronted with them. The best example of this is how in China, before the Han era, there was no religion, in the sense of believers and their one god, or many gods—a religious concept such as that appears only with Buddhism, a foreign religion which was explicitly made the state religion in the period between the Han and the Tang dynasties. This is just one example, which we can enlarge upon, and we can confidently state that the encounters with the surrounding peoples in China's cultural sphere were always quite cordial. So why be unfriendly today to the modern civilization of the West? If you look at the twentieth century, superficially you could think that modernization was a movement aimed against tradition. This is not true. The true goal of modernization is for tradition to live within it but to live in a renewed form. Those whom we respect as the outstanding figures of this movement, such as Lu Xun, were as well versed in classical culture as the literati of the eras before modernization.

Stein interrupts, and he says that, leaving aside what Yao just said about irreligiosity in the pre-Han era, inasmuch as he can judge, at the end of the nineteenth century and the beginning of the twentieth, the idea of modernization—namely, the unconditional demand for the renewal of culture and society—was fundamentally and precisely brought about by a deep dissatisfaction with tradition. Of course the greatest figures of this movement, he adds, received their classical erudition through traditional instruction, as other forms of instruction did not exist, but the entire goal of the movement they initiated was the creation of a modern culture in place of the traditional. And not some kind of combination of the two.

YAO. I acknowledge that the process towards a modern Chinese culture was at the expense of traditional culture. But that didn't mean, and it doesn't mean today, that the relationship of Chinese intellectuals towards traditional culture has changed. The basis of the culture of Chinese intellectuals is traditional classic culture, even today.

But Yao Luren can't really think this, Stein looks the interpreter and indicates for him to translate precisely. Here is Shanghai, he says. We look out of the window, we walk along the streets, we talk with people. Everyone, with no exceptions, toils ceaselessly . . . for the sake of the creation of a modern China. He, Stein, sees only masses of people who are curious about the consummated processes of the modern world—this is what they study, imitate and conform to. In his experience, he continues, going by the statements of intellectuals, they are fundamentally interested in what is going on in America, Europe and Japan. And you, Stein looks at his partner in dialogue with the most candid of gazes—like someone trying to encourage the person sitting across him to a similar expression—you say that intellectuals here live in a traditional culture? That the basis of their culture is tradition? His impression, says Stein, after every single meeting, is that intellectuals no longer have any connection with their former culture, they only react to it with meaningless statements. He feels that this is so obvious, especially here in this gigantic city modernizing at such hideous speed, that he doesn't know what to say!

He apologizes—Stein starts to make excuses—for he knows that he is upsetting the rules of polite behaviour in contradicting his host, but to say to him that these intellectuals—who clearly fill their days with the practical acquisition and the psychological assumption of all the values of the modern Americanized world—respect tradition, is not something that he can leave unmentioned! They really know classical Chinese culture as their own?! They really live it as their own?! He can only imagine that Yao would say this to someone who he thinks doesn't understand anything about Chinese culture or Chinese modernization, but he can't imagine that Yao himself believes what he is saying.

The interpreter is clearly in anguish, but he translates accurately. Yao hears him out, but he can hardly wait to speak.

YAO. You make no difference between the culture of the educated classes and that of the wide stratum of the population. And you have not taken into consideration that there were always mutual influences and connections between the two layers of classical culture. I'll give you an example. It is not just the intelligentsia who are fond of the kunqu theatre—the population at large also really enjoys it. And you can see not only older people in the audience but young people too. There is a Kunqu Research Society which was founded after the Cultural Revolution.[65] This is just one example. Classical Chinese culture can be researched from very many angles.

Stein is thinking that if he continues to refrain from polite circumlocutions, eventually Yao will be forced to open up. And so, after apologizing again, he continues by saying that Yao has not answered his question. Otherwise as well, he adds, living and researching a culture are two very different things. In China, just a few decades ago, it was fantastic, even formidable, how a person could feel that classical Chinese culture was truly a daily reality, because in its depths it was indestructible. And he, Stein, started off in this secret hope—because, he says, one always starts off with some secret hope in this country— but, well, these few weeks since he has been here have made it thoroughly impossible for him to nurture this hope within himself any more, because to state today about this society—that it would have any sort of connection at all to its own traditions, that this would be its daily reality in the depths—is simply absurd. The unbelievable hunger for the creation of a market economy in recent years, the hunger for the acquisition of money and possessions renders such statements ridiculous, even retroactively. And as far as Yao's example goes—Stein looks at him more decisively—surely he does not wish to prove, by citing the founding of the kunqu societies, that the kunqu theatre is alive and flourishing? The kunqu societies are dying out because neither the intelligentsia nor the 'wide stratum of the population' is sitting there in the audience. No kind of wide stratum of anything sits there at all. It's a miracle if there are even a few spectators. If there is even a performance being held somewhere.

YAO. Classical Chinese culture lives on in the depths. On the surface it may seem that while the construction of an industrial society is in progress, classical culture has been pushed into the background, but if this indeed has occurred, then once again classical values will regain their significance—these will be the values to which people reach back, because they will have need of them, we will have need of our own culture, the essence of which cannot be anything but classical culture. This cannot change.

Stein asks Yao what he actually means by the term 'Chinese classical culture.'

YAO. For me it signifies a belief. Others think that it is the practice of life according to the highest principles. You cannot understand this, but that's how it is, and the young people of today endeavour to not just live an everyday life.

Why couldn't I understand, Stein spreads his hands apart. He would like nothing better, he says, than to encounter some facts which would allow him to think the same thing. But he doesn't find any such facts, he lowers his hands. The young people of today?—He echoes the expression. For surely Yao himself is one of these youths, and he knows very well how young Chinese people spend their time in the cities. So why is he saying something different? They are endlessly dangling at the teats of the computer or the television, in the much better cases in the bookshops and libraries, trying to become acquainted with Western mass culture, amusing themselves with that, or, in the very loftiest of instances, trying to become acquainted with the more valuable accomplishment of Western culture and adapting it to the apparatus of their own intellectual lives.

Stein looks at Yao who, he senses, is eyeing his arguments with an ever-chillier glance. As a matter fact, here is where he should stop, but he doesn't give up, trying to retreat a little, seeking some principle, some point in common, and he begins to interrogate Yao: What does he see in general as being the essence of culture?

YAO. Culture is that strength which helps one discover the essence of life. It is enchantment. Chinese culture was always a continuum, it never became Westernized. Nor will it now. Because tradition is stronger than you realize.

Stein feels that their conversation is a kind of free fall where, however, he is the only one who is falling. He begins to lose his patience;

he begins to forget that this is exactly what he should not do—if he wants to make himself understood—so that, well, he confides to Yao that he would be ecstatic if he could sense the strength of this tradition. It's just that, he answers woefully, he only experiences the opposite. Everywhere. It is so obvious here in the big cities that there is no point in even trying to demonstrate it. And in the villages, well, what else do people want, especially the young people—and again he looks at him with that sincere gaze—what else do they want than to be big-city dwellers in this modern mass culture, because that's what we're talking about here—or in the case of the intelligentsia, to form connections, amid the advantages of the big city, with the elite culture of the West and to assimilate that culture fully? And, moreover, as quickly as possible and in ever-greater numbers . . . In every city, with every acquaintance, every friend, in every conversation, Stein raises his voice, this is his experience. And as Yao knows, he adds, the goal of his journey is not to find out if the Chinese intelligentsia respect their tradition with their words but to see if they live it. It goes without saying that they respect it. But do they live it? Or if this is no longer possible, what would you do, practically speaking? Do you stand— Stein flings out the question in bitterness—in front of the temples when these know-nothing 'preservationists' show up to protect the treasures with your own bodies? Do you safeguard artistic objects all over China? Take them into the museums so that they can find refuge? And then go with children into these museums to look at them? No, he shakes his head, Stein doesn't think Yao does this. These original artistic creations were destroyed by the civil war, or the Maoist era, or the tourist gangsterism of today, or by time itself or, worse, they have been counterfeited and sold as if they were real. What he has seen, Stein points to himself, for the most part during the past 10 years, as he has travelled through the provinces of China and viewed temples and monuments, is nothing other than the destruction of these exquisite objects in the hands of those who are not worthy. Wherever he has gone, he has met with forgeries and fraud. Because, he continues bitterly, temples are counterfeited in the name of reconstruction. Ancient monuments are 'saved' but they are not—these monuments are needed, so instead they are destroyed on the basis of purely material considerations stemming from a cheap dilettantish approach. And so he perceives—he slows down, because he can sense that he's speaking too quickly for the interpreter—that the only goal is to sell something that used to be an authentic temple, an authentic sacred place, an authentic statue of the Buddha; to sell it as a counterfeit, whether made new 'like magic' or daubed up again—and, sadly, even to unsuspecting Chinese tourists. This is what's happening, this is his experience—and Stein now feels he has been able to regain a calmer tone. And so, he explains, trying to persuade Yao of his good intentions through his glance, what the Chinese are annihilating is their very own culture which they could, in fact, be living. But you don't want to live this tradition, you and your compatriots, says Stein, and he gestures, pointing to the clamorous room, you and your compatriots live the second-rate mass culture that goes with the so-called modern market economy as well as so-called elite culture, dredged up from the squalid vortex of the market; and you do so of your own free will—just like us, by the way, in Europe. And he asks the interpreter to once again, and continuously now, add an apology. And the interpreter says that he's been doing so constantly. Practically after every sentence. But he signals to Stein that there is no way now to get the conversation onto a more friendly level. And he is right. Yao's face is rigid, his voice descends from ever-greater heights. It is clear by now

that he hardly has any statements to make that this European would
be worthy of hearing.

YAO. You are mistaken. Traditional culture plays a decisive role in
the life of China today—despite capitalistic tendencies.

They remain silent for a few moments, Stein thinks, Yao eats.
What should he do? Continue? Stop? Stein decides that he will not
stop, and so he asks if in the conditions of today the intelligentsia has
any opportunities to take part in any decisions? Do the intelligentsia
have any kind of importance in terms of influencing what happens
in China? Because he knows—he tries to draw the other's attention
to what is unconditionally shared between them—in the world's
other, so-called developed societies, the situation is tragic: the layer
of society known as the independent intelligentsia has collapsed, it
has no influence on anything at all, what it has to say is not important,
it writes about the state of the world, but no decisions are made with
its influence or input, things are decided on a level with which the
independent intelligentsia—in the former sense of the term—has no
connection whatsoever. The overwhelming majority of them have
chosen a non-critical role in terms of the structures of power in order
to have some access to real decision-making. And when that idea
occurs to him, it's as if he could engage Yao in the conversation again:
erudition itself has disappeared, Stein says, and with that the concept
of erudition itself. And—if even for a brief moment—some kind of
interest finally glimmers in Yao's eyes.

YAO. This is a specific question. The opinions of the intelligentsia,
its judgements, its influence, do not affect the processes of society
directly. The intelligentsia can affect reality through the transmission of culture and education. In imperial China, for example,

the intelligentsia were themselves the emperor's instructors. They were able to influence rulers by founding schools and through the instruction that took place there, even if they did not have a direct political role. There are no examples similar to this anywhere in the world, this only existed in China, and since then there has never been any kind of similar institutional mechanism . . .

Stein concurs approvingly, saying that, yes, this past was truly wondrous. This is why, he says, the entire world respects to such an extraordinary degree the former societal order of Confucianism[66] or, more precisely, the role Confucius himself intended for moral precepts. The image of such a system, which could even be said to be ideal, can be seen in China's millennia-old past where erudition in its essence meant a life lived according to moral precepts which had the highest possible value and which were built into the structure of society: society was a structure built upon the belief in morality. Stein doesn't continue on this point, for surely—he indicates with a movement of his hand—Yao is aware of this much more precisely and profoundly; so Stein only poses one question: What has remained of this? Nothing, Mr Yao. Do you agree?

YAO. No. Absolutely not. The role of the intelligentsia is just as important today. You have conveyed to me what happened to the intelligentsia in the developed Anglo-Saxon countries. This, however, will not happen in China.

It is clear from Stein's disappointed countenance that he was not counting on this reply. And he expresses his disappointment or, rather, his incomprehension, wondering if Yao can really think that the constellation into which China entered with the authorization of market relations is not everywhere the same? Does Yao really think that the effect of the legitimization of investment, currency markets and the laws of global finance could somehow lose its potency in China, and only in China, and somehow function differently?

YAO. China is not the same. China is different. China cannot be compared to any other country. Legalities are different here, specific. For example, the tradition of the social relevance of the intelligentsia, their extraordinary significance, the vitally important and well-known role of the literati, is very strong.

It is clear that Yao wants to expound upon this unconditionally, so Stein merely interrupts in a helpful manner, indicating that he shares Yao's opinion, and he asks how this prestigious societal role can be explained.

YAO. Chinese writing—with its outstanding role—cannot be compared to anything else. Ever since writing has existed, Chinese writing and the lettered have possessed decisive relevance in the history of the Chinese spirit and society. Never in the world has writing or a system of writing had such crucial significance. It is only thanks to the innate respect for writing inherent in Confucianism that caused China to be governed according to Confucian principles and to be built upon Confucian tradition— a tradition that remains until today. Chinese writing was sacred, irrevocable, absolute respect towards it was mandatory, thus the tradition of classical culture, preserved in writing was exemplary and indisputable. I do not claim that there are not and were not damaging influences stemming from Confucianism—it made society too rigid, everyone recognizes this. But its stance of respect for writing, and through it the creation, unique in the world, of a culture extant in writing is important—it has always been and is still highly worthy of recognition . . .

Stein interjects that he, along with many others, does not see in Confucianism or, more correctly, in the teachings of Confucius, an instrument by which society is made overly rigid but, rather, a theory of society which can assure continuity to that society. It did not make it rigid but offered it continuity. Or perhaps it did not even offer this continuity but simply articulated and codified the idea that society was something continuous. And he asks Yao if in his opinion any kind of renascence of Confucian thought could be possible?

YAO. The state of change today is immeasurable. But I feel that these changes are external. Tradition is at work in the depths. And one of the most decisive elements of this is Confucianism. I do not believe, however, that it could be revived in an unaltered form. It is indisputable, though, that it will have a crucial role in the future. Society today is restless. If tranquillity returns, then China will return to its own traditions as well. In my opinion, the opposite will occur here in China in relation to what happened in Eastern Europe, in the former Communist societies. In Hungary, the intelligentsia played only a trifling role, there is no way to compare that with the role of the Chinese intelligentsia. In China, this role can never diminish. Because it was always very strong.

Stein has serious doubts about such an argument but, in order to not disrupt what has begun, he asks if the intelligentsia of today has not distanced itself too much from the so-called wider stratum of society.

YAO. Traditionally, this relationship wasn't too wonderful—that is, it was always bad. The intelligentsia always thought that the fate of the world, that is, China, was in their hands. This was one of the most negative traits of the Chinese literati. They didn't bother with any kind of real connection with a broader spectrum of the public, they believed themselves to be unique and so they looked down upon the lower classes. This will have to be changed in a democratic renascence.

This last sentence, and its obvious empty demagogy or, rather, its immeasurable deception, once again defeats Stein, so he quickly tries to move on to another topic, or to approach the same topic from a different angle, because Stein can't give up, he can't stop, he is plunging down the hill now, and so he just asks and asks: he asks, for example, what kind of hope could there possibly be for a young person who would like to become acquainted with his own classical culture. Because from where, from what kind of sources could this be acquired? For classical culture is not a real, living element of every-day life or festivals—instead, there is the culture of modern China. So where can a young person find out anything at all about his own original culture? Is the situation not impossible? All the artworks are fake—instead of restoring ancient monuments, a kind of fraudulent trade is going on, so that whoever wants to understand classical Chinese culture by contemplating its material objects has no chance. As for the knowledge of classical writing and classical erudition—it seems very apparent that it is not the centre of interest for the younger generations. They are interested in completely other things, no?

YAO. There are certain requirements if someone wants to become acquainted with classical culture. It's true that the historical chronicles always mirrored the worldview of a certain dynasty in an extraordinary manner, and so the individual dynasties were continuously rewriting the past. But there was always one part of the intelligentsia that preserved its independence and wrote the truth in secret. These works are available for any young person who wants to read them.

But, Stein asks, can they actually read those old texts? Indeed, he raises his voice a little: Do they want to read these works at all? If we go into a library, will we see these classical works prominently figuring on the list of borrowed volumes?

The resignation which can be heard in Stein's voice makes it clear to Yao just what this European visitor thinks of him. His response is as cold and as short as possible.

YAO. They are more and more involved in reading these ancient writings.

Stein asks him if he means this seriously. The interpreter, turning red, translates his words. The evening cannot be salvaged.

YAO. Yes. More and more. And there is ever-more interest in classical culture as a lifestyle.

Stein feels another outburst of grief, so that he no longer feels it necessary to try to save what could be saved. And because he feels himself to be impotent, he begins to mock, and he mentions that his, Yao's life and lifestyle does not appear as if it would confirm everything that he just said. At least, looking at him, everything about him is reminiscent of an intellectual living well in a modern, industrialized society.

YAO. That is just the appearance. Now I'm wearing jeans. But at home I have traditional Chinese clothes.

And do you wear them sometimes, asks Stein.

YAO. Yes. And when I'm at home I always drink traditional Chinese tea.

So, not Cola, like now?

YAO. No, tea.

And what do you read? The classics? When you lie down at night, do you take out some classic from the Tang era and go to sleep with that?

YAO. I do have classical books. And I do read them sometimes, if not every day. Or I could say something else—I travel a lot. Very often I'll stop in the middle of a beautiful landscape, and then I feel the same as those who were raised in the classical culture. A classical line of verse always comes to mind. And I love traditional music and theatre.

The interpreter tries to stop him but this is no longer possible, so Stein interrogates Yao, asking him: Just how does he keep alive the connections with all of this? Does he find concerts to go to, classical performances? Because you really have to hunt these down in Shanghai, they are so rare . . .

YAO. I don't go to such events so very often. But sometimes I do.

Doesn't that exactly prove that he himself could not live according to the principles of classical culture, as a truly living world, even if he wanted to? At the very least, from reverence, he could try to just not give up on a relationship of acceptance and deference to these traditions, no?

YAO. It is not possible to live according to classical culture in every sense of the term. This is modern China.

Stein already feels joy that at least Yao has stated this. He would like to know if his acquaintances are just as faithful to tradition as he.

YAO. Not my acquaintances, no. The Western way of life is more convenient. At the present time, it is the ideal. It is not certain that a traditional lifestyle can be adequate for modern times today. This has to be understood. That's why we cannot speak of the usage of classical culture in the everyday sense of the term. For example, there is the traditional, long black coat, once much loved by the literati, with its characteristic buttoning. Traditional Chinese buttons. This is inconvenient, isn't it? It's hard to button up. The Western style of dress is much more simple and convenient. So why shouldn't we take it up? But that doesn't mean that I don't admire the old way of buttoning as a tradition.

Hearing this example, Stein tries hard to keep a straight face, and asks instead if this does not prove that tradition is already dead, in the best of instances it is something for the museums, the reason for a Sunday excursion with the children who 10 minutes later want to go to McDonald's. Otherwise: How could such a dialogue take place? Does he raise his children according to the principles of the classical tradition?

YAO. Of course that is not possible today.

So then where can the viewpoints formed through classical culture—his own culture—be validated? Can he transmit it to his students in the university, if not to his children?

YAO. My sense is that ever-more students are interested in traditional Chinese culture. In my view, there are very few who are not.

Once again there is silence at the table. The clamour in the restaurant is getting louder and louder. For a while they eat silently. The interpreter secretly nudges Stein to say something. He wipes his mouth, puts aside his chopsticks, and not worrying about whether what he is about to say has any connection to what they have been talking about, or if he has even mentioned it already, he says that he's been in many Buddhist monasteries but every single one has been handed over to incompetents who have ruined the structures and created forgeries in the name of restoration. They have made trash out of the sacred. And there is no place for the Buddha in a building like that.

YAO. You, sir, have only been here a few days, and you only see the surface.

Stein replies that he has been here for months, and not for the first time, and that he didn't even begin the past few years but that he has been coming here since 1990, and he sees an unrelenting process, in addition to the destroyed monasteries he just mentioned there are, for example, the expensive entrance fees, the uncommonly aggressive merchandising, deception and lies. And the Chinese are doing this in the name of their own culture.

YAO. That is just the surface.

Stein looks at him with innocent eyes. So what can he do so as not to see just the surface, if that's what it is?

YAO. There is no chance for you at all to understand anything about Chinese culture.

So—Stein hangs his head in resignation—nothing.

YAO. You would have to live here, and you would have to know Chinese life. And something else: you do not know Chinese writing. The foundation of Chinese culture is the knowledge of Chinese writing. You will never know anything at all about Chinese culture.

It's as if this thought had come to Stein from time to time, he concurs, and he acknowledges to Yao that what he has just said is very thought-provoking. Because he too feels the consequences of this lack. And he has even begun to study. Maliciously, he asks whether Yao is familiar with European culture.

YAO. Of course I am. I'm seen as someone who knows European culture extremely well.

How much time have you spent in Europe?

YAO. I've never been there.

Stein now frankly doesn't understand, but propelled by a new idea he poses a further question: How many languages does Yao speak?

YAO. Japanese and Chinese. That's enough. Everything that is important is translated. Especially in recent years.

Cautiously—so as to not risk obliging their host to bring the evening quickly to an end—Stein asks him whether he does not consider that in getting to know Europe and European culture, Yao would not have to follow the same principles as he has just pointed out to Stein?

YAO. No. A Chinese intellectual is different than a European one. And China has at its disposition a rich and tremendous cultural background. So what we understand from other cultures is quite enough for us to form our own opinions. China is interested in China, and our task is to lead China back, through its own traditions, to its former prominence in the world.

And this is the point from where there is no going on. Stein senses that if he does not want to irrevocably offend Yao, it would be better for him to stop. The clamour of the hordes of guests in the restaurant almost causes him physical pain. They have hardly touched their food. And clearly Yao has had enough of this conversation. Through the interpreter they discuss the weather, the unbelievable speed of Shanghai's development, Yao asks if they have seen Pudong yet, yes, of course, we've seen it, he asks if they have bought any fashionable clothes or electronics yet, because this is the place to do so, the interpreter says, no, we haven't; you should buy something, at least something for yourself, Yao banters with the interpreter a little, he is a young man who would definitely be interested in the goods of Shanghai, known all over the world. The interpreter answers that he is very grateful for the advice.

He lives here. He knows it's hopeless.

3. In the Captivity of Tourism

In the province of Jiangsu, south of Taihu,[67] roughly in the territory bordering Shanghai, Hangzhou, Shaoxing and Taihu, exists an enormous, timeless empire. It is entangled with canals and rivers and innumerable villages, and the entire area is so densely interwoven and so complicated that, apart from the locals, no one can find their way. If a foreigner sets off in this region, he immediately encounters these canals winding back and forth, and the tiny lakes turning up here and there, so it is no wonder if after the first few kilometres he loses his way and, after a short time, he has absolutely no idea where North and South are situated: he has no idea, which means that—due to the unbelievably complicated bus routes, incomprehensible to the uninformed—only quick perception can come to his aid; not to force any earlier-planned destinations, whether gleaned from maps or friendly advice, but to be content with whatever happens to fall into his lap: because behind nearly every third bus station is concealed a little village, and that village is evidence that time is not continuous—László Stein and his interpreter gaze upon the first such village, dating perhaps from the time of the Ming dynasty, and *having remained there*; because, as the saying goes, time has stood still for this village, so they can arrive at about six in the evening, twilight is falling, the weather is uncommonly mild and . . . there, right in front of them, is the end of the Ming era, Stein thinks to himself, and my God, he says to the interpreter, as they gaze at the roofs of the tiny houses snuggling up to one another— seen as yet from a distance, from the bus station—they gaze at the rhythm of the densely set blue and grey of the ridge tiles, my God, he keeps repeating, but he can't bear to continue the thought, because he simply cannot find any words, because he can't believe that this is possible, that here is Shanghai only 80 kilometres away, here is Shanghai 60 and 40 and 100 and 120 kilometres away, because Shanghai is everywhere, the empire of Shanghai is all around, with its dazzling speed and its distressingly incorrigible corruption, and yet this is here: they set off on a well-trodden footpath along which a young local woman with a little girl by her side amiably guides them; here is the Ming dynasty—or 'at the max', the interpreter says, correcting his enthusiasm, the beginning of the Qing![68]—come this way, the woman shows the route smilingly and then says something which the interpreter doesn't completely understand, but never mind, the two Europeans are incapable of engaging with this friendly young woman and even more friendly sweet daughter who is enchantingly shy, because there is the Ming dynasty, frozen in time, or 'at the max', the early Qing. This world had existed only in Stein's imagination, as for him there never could have existed a place—down to the last minute detail—such as he is looking at right now: it existed only and exclusively in his imagination, constructed entirely in his head, building by building, gate by gate, street by street—constructed from the fairytale vistas of novels, poems, stories, drawings and paintings—so that, as a matter of course, he never believed that it could be possible that one day, taking the bus from somewhere, as it happens from Shanghai, because he happened to hear from Yang Lian at one point that, not very far from where they were staying, the so-called water-town pearls could be seen tucked away amid the canals, he never believed that this could all just suddenly emerge from reality, and he is hardly able to grasp this, they make their way among the little houses, and they set off on the narrow walkway, and, really, it isn't as if they had simply arrived in a village of the Ming or Qing era but as if they had wandered into a marvellous dream taking place exactly at that time, the time of the Ming or the Qing, because nothing has changed here, says Stein to the interpreter who is just as astonished, well, how is this possible?—they look at each other and then they say goodbye to the young woman and the little girl who have just arrived at their own house, and who amicably invite them in for a visit, but for now they decline the invitation, since they want to remain outside, that is, remain inside the dream, because that's what it is—no matter how much they touch the saltpetre walls, no matter how much they sense the smell of the water from the canals running through the middle of the narrow streets, no matter how much they see the locals lingering in front of the houses, or as a woman, just now, washes clothes down in the canal, because even then it is only a dream: László Stein looks at these enchanting tiny streets on either side of the narrow canals, he looks at the strongly arched, tiny stone bridges under which long black small boats are borne away, real and yet not of this world; he looks at the decaying doorways, the open gates and the corridors inside, not even a metre wide, yet unbelievably long, dark and enclosed, in which light appears only as a tiny rectangle at a distant end, so tiny and so distant, light coming from a courtyard or who knows from where; he looks at all this and he immediately informs the interpreter that they should stay here, every other plan is senseless, they are not going any-where, yes, they will stay here, replies the interpreter in the greatest agreement—and they just walk on and on in the long evening in this village known as Zhouzhuang, and they fall into the sweetest kind of melancholy as a woman comes out from one of the houses and calls out to her children playing on the banks of the canal that dinner is ready; there is some kind of inexplicable unearthly peace in Zhouzhuang, old people sit on a bench, and not with the usual suspi-cion but, in the friendliest of cases, they take a good long look at the two Europeans, as perhaps could only be natural in a dream such as this, they look at them, then serenely acknowledge their greeting—Where are we? Stein asks the interpreter, is this possible? and they go on, evening begins to fall, the streets slowly begin to empty, and they too are left to themselves, but it is still not completely dark, the sky is clear, there is a full moon above them and a mild breeze is blowing, they can see well in the obscurity, and they cannot stop looking and looking at the end of the Ming era, or, as the interpreter now banter-ingly adds, 'at the max', the early Qing. They find only one place open, a teahouse where, instead of walls, a wonderful glazed lattice-work wall, varnished crimson-brown, faces the canal and the walkway of the tiny street, and inside an old couple sits idly behind the counter, watching television, and they look up as soon as the guests come in, and then place a pot of excellent, if expensive, Longjing tea in front of them, and the two guests happily sip away from the beautiful teacups and listen to the owner, Zhang Jihan, as he begins to relate:

Zhouzhuang, well, yes, Zhouzhuang is in its essence untouched, they can see—he points all around—that this doesn't mean his little tea-house but the entire village, no one here would think of damaging what is old, ever since the time of Shen Wanshan, that was a long time ago. But still, since when exactly? interjects Stein. Well, a very long time ago, the old man smiles, so this Shen Wanshan began to supply grain and this and that on River Baixian to the northern part of village—the old man points to the north—well, since then our life started up here, he nods a little wearily, as if he has been sitting here since then, then people diverted the water from the Great Canal to the west, he continues to relate, and the water from River Liu to the north-east, and that is how we got going here, that is how the Ancients founded Zhouzhuang, and so it is until this very day, he says, and very great gentlemen built such houses here that they came from Yangzhou and Suzhou to admire them; Shen, isn't it, he says as if to himself, then the Zhang family, then the Xu family, then came Liu Yazhi or Chen Qubing, or famous scholars such as Zhang Jiyang, the old man fluently narrates, as if he were the local chronicler familiar with every detail, the two guests happily sip the steaming, aromatic tea, the old man gestures that there is no need for them to pay this time, and brings new leaves and fills the cups again, and they don't have the strength to get up, and he leaves them to themselves, for they have no strength to leave this person here with his wife, with his stories, to leave this magical building with its doors open onto the canal and the village, darkness has fallen now, and they dare not budge an inch lest it should emerge that the tiniest movement is enough, that this is all just a dream, and—poof!—it will be gone.

The first air-conditioned luxury bus arrives at eight o'clock in the morning from the main highway, and then the buses pull in and pull in and pull in, one after the other, without stopping, they begin to stream outward as if from some bottomless sack, and tourists begin to flood in, inundate, fight their way inside, as hundreds and hundreds of newer groups, arriving relentlessly like an attacking army, in an unbelievably short amount of time they occupy the end of the Ming era, or the beginning of the Qing, and the tour guides begin to yell, they begin to yell in that loathsome, thin voice into their megaphones and, by the time the two visitors realize what has happened, Zhou-zhuang is already full, so full that by eight-thirty it is impossible to move in the narrow streets, they are terrified, they don't know what is going on, they've hardly woken up, they are sitting in the same tea-house as last evening and suddenly they are struck by a hideous clam-our: the tourists are cheerful, they are yelling and screaming and making a rush at whatever they can, descending upon the marvellous little houses, completely denuded now of last night's tranquillity, and it seems that they are happy to see daytime arrive, inside there are shelves and countless goods: food, sweets, souvenirs, genuine pearls, dried fish, folksong CDs, hundreds and hundreds of trinkets: What has happened here?—the two visitors look at each other, and then say goodbye to the elderly teashop owner who urges them not to miss out on the Zhen, Zhang and Shen residences, they will be open very soon, he says, but they are trying to struggle through the dense crowds to somewhere outside, they haven't the slightest idea exactly where this outside is, in any event, they try and push themselves forward against the crowd, because they have deduced from the crowds' move-ments that they must go to wherever they, the crowds, have come from; Zhouzhuang is small, so they reach the highway in a relatively short time, they stop at one point and, as they have seen the Chinese do, they wait there, they wait patiently for something to arrive, a bus which they can wave down and which will then take them onward, even if they are not able to say right now when a bus will come or where this onward is; the interpreter is asked: Where are you going, and he has to say something, so he looks at Stein—where?—and Stein pronounces the single place name he can recall from Yang Lian's account, Zhujiajiao, at which the bus driver shakes his head, he doesn't go there, that's not in this direction, but if they want he can take them to Tongli. Tongli?—the interpreter looks at Stein unhappily, and he says fine, let's go to Tongli, so that after half an hour they're in Tongli, the bus lets them out again by the side of the highway, and for the time being everything is quiet, the region seems relatively uninhabited, this is a good sign, they reassure each other, Zhouzhuang is like a prison, it opens at eight in the morning and closes at six in the evening—they had gleaned this from a sign as they were fleeing—and maybe, the interpreter adds, that woman who led us into the village last night was trying to explain to us that we had come at a good time, because it was after six o'clock, and Zhouzhuang is completely different then, maybe that's what she was trying to say, the interpreter suddenly realized, but maybe Tongli is different, he says, maybe Tongli is just a simple village and we won't have to encounter any kind of barbarian attack as in Zhouzhuang—Stein is silent; 200 metres away from the road a few tile-ridged roofs can be seen, so they set off in that direction, and they are not mistaken as far as the direction is concerned because it immediately emerges that Tongli is indeed that way; the direction, however, is the only thing in which they have not made a mistake; as for their own selves, they are very mistaken because, after 200 metres, the brutal truth swoops down upon them that here too there is nothing for them to seek, once again they have miscalculated, once again they have rushed into something, because if they would have to state that Zhouzhuang— left in peace only at night—was firmly in the hands of the tourist industry, then Tongli—this little water-town, just as enchanting—is manifestly the general headquarters of every tourist office for all of Jiangsu as well as the centre of touristic dreams of the province and half of China, once again a wondrous settlement from the past, the same narrow streets, the same narrow canals with the same black, slowly drifting boats, the same saltpetre walls and the same gateways and teahouses and the same enthrallingly carved crimson-brown lacquered pavilions, facing the water, but the swarming hordes seeking entertainment, the sheer havoc-wreaking number of tourists surpasses every conceivable measurement here, surpasses even the ruinous crowds of Zhouzhuang, and what they at least did not have to per- ceive while escaping from that latter place here surrounds them: that everything here is for sale, and this everything must be sold, this can be seen on the hunted expressions of the locals, or whoever they are, as at the same time from the other side comes the response that every- thing must be bought, that we will buy everything, this is what radiates from the expressions of the tourists, what is taking place here is unspeakably repugnant, so they decide to take a look at the three residences mentioned in the tourist guide vitrines, which they had failed to do in Zhouzhuang, so they pick themselves up and conclude their excursion. What they see is exquisitely beautiful again, the wondrous Tuisi Garden, the wondrous Jicheng and Feigong resi- dences, the wondrous canal banks, the houses, the bridges, everything is just as dazzling as it could possibly be, but they must escape because they cannot bear what is happening here, they cannot bear the unspeakably repugnant merchandising of these wondrous enclosed strata of ancient times; once again they stand by the highway, once again they don't move from that spot, and then they begin to think a little bit, and then they both reach the same conclusion: that there is no mercy; if this is how it is in Zhouzhuang, if this is how it is in Tongli, then this is how that will be in Wuchen, in Lili, in Xinshi, in Linghu, in Doumen, in Nanxun, in Xitang, in Dongyang and in Wujian and everywhere in this formerly enchanting landscape, so then they slowly trudge across to the other side of the highway, they begin to watch the buses going back, then they get on to the first vehicle returning to Shanghai, and in the days to follow they do nothing but gape at the ultra-modern buildings of Pudong from the railing of River Huangpu, and they try to remain awake, to clutch at reality, and to forget, forget—to forget what they saw, to beat out of their heads the fact that they saw anything at all.

4. Requiem in Hangzhou

In one of the world's most beautiful cities, in the unparalleled administrative seat of the Southern Song dynasty,[69] from the first moment until the last, they never feel any sort of disappointment. Hangzhou does not lie. It can be seen that there *was* splendour and brilliance here, there *was* erudition and intellect, it can be seen that the current conspicuous and exceptional wealth of the city is not due simply to the new era of Deng and Deng's followers but that it follows upon former wealth; Hangzhou, nonetheless, does not claim for itself, among all this new prosperity, any connection to the past which, of course, is indestructible in the same sense as the scene of a murder or an obstinate memory in the brain—no, Hangzhou announces, you won't find that here, no point looking for anything—and the fact that people keep coming is due simply to the present of the past that was once here, but Hangzhou doesn't say anything like that, it doesn't deceive because it has no need of deception, it propagates its new name in place of the old, and it has the right to do so from pride, from self-esteem: here is the new, the wealthy Hangzhou, and it does not wish to display itself in any kind of role that would tie it to the old, it has accepted that the old is gone, and it is happy for whatever residue has remained, this is Hangzhou today and, thanks to this, they feel above reproach for the first time, that is, they would feel above reproach if the rain were not constantly pouring down, if it wasn't cold, if the sky wasn't eternally cloudy, meaning that the other side of the lake was never visible, not even for a single hour, but fine, in spite of all this everything is fine because they have no expectations, and they are not obligated to take anything to task here, because in the Hangzhou of today there isn't anything to take to task, they enjoy the former splendour dimly glimmering here and there, they enjoy it, and they are satisfied with that much, and if in the meantime the thought arises in Stein: God Almighty, what astounding beauty there must have been once in this city, if after so much definitive destruction you can still sense something of it, like a draft of air where an amputated leg used to be. Because that's what he feels, László Stein corrects the explanation of the interpreter who has got entangled in this, when after a few days he asks what the problem is: he finds it unusual that Stein is so silent—he tends to feel, Stein says, that it was beautiful, that it was so incredibly beautiful here, that China's most eternally famous lake was beautiful, the Xihu[70] or West Lake, celebrated by the greatest poets more beautifully than anything else, that Gushan island ('Orphan Mountain Island')[71] was beautiful, and the two dams, Bai Juyi,[72] in the lake, that the Chan Buddhist[73] Jinci temple[74] was beautiful, that Feilai Feng ('The Peak That Flew Hither'),[75] and Yuhuangshan ('Jade

Emperor Mountain),[76] and Leifeng Ta ('Storm Peak Pagoda'),[77] and Yuquan ('Jade Spring'),[78] and Hupaquan ('Running Tiger Spring),[79] and the tea plantations of Longjing[80] were beautiful, indeed breathtaking, and that something has remained of everything here, like a kind of hint, is beautiful as well; in fact, they could even say that *many things* have remained and, with the help of a tour guide, contacted through Tang Xiaodu, they are seeking out these many things, although they don't feel any amazement at all when their guide takes them first to his own secret lookout, in the freezing rain, to the slippery cliffs atop the mountain in Gushan, promising that from there, from above, from that height which he has loved greatly since his childhood, they will see all of Xihu and all of Hangzhou, and it never even occurs to them to ask him where these things are, because from up there nothing but nothing in the entire God-given world can be seen, the lake and the city are enveloped in thick fog while the sky is covered by heavy clouds; their newly found friend is sad, Stein, however, is not, because he is aware that to *see* Hangzhou would not be possible even in bright sunshine, but he does not try to explain what he is thinking, he just consoles his friend that even like this it is beautiful, and that he is being very kind and what they can see from of the lake is very pretty: the fog, and the clouds above Hangzhou, this is enough, enough just to be here, and to be able to see the former Longjing tea plantations and the little village where the tea planters lived and live even today, just as they realize with joy that they can see the city's most famous temple or, rather, what has become today of Lingyin Si temple,[81] a soulless place of pilgrimage, victimized by its restoration, because that was the place where . . . but chiefly what makes them happy is when their enthusiastic guide takes them to the magical Feilai Feng, the mountain known as the Peak That Flew Hither, he takes them into what is undoubtedly one of the most significant—and hardly known—works of Buddhist sculptural art in the world, and it has an enormous effect upon them, here and now, beneath the earth, standing face to face with them: no one was able to destroy these Buddhas and bodhisattvas and luohans and monks, carved, in their immortal beauty, into the walls of the interconnected watery caves, but—and this is the thing that is really breathtaking—no one was even able to disturb them, maybe these statues carved into the walls of appallingly hard rock could have only been detonated, but no one got around to it, and now it's too late, now they are protected by the so-called dominant trend of the preservation of national culture as well as by the significant proceeds originating from the armies of tourists flooding this place, in short, here they are, perfect, undamaged, drenched in the water dripping from the ceilings of the caves, and nowhere else, not in any other temple cave, can such terrifying faces be seen, nowhere else can such uncanny suggestive gazes be seen, such an unearthly radiance from the eyes, not in Longmen,[82] not in Datong,[83] nowhere else, just here, beneath the earth, in the depths of the mountain, so that when at twilight their young guide takes them to Gushan to see a friend, Ge Youliang, who, as the owner of the renowned Louwailou pavilions,[84] opens up the magnificent lacquered doors, looking onto the lake, and in his teashop graciously invites them to sit down and offers them a cup of the very best Longjing tea, Stein's happiness is genuine, because he wasn't hoping for anything from old Hangzhou, and he didn't get anything, it was good on that cliff peak, though, he reassures his companion later on, it was good in Longjing, it was good below Feilai Feng and it was good in the tea pavilion on Gushan, and Xihu, says Stein, was beautiful, as its motionless mirror-like surface, from the breath-like touch of the thousands and thousands of raindrops, glittered in the twilight thousands and thousands of times; so that everything is perfectly fine, he reassures the interpreter, and in a few days they set off to meet one of the most outstanding figures of artistic life in Hangzhou, the deputy director of the kunqu theatre, they set off in order to somehow entangle themselves back into reality, back into forfeitous reality, back to where they had been led by their own superfluous interest and their own faulty presumptions, back into disappointment, the disappointment that what they believed to exist, to be alive, is gone, is not alive, back to the feeling—in the embittered words born of human dignity and serenity—that for them here, in this China, with their own great love for the exquisite treasures of this culture, there is nothing, but nothing for them to look at any more.

The theatre is situated among bare, prefabricated housing estates with cracked facades in a remote, hidden street which the local taxi driver can barely find—kunqu theatre? he asks, irritated, twisting the map in his lap; they are almost late because it is so hard for him to find the spot, and finally, after much meandering and an exorbitant fee, he discharges the two foreigners at the requested location. They are in a cul-de-sac, of course if this little stretch of road leading to the front entrance in the middle of a soulless housing estate could even qualify as such, and if a cul-de-sac can be something that leads inward, but behind the ugly concrete building of the theatre some kind of abandoned electric works or transformer essentially closes off the road and does not permit any further passage.

The deputy director of the kunqu theatre is a skinny person of average height, wearing—even today—the uniform of impoverished public servants, a dark-blue suit, shabby, worn through at the elbows and the knees, a crumpled white shirt, a knotted tie; a smouldering cigarette is eternally in his hand. He smiles, and offers tea to his visitors in the rundown office in which there is only a ramshackle table and a few chairs. The walls are grimy, hardly any light comes in; a thick set of bars closes in on a tiny window. They listen closely, but from the outside, from the building, nothing can be heard, from either the floor or the corridors—something, anything, a bit of noise, human speech, a shout, something that would confirm that they are not here alone.

But—they are alone, says the deputy director smilingly. Just at this moment—he clears his throat, embarrassed—there are no rehearsals. Maybe later on there will be some. Maybe?—Stein looks at him questioningly. He just smiles, listens to the introductory words of the interpreter, why they are here, what they are looking for, how they happened to find him, what they wish to accomplish with this conversation, that is, they would like to know if it is possible that—in this era of the final dying gasps of Chinese classical culture—the kunqu theatre, as a forgotten, neglected genre, might have preserved something from this culture precisely because it is forgotten and neglected; perhaps—through its methodology or its special means of conveying tradition—perhaps hidden away, concealed in some minuscule fact—is the whole . . . Because an era, says Stein, or if you will, a succession of eras, can eliminate the kunqu theatre from the face of the earth, can annihilate the kunqu texts, can expel or retrain the kunqu actors and musicians, but maybe what it can't do is to beat the knowledge out of the master's head, knowledge which—if he can survive the difficult times—he can transmit to his disciples. The deputy director nods, he understands, but he does not say anything for a long time. He pours the tea, and then he pours it again. He is preparing not for a dialogue but for a performance. He clears his throat again, and begins to speak.

LAI GUOLIANG. The kunqu is not only the oldest kind of Chinese theatre but is also, next to Greek tragedy and the Sanskrit drama, one of the three most ancient theatrical forms. The Greek and Sanskrit theatres have not existed now for over 2,000 years but the kunqu has, and so it is one of the sources through which the Chinese spirit has been preserved and safeguarded. We refer to it as ancient, and we consider it one of the fundamental forms of archaic theatre, although what we know and practice today is a variation in continuous development from an ancient original, directly created during the Ming era by Wei Liangfu[85] in Kunshan, to the north-east of Suzhou. The connection between the novels of the Ming and Qing eras and kunqu is extraordinarily close. You could even say that the classical Chinese novel came about through kunqu. For example, *Mudan Ting* ('The Peony Arbour')[86] by Tang Xiandu,[87] *Chang Sheng Dian* ('The Palace of Eternal Life')[88] by Hong Sheng[89] or *Feng Zheng Wu* ('The Kite's Mistake')[90] by Li Yu,[91] well, these famous kunqu plays are all part of classical Chinese culture. We must always approach kunqu through the classical Chinese novel, through classical Chinese literature, because kunqu itself represents the most exquisite classical literature.

They look at his crumpled dark-blue suit, they listen to this skinny individual and they sense a kind of elation behind his words, a kind of mirth for all his seeming broken down. They can see that he would very much like to continue talking, to say more about what he started, but they need to try and bring him back to the concrete question, so they repeat that almost nothing has been able to remain today from all that was classical culture. And yet here is a kunqu theatre. Kunqu was a part of classical erudition. How is it possible that it survived?

LAI. I'm not sure that it has! In any event, in terms of the preservation of the genre or, rather, its resurrection, it is precisely this theatre of ours, right here, which always played a very important role. We are the Kunqu Company of Zhejiang Province. And this place, where you are now sitting, is the director's office. Well, the deputy director's, because we have no director right now, just a deputy director, and that's me. Well, so, you understand now. In 1956, the Zhejiang Provincial Society performed a traditional piece in Beijing, the title of which was *Shiwu Guan* ('Fifteen Strings of Copper Coins').[92] After the founding of the People's Republic of China, this was a tremendous event from the viewpoint of kunqu—because the entire country took notice of this performance of ours in Beijing. Zhou Enlai[93] convened a special conference to debate the success of this performance. Zhou Enlai! And then an article appeared about it in *Renmin Ribao*.[94] Our society became the first state Kunqu Company. Honour was restored to kunqu.

Stein senses that the conversation is beginning to meander away from a promising path, so as a way of trying to get back to the subject of the ways of transmission of tradition, he recalls Lai's words: that kunqu is a very ancient genre. It cannot be taught just like that but must be transmitted in a special way. How does the instruction of kunqu take place?

LAI. Kunqu is passed on from generation to generation, as you very correctly noted. In the 50s, the greatest master, Chan Zibei, was still alive. All his students performed in our society. That is why the Kunqu Company of Zhejiang Province was the most renowned. The performance of *Shiwu Guan* and the pieces that followed were all filmed. Our activities were very highly valued.

But how did the instruction take place? How did Chan Zibei teach?

LAI. In the ancient manner of transmission of tradition. Like artisans, or Chinese doctors. Look at traditional Chinese medicine. How does that work? There are medical prescriptions, or acupuncture. Your head is hurting but the needle is stuck into your leg. How do they know? There is no interconnected theory, as in Western medical science, but the accumulation of experiences which leads to an interconnection of practice. It is not possible to master Chinese medicine at a university. A master is needed, a master who knows. And this master transmits his knowledge to his students through practice, who then become masters and continue in the same way. Kunqu too can only be taught this way. A master is needed. He is the one who shows, rehearses, practices, enacts; and at the beginning, the students do nothing but imitate the master. They don't ask any questions, they don't read books, they don't go to kunqu school, they don't write papers on the theory of kunqu nor take exams in it, they only watch and imitate. After many years, their individual styles begin to emerge. The modes of performance change, of course: these change with the era, the circumstances of life, peoples' sensibilities towards the beautiful and with the material at hand. All these changes are reflected in the history of kunqu. In the instruments of its expression. But

I must say that kunqu does adhere to tradition very strictly, to the texts of the written plays, to the continuity of characteristics manifest in those works, and if the individual eras have always— as they continue to do—left their stamp upon the genre, there still remains that which never changes and never can change— the kunqu concept of space and time. Western theatrical performance is very highly respected here, but bear this in mind from your perspective. Think of Shakespeare. The action is taking place in a castle, so on the stage a castle is built. And this creates a definite idea of time and space in the mind of the spectator. But this limits the actor—in our tradition. In Chinese theatre, in particular on the kunqu stage, you won't see any castles. The kunqu actor has to create it by his own means. He uses every instrument, every skill, every movement, every modulation of voice at his command, and the public *experiences* and *understands* that the action is, at that moment, taking place in a castle. The actor creates time and space. This is the foundation of kunqu and all Chinese theatre. We call it xuni, 'empty mimicry'. And kunqu is the only tradition which has preserved this ancient essence. It has preserved the colours of the costumes, the regulation of the movements, the order of the gestures of expression, the symbolism of the face painting . . . Let us take face painting. Why did it develop like this? And why did it develop at all? I am not a professor of kunqu, I am just a deputy director at the Kunqu Company of Zhejiang Province, but I have thought a lot about this while taking care of the theatre's affairs. I am in charge of the lighting at our performances. And maybe it is precisely because of that—I know something about lighting—that I came to the following conclusion. In the old days, across the many centuries of kunqu, there were no spotlights. There were only flaming torches, and the performances took place by torchlight. The light of the spotlight makes it possible to see the tiniest quiver on the face of an actor. This is not possible by the light of a torch. The tradition of kunqu also took into account that, in our civilization, people always attribute definite meanings to certain colours. Look at red. Red is the colour of honour, of smouldering feelings, of passion. White is the colour of intrigue and unscrupulousness. When the kunqu actor stepped onto the stage, people immediately knew from his make-up that this was a good person, this was an evil person. This was visible by the light of the torch. Now we use spotlights but we remain loyal to our face painting. The spotlight does not change anything of the essence. Nor does it change anything about kunqu. Nor does it alter anything in the meaning of the make-up. If it changed it in any way, then we would still be performing by torchlight . . . !

Do you perform exclusively old pieces here?

LAI. We perform new pieces too. In a new piece, there is no longer any meaning to the make-up. You know, comrade, the conceptual abilities, aesthetic sensibilities and intellectual capacities of the people today are much more advanced. Because our predecessors lived somewhere among the mountains or in a river valley. And they never left, they never travelled, so they never knew the outside world. Things are no longer like that. People travel. The public is very well acquainted with the outside world, so their faculties of discernment are on a much higher level. So that theatre will also be different, will demand something different now. Only one thing cannot change—kunqu. I understand that theatrical performance has to change with the modern world, because people have changed, but there is one very important thing which I would like to emphasize—kunqu cannot change. It cannot become jingju[95]—the Peking Opera. Kunqu originates from Kunshan, kunqu is Kunshan opera, it cannot be anything else. Because then it will no longer be kunqu. That is my opinion.

Lai fills the cups with tea, nodding, hemming and hawing, then nodding, hemming and hawing again, then he clears his throat and looks deeply into Stein's eyes.

LAI. All of Chinese culture is facing tremendous challenges. I am in charge of this theatre, but I could also say that I am just a lighting technician at the Kunqu Company of Zhejiang Province. However, I do have an opinion, because I think about these things. And I see that it is not only traditional culture that is endangered. I believe that we do not even know now what kind of role culture can play in people's lives. We do not know, no one knows. And there is a great need for this problem to be solved.

We here, and maybe you too, in Europe—maybe everywhere in the world—are living through a very difficult time of economic development. And this era of economic development, in my opinion, presents the gravest of problems for national culture. What happened in Japan after the Second World War? Kabuki went through a very sad epoch, as well as noh. Later on, standards of living improved in Japan and the sense of responsibility towards their national culture arose in them. So there is hope that this will happen with us as well. Right now, it is truly difficult. Today, we do not know how to grant status to culture. For kunqu, this is the most difficult of times. You know, Comrade László, I do not say that there is no hope. Culture in Japan has thrived, and now a ticket for a performance of kabuki or noh is very expensive. A kabuki piece can run for weeks and months. That could happen here as well. But we must be aware of one thing—kunqu will never be a theatre for the masses. Kunqu was always for the few, for the erudite. Now, and perhaps never again, can we wish for young people to come flooding into the kunqu theatre. They envisage entertainment as something and someplace else. This is fine, we cannot deny them this. But we can expect one thing from them—not to deny the culture of their ancestors. At least a few of them.

Stein now asks about his personal life. Mr Lai is silent for a long time; he turns his cigarette around in his hand.

LAI. I originally did not study to be a kunqu actor. Before 1979, I was a part of the Zhejiang Song and Dance Ensemble. I wanted to be a dancer. I studied dance, and my wife studied kunqu at the provincial art college. And in Zhejiang I was very lucky—at that time, they taught dance according to the traditions of the Russian ballet school. They also placed great emphasis on a complex training, so I had to learn kunqu too. So I learnt traditional singing, traditional music, even anatomy. My wife and I had the same master. How did this work? A person had to observe the master, observe the pieces, then imitate the master until, without any instruction, in the recognition of his own personality and among the givens of his own cultivation, he could somehow, step by step, understand *the figure* that had to be created. This is the decisive thing—the comprehension of the figure to be portrayed; the rest is theatrical performance and so on. It helps only partially.

What that figure—which a person will create across an entire life—will be like depends on many things. First, it depends on his age, his talent, his education, his sensitivity and other accidental factors. And an actor, in kunqu, does not simply play a man. As you perhaps know from jingju, from the Peking Opera, there are differing male roles. For us as well there is the xiaosheng, the young man; there is the laosheng, the old man; there is the man with a painted face, the da hualian; the clown, the xiaochou; as well as the wusheng, the warrior. During basic training it doesn't matter what kind of role you are playing or will play, you must learn the most important theatrical abilities. You must learn the theatrical steps, the practice of the 'bent shoulder', the lowering of the long silk sleeve, the basic modes of singing. Everyone learns these. Then if, let us say, you will be a wusheng, from that point on you will complete the training necessary for that set of roles, or if you will be a xiaosheng, you train for that. So we say that the wusheng follows the wusheng master, and the xiaosheng follows the xiaosheng master. And it is always the given master who decides if you are suitable for this group of roles. He picks out his students.

Should it really be imagined as such, that there is really nothing: Neither book, no description, nor secret handbook, nothing at all, just the master?

LAI. The student learns from the master. Naturally, certain pieces have to have their own texts. There are role books as well. And each kunqu drama text contains, of course, dramatic instructions. It looks something like the texts for the noh pieces in Japan. Where, for example, a single book contains the score and the text. In the old days, this was known as the gongchi[96] score.

They have been sitting for more than two hours in this shabby office, listening to this bitter, cheerful person. They make their excuses and, slowly, their farewells, but as Lai leads them out of the office he offers to show them the theatre. He has two rooms at his disposal, which in Europe would serve as a rehearsal room for a studio theatre: at the front is a stage of a few square metres, a spectators' area also of a few square metres by the entrance, for five rows of chairs, and in between certain empty places, the function of which is unclear. Lai jokingly shows them everything they have, it is not too much, he says, still, there's plenty of room for the public, he winks at his visitors with his own bitter serenity, then stops before the pictures on the wall in the miserable, half-lit, chilly corridor, points at them and recites the names of each famous kunqu actor, and finally accompanies them to the front door. They do not leave immediately because they would like to know something.

Mr Lai—Stein leans in close to him—would you permit a confidential question? So much has been said about kunqu, but what does kunqu mean to you, personally? He has been truly moved, Stein says, by what he has heard and what he has seen of the theatre but he has also grown rather sad. Mr Lai—Stein gestures, to the outside. There are so many rich people in the city . . . You could do so many things to make a lot of money . . . You sit here in this office, you take care of the affairs of this poor kunqu theatre, and in the evenings, if there is a performance, you do the lighting. Tell me, why?

LAI. I am a kunqu actor. And I am not completely alone. That is, I speak in the name of those with whom I can say that this is the Kunqu Company of Zhejiang Province. Of course there aren't too many of us, but all of us work for kunqu. And if I say that I am proud of our culture, proud of classical literature, music, painting and of course theatre, then that is true as well. But I believe there is something else. I love kunqu. I love classical culture. And I love China. So what does it matter if I am poor, that I will never have even a penny to my name?

He shakes the hands of his visitors, closes the door after them, turns around and disappears from sight.

The next day they leave Hangzhou.

5. If Forgotten, It Will Be Saved

In their hands is a slip of paper from their friend Tang Xiaodu, and on it is written the eight things they must see if they are really serious, and so they go there; then there is the page in the unbelievably crappy Lonely Planet guide to China from which nothing at all can be discerned about the place they are preparing to visit; nor have they been able to obtain any serious information, from Yang Lian or from Tang Xiaodu or from anyone else, as if all their distant and less distant advisers implicitly wished to talk them out of this destination, so that when they sift through and examine the scanty materials at their disposal on the highway leading to Shaoxing, they take it for granted that Shaoxing will be exactly like Yangzhou, or exactly like Nanjing or Zhenjiang, because why would it be any different, there will be a few monuments in this or that specific stage of restoration, there will be a few dreadful hotels according to this or that woefully starred standard, there will be 10,000 tourists, and everywhere there will be high entrance fees and cheap junk and the swarming masses of vendors, unavoidable and unbearable, in a word, there will be everything; and so their friends try to persuade them that to come here, to Shaoxing, really isn't worth it, they should forget it and go somewhere else, anywhere else, just not here, because not only is there nothing here, there never has been anything interesting here—they, however, go there, Shaoxing is nonetheless the subsequent goal of their trip, Stein has absolutely no idea as to why he is insisting on this so much, why he isn't changing his mind at the last moment, when he could have, in the eastern bus station of Hangzhou, maybe because the sun began to shine?—he really does not know; in any case, there they were in the bus station, standing in line in front of the ticket counter; suddenly the skies, which had been overcast for weeks, cleared up, and the sun came out so quickly it was as if it had been switched on, it began to shine outside, and inside as well, they noticed it while standing in line, because the rays of the sun suddenly burst in, falling obliquely across the glass windows of the bus station, Stein pointed it out to his companion: it was like a bundle of kindling, like a fine, lukewarm rug that spread out before their feet for a couple of minutes, then it withdrew and faded away into the grimy flagstones—in a word, nothing, but nothing else came up which could have influenced his decision, only this sudden sunlight in front of the ticket counter; so he got the ticket on the basis of a feeling, two for Shaoxing, he said, gesticulating, just one way, the interpreter explained from behind him, smiling apologetically when the women at the ticket counter really didn't want to understand why the European with the big nose who knew how to ask for a ticket refused to answer the question: just one way, or round-trip; yes, just one way, one way, he kept repeating when he understood the question; then they got onto the bus, and set off from the single slum in Hangzhou in a southerly direction, and the route was to Shaoxing, the one-time Shanyin, the definitive name of which was settled upon by Emperor Gaozong[9]—in his happiness, as is rumoured, at the victory he had reaped over the Jurchens: Let the name of this place be Shaoxing, he proclaimed, and the imperial clerks were writing it down with their wondrous brushes onto the wondrous imperial documents, let its name be 'Resurgent Prosperity', dictated Gaozong in 1230 CE, and so it became, from then on, the name of the city, to which—for reasons unknown, in the characteristic good cheer of aimless, careless, thoughtless decisions—he became so attached, suddenly, just like the sunshine, explained Stein, but, well—the interpreter asked—What do you want so much in Shaoxing? and Stein just pointed outside, through the bus window, at the sun that was shining, and spoke not a single word, like someone who knew something; he did not, however, know anything, he just kept smiling, and enjoying the warm sunshine after the torturous weeks of cold and dark, enjoying the fact that the sun was shining at all, and warming him up, as he said happily when they arrived and asked enthusiastically, Can you feel it? he asked his companion who also was growing ever-more cheerful, can you feel the warmth?—and, really, it has grown warm, so that when, having picked out a hotel and settled down, they quickly start off towards the city, to Jiefang Bei Lu, they slowly begin to take off the outer items of clothing, at first the raincoats which no longer make any sense, for the pure sky was shining above, then the sneakers, intended for mountain climbing and against the cold, which they have been wearing for the past few weeks, since their arrival in Nanjing and the exasperating experience of the unusual May conditions, so that when they reach the first significant structure near the city centre, both are wearing T-shirts, and to their greatest surprise, as far as the residents of Shaoxing go, all of them are dressed just as lightly, as if it were May; they look around happily, as if it were really finally May here, to the south, quite a distance below the Yangtze. That certain first significant structure is hardly 200 or 300 metres from that point where they had just turned out onto the main street, having left their fairly shabby hotel, and it is not merely significant, but they are at a loss for words, they are struck down, as they find the Dashan pagoda[98]—for this is what they see—in a state of perfection, the seven graceful storeys built from brick still standing, have been standing since 1004 CE; they gape at the walls, originally painted white but, of course, due to the city buses continually passing its perimeter—ornamented at a later date—now nearly completely blackened: it stands, they stretch their necks upward, it stands, in the most beneficial neglect, which means that the Dashan is quite simply a part of life here; this will be immediately clear to them: it is not partitioned off, it is not promulgated, it is not cordoned off, there is no ticket booth out in front, and this is betrayed by the fact that, in addition to the bus routes passing right by, the local youth—possibly coming here from the outskirts of the city—have scribbled all over the inner walls, and that these youths, judging by this, possibly spend their evenings here as well, perhaps stroll around here on those evenings or those days, because there is no fence nor is there a doorway on the ground floor, only four openings in the octag-onal ground plan where the entrances would be, so one can go in and out freely, everyone, including the local youths from the outskirts of the city, who, without the slightest idea of what they are doing, have scribbled all over the walls—until someone will dare to say out loud, beneath these dense scrawls, what has been carved into the plaster:

namely, that the Dashan pagoda has remained a part of everyday life, and, looking at the walls, that this everyday life is full of all kinds of dangers, it has remained a part of this life, they determine, and it withstands those words on its walls just as it withstands the grime of the filthy exhaust fumes from the immediate area, it withstands the fact that anyone can go inside and anyone can roar past at full speed, just as it has withstood, for the past thousand years, how the outer precincts—with its crude emissaries and its grimy and stinking buses—have permeated within and rumbled alongside it, for a thousand years. They go on, and over the next few days they visit everything listed on the piece of paper pressed into their hands at the eastern bus station of Hangzhou when they said goodbye to the friend of Tang Xiaodu: they go to the house where Lu Xun, the great reformer, was born, then to where Lu Xun later lived, and finally to the private school where Lu Xun finished his grade school studies at the end of the Imperial era; they visit the atelier of Xu Wei,[99] the Ming-era painter, they take the No. 3 bus to the Orchid Pavilion of Wang Xizhi,[100] they look at the imperial tomb of the Yue Kingdom,[101] recently excavated and to this day the only proof of its existence, then they take the No. 2 bus and look at the presumed burial place of King Yu,[102] the legendary water conservationist, they go up to the roof of the Song-era Yingtian pagoda[103] in the city centre, they stroll through the living alleyways of the city densely interwoven with canals, they examine everything, they look at everything, they go to all the places on the list, and then they lie down in their beds in the hotel at the end of one day or another because, although they are dead tired, they cannot sleep, for they simply cannot believe on the first, on the second or on the following days—although, it is obvious from the very first instant—that Shaoxing has been forgotten, that Shaoxing has been left out of the Great Modern Revival, it has been decided that Shaoxing is not needed—that Shaoxing is intact, that Shaoxing has remained: a very poor, an enchanting, a left-behind, peaceful and modest stratum from the past, sunken into quiet provinciality, Shaoxing has remained, even if it is difficult to determine—as they try every evening in the hotel room—exactly which stratum of the past it is; because when they were outside by Chi Brook, in the valley of Kuaiji Mountain,[104] south-west of the city, where they spent a half day in the shrubbery garden of the Orchid Pavilion of Wang Xizhi, the greatest calligrapher of all times, giving themselves over to the nearly natural tranquillity of the unforgettable beauty preserved on the steles commemorating the mountain, the brook and a former poetry competition of world renown,[105] they felt that Shaoxing irrevocably belonged to the fourth century. But on the following day, when they again visited the buildings associated with Lu Xun, and were enchanted by that noble simplicity of Chinese tradition created by the internal order—maintained until the great downfall—of the noble houses in the provincial small towns south of the Yangtze, then they said, no, Shaoxing was the seat of China before its downfall. And it was like that afterward too—if they were in the tiny studio of Xu Wei, with its delightful garden, then they felt that everything had come to a standstill in the Ming dynasty; if every afternoon, as it faded into evening, they walked, until they were exhausted, along the alleyways lurking alongside the narrow little canals, if, on these narrow streets, they mixed in with the thronging multitudes, if during these strolls their hearts stopped at one or another sight, so that they were not able to move on in the crowd for minutes—for example, they could not bear to stop looking at an old man who came out of the door of his wretched little house in his underwear and T-shirt, carrying a wash basin filled with water, because he did not wish to splash around inside, or because inside it would have been too small for splashing around, he began his evening wash, amid the people thronging here and there, and thoroughly, from head to toe, as if he were outside completely alone: that day they had to say that that man with his wash basin had come from the Qing dynasty, and when he finished, he dried himself off with the towel and went back inside— and it was always like that, that is how things were in Shaoxing, because everywhere they went something perpetually occurred that stopped them in their tracks: another time they watched, amid a group of old people, near the mausoleum of King Yu, a performance of an itinerant opera society; they came upon it completely by chance; afterward, these old people from the neighbourhood—as the last aria died away, and the actors began to disassemble the stage—they quickly picked up their chairs, put them on their backs and, bent a little under their weight but with, what was, for Stein and the interpreter, unforgettable tranquillity, they began to trudge home in the twilight; yet another time they observed the smaller landing piers of the narrow, oblong-shaped water vessels, half-canopied and covered with tar—originally used for transporting cargo, they somehow seemed more like transporters of souls, and so they referred to them as 'death gondolas', and they realized that the sculler lads were looking at them as if they were not used to foreigners, that is, every single day, every single hour they experienced something that brought them joy, the profound recognition of which could be formulated by saying that Shaoxing lives but its life is not connected to the year of the second millennium, not even to the twentieth century, but to the China of old in which, from King Yu until the late Qing dynasty, somehow everything is there simultaneously—and in wholeness, the interpreter says, now having decided to put off their departure, to remain one more day, they set off into the city, but now they do not want to see anything new, only the grave of King Yu and the Orchid Pavilion and the Dashan and the houses of Lu Xun and the scullers and the atelier of Xu Wei again and again, they do not want anything new now, only the old, the things they know already, they traverse the same little streets over and over again, and then one day they are struck by the feeling that they have begun to step in those same places as if they were at home, they nearly begin to turn a corner without looking, as if they do not need to think what is there where they are going—and then Stein says to the interpreter: Time to go, they must pack up, they leave, finally depart, take their backpacks and disappear, but never, never should they speak of this place to anyone, nor should they be silent about it too conspicuously, but they must faultlessly conceal the fact, they must perfectly dissimulate, so that no one will ever realize— that Shaoxing exists.

6. Redemption Omitted

Standing amid the natural beauty of Tiantai Mountain[106] is the Guoqing Si monastery,[107] founded during the Sui dynasty; it takes its name from the mountain and belongs to the Tiantai school as well. The Tiantai school was established by an extraordinary individual, a monk by the name of Zhiyi,[108] who—with the help of a particular doctrine, according to which everything in the world is of equal significance, and this equal significance is comprised of minuscule elements all containing the Buddha—recommended an unusual solution to the problem of Chinese Buddhism, already in profound crisis at the time of the early Sui dynasty: how to trace the confusing multiplicity of the remaining texts, often diametrically opposed in meaning, back to the Buddha's actual words. Zhiyi regarded the sacred writings of the Hinayana[109] and Mahayana[110] as connected to various epochs of the Buddha's life and expressing various stages of his teachings. Hence he put all the sacred writings translated into Chinese at that point into chronological order and, connecting them to concrete points in the life of the Buddha, ultimately laid particular stress on one, the Lotus Sutra, as the sutra most deeply expressive of the Buddha's thoughts. So it was Zhiyi who was the first to attempt to standardize the scattered variations of Buddhism; in the meantime, he tried to make peace among the different contending schools of thought, as if the question weighed heavily upon him as to whether there could ever be a way to have some presentiment of what the Buddha might have said and thought—in reality. For very many, this remains an insoluble problem: the Buddha's words were put into writing only several centuries after they were heard. Coming close to that place, where Zhiyi lived, and aware that the founder of the distant fraternal sect, Saicho,[111] who established the Tendai[112] school in Japan, lived here in the ninth century so as to study the spirit and the teachings of Zhiyi, László Stein and his interpreter arrive at this mountain in the hope that chance will lead them to a monk in the monastery with whom they can clear up the question.

So stepping into the inner courtyard of the Guoqing Si, they do not hesitate for long. They address the first young monk they see, and without hesitation ask him if he would have the time and the disposition to talk to them. He gestures for them to wait and then goes off somewhere. Not long afterward he returns, motioning for them to follow. Fate has not made it possible for him to be able to converse with them. Fate has led them to one of the directors of the monastery, Abbot Pinghui. They end up in an office crammed with people coming and going, where Stein is seated in an easy chair and the interpreter in a plain wooden one next to him, slightly to the back. A

cell phone is constantly ringing; someone picks it up, perhaps a secretary, says something quickly, then puts it down. But it rings again.
And it rings almost constantly as they sit there in the armchair and
the wooden chair, it rings eternally while they hope that Stein will
be able to get a sympathetic response from the person who is slowly
lowering himself into an armchair, padded with heavy blankets,
across him.

A middle-aged, serious, severe and, as it quickly emerges, busy
person sits across him wearing the orange robes of a monk and enormous metal-framed glasses. His glance is penetrating. During the
introductions, which the interpreter transmits in a rather moved state,
he does not cease gazing at Stein. Nor does Stein cease gazing at him.

Stein begins by saying that the reason he has made this long
journey to Guoqing Si is not because of some kind of poetic task, as
one could think due to his occupation. He does not wish to write
any kind of poetry here: it is not poetry at all that he is engaged with
but altogether another question, a question which is for so many the
most troubling or the most tormenting, and to which he hopes to
obtain an answer from the abbot.

Once again the din strikes up in the room, the telephone rings,
someone runs out, someone else runs in. Stein stops speaking, the
interpreter looks at him, confused, what should he translate, but Stein
cannot continue, because as he looks into this pair of eyes in the midst
of this chaos, he suddenly understands that he has either come at the
wrong time or that he will always come at the wrong time, so he must
put an end to it now, even before he begins, because these two eyes,
the gaze of the abbot of Guoqing Si, in spite of all the implacability
of this being, is, in reality, impatient. Stein wants to stand up, wishing

only to say that even to have met the abbot is a tremendous experience and, as he sees that he is busy, he will ask him another time. Perhaps he will come back later, on another occasion.

But the abbot, with a gesture that brooks no dissent, motions to the interpreter.

PINGHUI. Absolutely not. I am listening.

Stein is now completely certain that they must leave. He thanks him very much, he says, but asks the abbot to tell him if he does not have time for a more tranquil discussion . . .

PINGHUI. No, just say it. Say it.

Stein remains seated, trying to find the right words, if after all there might be some hope of a discussion. He starts with numerous courteous formulae, and relates to the abbot, as is necessary on each occasion, by way of introduction, who he is, what he wants, what he is looking for here and what he has not found. He has attempted to seek out every remaining Buddhist temple and monastery. And he is appalled by what is going on so often in these temples and monasteries. Everything reeks of money. High entrance fees are collected— entrance fees! At the gates, impossible things are for sale, fake rubbish, the basest religious kitsch, the faithful are made to throw money into the collection box, and in the evening they spill it out and count it up nicely and accurately, they count up the takings . . . ! And these are not simple vendors but monks . . . ! Venerable abbot, László Stein involuntarily lowers his head, this is so sad.

PINGHUI. Zhiyi was the founding father of the creation of our temple. After he died in 597, his body was buried here. That is why the centre of our faith is here.

Stein looks at the interpreter: What is going on here?—but the interpreter indicates that he is translating exactly what the abbot is saying. Stein tries to interrupt but the abbot does not let the interpreter get a word in; clearly, he views all interruptions as impossible.

PINGHUI. Zhiyi lived here, and there is a sutra, the Lianhua Jing or the Lotus Sutra which he studied with extraordinary profundity, and it was upon this sutra that he established everything that . . .

A cell phone rings again. Abbot Pinghui stops speaking, looks at the secretary, nods once, and the secretary hands him the phone.

PINGHUI. Hello. Yes, that's fine . . . No problem. If they come, we can talk.

He gives the phone back to the secretary who ends the call. Stein does not continue, and the abbot does not expect him to. He looks at him penetratingly, like someone trying to find his way back to his train of thought, then he pushes the glasses further up the bridge of his nose.

PINGHUI. Yes. The Guoqing Si, namely, the monastery of the Tiantai school, was built after the death of Zhiyi.

Stein raises his voice just perceptibly and says that perhaps there is a misunderstanding, perhaps due to the difficulties of translation, he does not know, but his question refers to something completely different—he wants to talk about how the meeting with the figure of Saicho and the Japanese Tendai school led Zhiyi to the idea of seeking out the place where it all began, and with the abbot's permission . . .

The abbot does not permit. He motions to the interpreter not to speak.

PINGHUI. Yes. That's what I'm saying. Not only Japanese but also
Korean monks arrived here. Even during the Sui dynasty,
there were Korean monks studying here. During the Tang era,
Jianzhen, who had turned up here, first brought the news of our
religion to Japan. Jianzhen studied here. His teacher was Hanyin.
We venerate Hanyin as the most significant figure of the third
generation to follow Zhiyi. Hanyin's teacher was Master Zhan'en.
Well, Jianzhen had acquainted all his monk companions with the
numerous sutras he collected before he reached Japan. As a result,
the Japanese monks began their pilgrimage. The most important
event occurred in 803, when Saicho arrived and began studying.
Later, he founded the Tiantai school in Japan. Saicho spent about
11 years here. But Kobo Daishi, another great Japanese Buddhist,
the founder of the Shingon school, also turned up here. During
the entire Tang era, innumerable Japanese monks came to us, at
least two-thirds of all the Japanese monks. This indicates the significance of the Tiantai monastery in Japanese Buddhism.

Stein gives up and, deferring to the abbot, tries to proceed in the
direction he is offering. He—lowering his head again—is very preoccupied with the figure of Zhiyi. In Zhiyi, he esteems that singular
figure, the very first to confront the question of what we can accept
as belonging to the Buddha's original teachings . . . The abbot, as
soon as he hears this, immediately cuts short the interpreter.

PINGHUI. This comprises exactly the most important sutras of our
school. Apart from the aforementioned Lotus Sutra, we should
include the Daban Niepan Jing,[113] the Dazhidu Lun[114] and the
Zhongguan Lun.[115] Zhiyi was the first to collect the essential
sutras, and then later, in his footsteps, the great figures of the

Tiantai school created the *Sandabu* or *The Three Major Commentaries* and the *Wuxiaobu* or *The Five Minor Texts*. The first part of the *Sandabu* is the most important for us.

There is something else which I must say to you. And I will say it now. In the beginning, there were greater differences of opinion between the northern and the southern Buddhists, theological differences of opinion. The northern Buddhists emphasized continual, persistently practised immersion, the unbroken meditation of ever-deeper concentration, the conviction that this lasting immersion, this persistent meditation would one day bring forth its own fruit, and that the monk, at the end of a long continuum, would reach nirvana. In contrast, the southern Buddhists believed they had found their leading principle exclusively in the sudden experience of the essential: they thought that nirvana could only be reached in an unexpected, irrational moment, one that cannot be prepared for. This is the significance of Master Zhiyi—he formulated the essence of this differentiation and combined the two schools. (*The abbot writes on a piece of paper*) The teachings of the southern Buddhists, who emphasize only sudden experience, is called chan ding,[116] whereas the tendency of the northern Buddhists is called zhi hui.[117] As you can see, each of these concepts is made up of two expressions. Master Zhi En used one character from each, thus expressing that the essence of unity is the equality of access of both the theoretical and the practical. He called this ding hui.[118] And this is how he wrote it . . .

He encircles, from each of the two words, the characters for ding and hui, then draws an arrow pointing downward and writes the new word: ding hui.

At that point, however, from the other side of the office, on a desk piled high with papers, a cell phone begins to ring: with a long drawn-out jingling, it shouts to be picked up. Finally the young secretary-like monk picks it up, then, putting it down, says something to the abbot who motions to him to bring it over.

PINGHUI. Hello? . . . Yes . . . 16 pieces . . . good . . . How many?! OK, fine. So, Thursday?

He gives back the cell phone. He looks at Stein, scrutinizing him at length again, and suddenly continues his thoughts.

PINGHUI. Zhiyi was an extraordinarily important person. Since the time of Shakyamuni Buddha, there were innumerable tendencies operating in the name of Buddhism, and order had to be created among them. We can regard the activities of Zhiyi as that turning point after which it was possible to attempt to find unity among the variations. He was the one who indicated the path towards the determinations of the wuji bajiao.[119] Whoever, after Zhiyi, perceived and taught Buddhism within the unity of this guidance was able to easily find his own way and method.

The great problem is—Stein tries to direct the abbot closer to his own question—what is the so-called correct approach to the teachings of the Buddha . . .

PINGHUI. Master Zhiyi summarized the remaining utterances of the teachings of the Buddha and classified them into five time periods and eight stages. The Buddha taught for 49 years. His teachings are immeasurably deep, so that if someone studies this through the system summarized by Zhiyi, he has a chance at reaching the correct approach. That is why we consider Master Zhiyi to be so great.

But how did Master Zhiyi arrive at the thought that there was a contradiction—to put it delicately—between the original teachings of the Buddha and the confusing variegation of Buddhist literature?

PINGHUI. There is no contradiction. At the very beginning, the Tiantai school came into being. Later on, only the Chan school was in operation. If, however, we look at the teachings of the Tiantai after this development, then we can state that the Tiantai also employs the knowledge of Chan. We must hold Chan in great esteem, because the Chan teachings were directly contained in the original teachings of the Buddha. The situation of today is such that, according to the teachings practised by the Tiantai, Chan and the theoretical basis are mutually complementary. The Chan sect does not respect this, and acknowledges only the experience of Chan. According to their school, it is not necessary to write down anything, the sutras have no significance. Chan has not left behind any writing.

There is no point to the conversation. Various people rush about the office, the cacophony is great. All the while, however, the abbot doesn't move, as if awaiting further questions—Stein must decide where to go from here. It occurs to him that well, they could talk about what daily life was like in this renowned monastery. Venerable Abbot, he asks, Zhiyi lived here. The monastery was built only after his death. So where did he live? In a cave? Was there some kind of building here already during the life of Zhiyi, which then became the foundation of the monastery? And in general: What was Zhiyi's life like? Moreover, if it is possible to ask: How did he spend his days?

But there is no hope that this cleric of great authority will ever give a reply to anything he is asked, and it occurs to Stein that there might be some difficulty with the translation, or some misunder-standing due to the dialect. The interpreter signals that he should not worry—whatever the abbot says is being faithfully translated.

PINGHUI. We wake up at three-thirty. This is followed by prayers in the temple until five-thirty. Then there is breakfast, then each monk attends to his own tasks: some read sutras, some meditate, some look after the affairs of the monastery, some take care of the hall. Lunch is at ten-thirty. From one o'clock to four-thirty the same schedule is followed. Evening prayers begin at five-fifteen. After that there is reading of sutras, meditation, each according to his own preference. In the monastery we also main-tain a Buddhist school where, for the most part, we teach the Tiantai doctrines as well as general Buddhist theory.

Stein attempts a kind of forced joking phrase, and interrupts, asking: So do they go to sleep today at the same time as in the time of Zhiyi? The joke elicits a very pale response, because the abbot smiles for a moment but then—as if the smile had been cut in two—that mercilessly administrative severity returns to his gaze.

PINGHUI. Generally, after seven . . . Ah, no, excuse me that's wrong, around eight-thirty or nine . . .

Stein is thinking: What would happen if he would just overlook everything? If he would just ignore the fact that the abbot visibly does not want to talk about why they have sought him out. He speaks to the interpreter softly: Tell the abbot that he, Stein, is not interested in any of this. But ask him, and don't let him not reply—would he take into consideration what is troubling Stein, what is oppressing him, what is making him feel that he is ruined—would the abbot listen to him then? Would he help him to solve this? Would he help him to find an answer? Would he let him into the monastery? Would he take him in here among the young monks? Is there a possibility of this? How does someone join the order here? How does it work?

PINGHUI. It's possible.

Stein has no idea why he got an answer to his question this time. Emboldened, he continues, and asks: How does this work? What are the conditions? Can anyone come? He, Stein, could also stand in front of the gates, wait for three days, get drenched in the rain, not eat, then on the third day the gates will open, they will let him in, and . . .

Pinghui raises his hand, silencing the interpreter.

PINGHUI. To begin with, there are three strict requirements: the applicant must be a believer, he cannot be involved in a court case, and we demand permission from the parents. If all this is in order, then there is a trial period of six months. We say that he can be a monk here whose 'eyes and nose . . . are in their place'.

And then, if these conditions are met and the six months are up?

PINGHUI. After six months we have a look, to see if all the conditions have been met—if so, we cut the novice's hair. Then comes the shoujie,[120] then the phase of biqiu[121] for the men and biqiuni[122] for the women.

Stein is completely emboldened, because suddenly it's as if they were really talking about something. Spurred on by a sudden idea, he says to the abbot that he has met with so many people in China, and he has always observed the forms of courtesy demanded by this country. Here, however, in this Buddhist temple, he does not consider this to be requisite. May he count on the understanding of the abbot? And may he say why he has come?

The face of Pinghui does not flinch for a second. He listens to the words of the interpreter without interrupting. He is thinking.

PINGHUI. Moments of prayer, when the believer stands in front of the Buddha with a pure soul, are extraordinarily important occasions. We have our festivals. For example, we commemorate the birth and death of Master Zhiyi, and every three years we have the Jiangjing festival lasting several days. Then, on the fifteenth day of the seventh lunar month, there is the Yulan fenghui[123] . . .

They have fallen back to that place where they keep falling: Stein is unexpectedly seized by an embittered audacity. He doesn't know what has suddenly come over him but, waiting after each sentence for the interpreter to render his words into Chinese, he takes no notice of what the abbot has just said and tells him what he thinks: that since he has arrived at this monastery, there has been deep sorrow in his heart. The interpreter stares at Stein. He tells the interpreter, if he can, to translate word for word. He has been full of pain, he continues, because what is important to him, the spirit of Chinese classical culture, its beauty, its strength, has disappeared—it disappeared a long time ago. Because for years he deluded himself that there was a point to his own research here, in modern China, and that he didn't want to acknowledge how ridiculous it was, how truly pathetic.

The question never really gets to Pinghui, at least not in the form of words, because he's already waving down the interpreter, this time clearly in great impatience when he gets to the part of Stein's statement which deals with classical culture. Stein is convinced that the abbot knows full well, in fact knows with dead certainty what he is saying; moreover, that he knows, even without words, what Stein wants.

PINGHUI. In my opinion, classical culture has not vanished at all. Once again, you can see the buildings, paintings and calligraphy, all from the classical tradition and now restored—from that I draw the conclusion that this culture is still alive. There are the traditional ceremonies as well. These too have remained, even if in a somewhat different form. In the Japanese tea ceremony, the outward forms are the most important. For the Koreans, the taste of the tea is essential as well as the ceremony. In Chinese culture, tea drinking as a tradition has remained but without the formalities. So I would express it by saying that there is no ceremony, no formalities, but there is the inner content, there is prayer.

Venerable Abbot, Stein raises his voice—the clamour in the room abates for an instant—he, Stein, cannot believe what he is hearing! Does he really think that the feelings of the monks of recent times, this inner content, more important than anything else, has remained unharmed? Does he really think that the souls of the ones who live here now are the same as they were in the days of old? His, Stein's, opinion is radically different. He thinks, says Stein—with clearly unforgivable discourtesy, he leans closer to the abbot—it's not that these monks of today with their cell phones and their businesses aren't like the monks from the Sui dynasty. Simply put, their hearts are not the same.

Pinghui doesn't budge an inch, he doesn't even adjust his eyeglasses which have slid down his nose a bit.

PINGHUI. There is an expression, suiyuan, which means something like 'according to predestination', 'according to fate'. During the Sui dynasty, Buddhists lived according to the suiyuan of their time. Today they live according to the suiyuan of our time. The form is different but the essence is unchanged.

So why is it—Stein spreads his hands apart helplessly—that his impressions are so different? Is it because he is European? But, well, Venerable Abbot, he says, lowering his voice this time, everything that occurs in the name of rebuilding the temples, everything that Stein has spoken of so far—the chase after money, even allowing money into the inner world of the monasteries at all, the deluge of tourists and the tourist industry based on that deluge, fully integrated into temple life, all this . . .

Pinghui cuts off his monologue.

PINGHUI. The monks study the same things today, the ding hui and the wuji bajiao. In the modern world, Taoism operates in a similar fashion. We use different words than the Taoists but we are searching for the same thing. That has not changed.

Stein leans back in the easy chair. He has seen the cities, he has walked along the streets, and here is a world which unfortunately he knows all too well. The supermarkets, the mega shopping centres—on the one hand, the fever to buy, and, on the other, the fever to sell, the desire to possess things, the empty rhythms in the temples. Venerable Abbot, he says to him confidentially, as if there were some kind of basis for this confidentiality—he, Stein sees the opposite of what the abbot has just said, that formally everything does proceed in the same way before the altars of the temples, but the inner essence has completely been lost . . .

The abbot adjusts his eyeglasses.

PINGHUI. In the schools, the study of classical culture is accorded an ever-greater role. Here, for example, in the Buddhist schools, we teach the classical Chinese language and the culture of the pre-Qing dynasty. The culture of the Song and Tang dynasties. Here, for example, we teach *Lunyu*,[124] *Yijing*,[125] *Zhuangzi*,[126] *Mengzi*[127] and *Laozi*.[128]

Stein says that this is indeed very praiseworthy, but what kind of effect does it have on what goes on in the monastery courtyards? And on the soul of a monk?

PINGHUI. The goal of classical culture—and within it, Buddhism— is to help people avoid the three evils. These three evils are in a person, and they remain, no matter how much development there is. Only with the help of tradition can we vanquish them.

Venerable Abbot—Stein lowers his voice, and leans towards him across the table as much as he can—he sees that there is a serious obstacle to their discussion. He knows he should get up, he knows it is time to go but he tries one last time, so he says: Yes, he will try one more time, one last time, to say why fate brought him here . . . A long time ago, many years ago, he was drawn more and more to everything the historical Buddha could have uttered. This unequalled perspective became ever-more important to him from one year to the next. He would have liked to have studied it, he says to the abbot, almost whispering now, to get closer to it, to turn over the pages of the *Tripitaka*,[129] but he began to ask people about it and he never got closer to the original thoughts of the Buddha but to the original teachings of Buddhism. And here, he felt was a dramatic tension. As is well known, the Buddha never wrote down his teachings. Despite all the refined, and unparalleled, techniques of oral transmission, what emerged later on were actually translations—into Pali and Sanskrit, respectively, later on into Chinese and Tibetan, then into Korean and finally into Japanese. The question concerns him very deeply—he looks at the abbot with those two sincere eyes—and he asks for help:

Where can someone find the right approach to lead him to the Buddha's original train of thought?

PINGHUI. It's true that the Buddha never wrote down his teachings but after his death, at the time of the First Council, his most loyal disciple, Ananda,[130] faithfully quoted the words of the Buddha at the council's request. The council asked Ananda to say them again, word by word. And then they were noted down, and from that came the Buddhist canon. This cannot be doubted.

In Stein, however, the doubts are huge. As far as he knows, the story about Ananda's words being written down is of far later vintage than the period immediately following Buddha's death; and the Buddha's words were not written down for the first time then, actually not until the first century before the Common Era. And it wasn't in Magadhi, the language in which these words had sounded from the Buddha's mouth, but a translation, into Pali and Sanskrit. It is unimaginable that everything that the Buddha said would not have been damaged, perhaps fundamentally! If one thinks of Mahayana Buddhism, Stein explains, innumerable elements differ radically from the material registered in the *Tripitaka*—which Stein particularly reveres as well.

Pinghui leans back wearily. The words of his visitor have clearly had no effect on him. They have no effect at present, nor will they in the future, Stein realizes, when the abbot begins to speak.

PINGHUI. Everything that has been put into writing in the canon, from the first words to the last, is as uttered by the Buddha. Both the Hinayana and the Mahayana schools go back to the original statements of the Buddha. It is like that.

Venerable Abbot, Stein points out to him despondently, the most important sutra of the Tiantai school, the Lotus Sutra, was not uttered by the Buddha, this is a Buddhist work from later, centuries later . . .

PINGHUI. Yes, but what it contains, its spirit—that is the original.

It is now patently obvious to everyone in the room that this European has transgressed every last rule of courtesy and is engaging in something everyone knows to be proscribed. He—the European—considers, however, that he should keep on and that he should disagree with what the abbot is saying. The Buddhist literature is very rich, he does not deny this for a moment. But it is completely clear, that these teachings—with the formation as Shakyamuni as a deity, the appearance of other buddhas,[131] the permission of the depiction of the figure of the Buddha, originally forbidden, with the introduction of prayer and so on—are very distant from what the Buddha could have thought and said.

The abbot is now at his most severe.

PINGHUI. The original teachings of the Buddha are in the Agama Sutra. The four Agama Sutras.[132] And in the Lotus Sutra, the Mahaparinirvana Sutra as well as in the Mahaprajnaparamita Sutra[133]. . .

On the desk near the window an old telephone rings. It jingles, then stops for a moment, then rings again, but no one picks it up. Stein doesn't speak, the abbot doesn't speak, the interpreter is in the grip of the most profound embarrassment. Then the cell phone begins to ring and, while no one is interested in the telephone on the desk—even though there are four or five people in the office—the secretary wordlessly hands the cell phone to the abbot.

PINGHUI. Yes. Thank you, thank you . . . No! Absolutely not—16 will be enough . . . Thank you . . . I said Thursday. Goodbye.

They are standing up in the office, Stein is helping the interpreter with his heavy backpack, and then his companion helps him with his. There they stand, two heavy, unhappy backpacks in the doorway. And at last the abbot finishes his phone call.

Venerable Abbot—Stein bows to him—he and his interpreter will not take up any more of his precious time. Would he kindly allow them to express their thanks for having received them? Now they are departing, as they have not yet seen the temple. There are leaving, he says to the abbot and they shall seek further.

Pinghui is not surprised by their departure. He seems somewhat relieved. He nods with cold ceremony.

PINGHUI. Take your time. Just go ahead and seek.

They walk around the monastery.

The bus which will take them down from the mountain leaves every hour.

They board the very next one, and leave Tiantai.

7. The Invisible Library

There, where River Fenghua converges with River Yao, and flows towards the nearby ocean under the name of River Yong, there is a city of approximately 6 million souls, renowned for its industry, and its harbour which in former times played a highly significant role in China's relations with Japan. All Stein's friends, left behind in Beijing, don't understand why Stein wants to go there, there is really no point, they admonish him, even Tang Xiaodu, who directs their every move with his own mysterious and benevolent attention, has nothing to say when they tell him that their next stop will be Ningbo, they don't get a response to their email, even if here, as nearly everywhere else, someone is waiting for them: a friend from Tang Xiaodu's wide circle of acquaintances, a dear woman writer named Rong Rong and her friend Jiang Yuqing—who makes them think of a half-asleep, clumsy and awkward little owl—who both immediately take them, after their arrival, to a Ningbo radically different from what they were expecting, because they are taken to the magnificent temple A Yu Wang Si[134] (originally named after the great Indian Buddhist ruler Ashoka), into the age of the Sui dynasty, where a piece of the Buddha's skull is preserved; because they are taken to the greatest and the most captivating Chan Buddhist temple, into the fourth century, towards the Tiantong Chan Si,[135] at the foot of Taipei Mountain[136]—and in the meantime they are fed with an unbelievable amount of genuine southern Chinese food, lunches and evening meals follow one another, the guests, in the surging and eminently congenial company of writers and poets, are giddy with happiness, in a convivial and alluring rusticity, far away from everything that is the world, far away from everything that they want to be far away from.

The greatest surprise of all is held in reserve for the very last moment, a surprise with which they are truly dazzled, even if from this dazzled state they must awaken to bitter sadness. On the day of their departure, the two Europeans are taken to Tianyi Ge, the renowned Ming-era private library, and things are arranged so that the director himself—a thin, tall, serious, learned young man— receives them. Gong Liefei leads the visitors through a gate, turns here and there with them, opens doors before them, then closes doors after them until, at last, they find themselves in a wondrous Ming-era reception hall, among wonderful curved furniture and beauteous paintings. The director has Stein sit in one of the places of honour in the middle of the hall, he sits on the other side while the interpreter and Rong Rong, who is accompanying them, sit off to the side. Stein cannot speak for a few minutes, so surprised is he by all this pomp, so unbelievable is it, that here, in the middle of nowhere, this exists, and he gazes, moved at the person who sits next to him, clearing his throat and waiting for him to ask the first question.

Stein begins by saying: Before one arrives in Ningbo, one gets the sense that even birds don't fly here. His Chinese friends kept asking him why he was going to Ningbo. There's no culture there at all, only wealth, trade, industry and a harbour. What he, Stein, is looking for, never even got there. It's the real South, there isn't anything there— end of story—and there never was. And then all around this city, Stein continues enthusiastically, fantastic monuments, temples! Now, however, he says, inclining his head upward, here he sits in a gigantic museum, namely, the most particular of museums, because this is the museum of books, as he hears and has read: the oldest private library in China. How did this garden, comprised of wondrous buildings, end up here? How did a private library end up here at all?

In the director is something of the schoolboy who has prepared his homework well. Breathing in deeply like a pupil, he starts the lesson, recited so many times before, with self-assurance.

GONG. As you are aware, this is China's oldest private library. It was built in the Jiajing[137] years of the Ming era. It was created by a government official from Ningbo, the deputy minister of defence. When he was 50, he returned to the region of his birth and he founded this private library. At the time of his death, there were 70,000 volumes here. These are comprised of two main collections. One contains the so-called local historical records—the historical chronicles pertaining to individual locales during the Ming and previous eras. The other is comprised of the archive of examinations. In imperial China, the examinees strived to reach the rank of jinshi[138]—'presented scholar'—and whoever gained this rank could become an official. This is known as 'distinction through examination'. And all the successful examination materials, the examination papers were archived. Thirty-five per cent of the Ming-era local historical chronicles are preserved in our library. As for the archive of examinations, 90 per cent of all the collections are located here. Among them are very many unique specimens, which means that there is only one in the entire world.

Here, in Ningbo?

GONG. Yes, here, in Ningbo. Due to this enormous value, we here at Tianyi Ge enjoy institutional cultural protection of higher significance, as proclaimed by the state. In all Asia, we are first among the private libraries.

Stein politely makes enquiries as to when exactly the library was founded.

GONG. Our archive is 440 years old, and from its founding has operated continually, without interruption. Of course, the Tianyi Ge of today is larger than it was then—even considering that of the 638 volumes lent to the Qianlong[139] Siku Quanshu, only a mere fraction, despite the court's promises, were returned to us, and thanks to the horrendous chaos and devastation which the Tianyi Ge, along with China, had to withstand during the catastrophic nineteenth and twentieth centuries, at the beginning of the 1950s, only 13,000 of the original 70,000 items remained. A remarkably fruitful collection effort has been underway since that time, however, and, thanks to local benefactors, we now have more than 300,000 volumes worth of material. Each a classical, original work, not a contemporary reprint but a woodblock print, bound in traditional Chinese fashion, fabricated from paper, printed without punctuation.

Stein is curious about how the library has been able to remain in existence. So many wars, fires, historical or family conflicts . . .

    GONG. Our library has been able to remain in existence for such a long time because it was preserved, and is preserved, in a particular fashion.

It is clear that there is a choreography to the the answers—determined in advance—so that, while maintaining the requirements of politeness, Stein tries to shift their conversation to the questions that interest him. So for the first time he interrogates the director about how the whole thing came about. At the time, was it common for a government official to found his own private library? What would have been his considerations? How exactly was this library formed?

    GONG. Well, now a little family story is in order: the owner of the collection, Fan Qin, divided his estate in two. One son could choose the library whereas the other could choose 10,000 silver liang[140] as a monetary inheritance. The father mandated that whoever got the library could not get the silver, and whoever got the silver could not get anything from the library. The books had to be kept together. And so it remained, and from that time onward, no matter what happened to the family, they were not allowed to divide up the books. Finally the entire collection was qualified as a common family fortune, the collective and unanimous responsibility for which applied to all, in such a way that while every branch of the Fan family had a key to the library, it could only be opened if the entire family was present. Or, for example, there existed a law which applied only to the Fans, stating that anyone from this clan who transgressed the rules concerning the library would be excluded from the right to be worshipped in the Hall of the Ancients—and in feudal China, there could hardly be worse punishment. Well, with these kinds of mandates, they succeeded in keeping the collection together for more than 400 years. There were other measures taken too. For example, it was not allowed to take the books away under any circumstance—not only was it forbidden to sell them but also to loan them. Then, every year, after the rainy season, every single item in the library had to be cleaned, aired out, the pages turned and, if necessary, dried out.

To keep a library intact: What does that mean exactly?

GONG. We are in Ningbo, and this is south-east Asia, where half the year is the dry season, and the other half the rainy season. It's called the mildew season. Every year, when it comes to an end, many people have to make sure that the doors and windows are opened wide, the rooms aired out and the mildew removed. Today of course there's air-conditioning, a ventilation system, shades to protect from light, dust guards as well as protection against insects, but in the old days other means had to be employed. For example, there was a plant, the yuncao. Although a medicinal plant, it proved to be excellent at deterring vermin, chiefly the woodworm, as well as in protecting paper from being damaged by moisture. A piece of this plant was placed between the leaves of every book.

Where? At the beginning? In the middle? At the end?

GONG. Anywhere. Between any two pages. They had another method: a white lotus petal had to be put somewhere into the book, it didn't matter where, and then the insects didn't chew it up . . .

Why is the library called Tianyi Ge?

GONG. The name originates from a well-known sentence from the
Yijing: 'Heaven first creates water,' in Chinese: 'Tian yi sheng
shui.' The word 'ge' means pavilion. The reason for the choice
of the first two characters of this renowned sentence is that
though many dangers lay in wait for the books, the greatest
danger was always fire. Accordingly, word for word, 'Tianyi Ge'
means 'Heaven-first pavilion'. A Chinese person, hearing the
first two characters 'tian yi', will immediately think of the quoted
line from the *Yijing*, and immediately realize that the granting
of this name is in itself a way of referring to the importance of
protection from fire, fire as an enemy, that is, the necessity of the
protection of water.

What should be understood by the designation of 'private library'
here? Does it contain only books?

GONG. Oh, not at all. The greater part of the collection is comprised
of books, but there are also 4,000 calligraphic works as well as
numerous traditional paintings. Most of these date from the
Song, Yuan,[141] Ming and Qing eras.

Four thousand calligraphic works and paintings?

GONG. Yes, approximately 4,000! But you should understand that,
in addition, the collection contains approximately 1,000 bei—
stone inscriptions from the Tang era until the period of the last
dynasty.

What does the entire library look like? For there are, are there not,
numerous pavilions, wonderful gardens, at times—with alarming sud-
denness—one encounters ancient statues of animals in the grass . . .

GONG. Those are from the Han era, and they are truly amazing. Altogether, the space of the library—I know this exactly, because a director has to know this—is 28,000 square metres. Of this, the area taken up by the older-style buildings is approximately 8,000 square metres . . . But this isn't really important. For me, the true importance of this place is not its scale but that this is one of the most significant book collections created across China, and without which—particularly, without the Ningbo library—classical literature simply would not have been able to survive. Every visitor is well aware of this. Because it is the great desire of every literate person of today to come here. And so, well, many do come, every year we have about 100,000 visitors.

Stein is alarmed at this number. A hundred thousand visitors, he repeats the fact cautiously. Won't this ruin the library?

GONG. We are not just some public library—the books can only be viewed by experts. We take the ordinary visitors through an exhibit so that they can get a general idea of the library, but they are not allowed to enter into the real rooms. Only scholars may do so. Not only may they enter, they may work there as well. But only in the pavilions, because even they may not enter where the books are kept, nor come into this hall where we are now sitting—this is exclusively a building for receiving guests of high rank. Before your arrival, I have welcomed ministers and leading politicians here. The last one, for example, to sit in that Ming-era chair, in which you are sitting, was the president of the Romanian parliament.

Permit me, Stein stops him, to bring up the subject again of the history of private libraries in China. Was this custom of creating libraries usual among leading government officials and literati? Should he imagine that, in China, any teacher, literate person, official, worth anything at all, had a pavilion at home with a book collection?

GONG. Many literati had libraries at home, but these were not well preserved. Some were able to keep their collection whole for a few decades or perhaps even a century. In the regions south of the Yangtze, we know of the one-time existence of approximately 500 private libraries, but they were not sufficiently protected. Now there are only a few left—the libraries in Hangzhou, in Beijing, and the largest, this one, the Ningbo library.

How widespread was this passion for collecting books, how should Stein picture it?

GONG. In traditional society, erudition and, above all, writing was granted extraordinary significance. Whether we are speaking of the wealthy or the poor, every family striving to better its circumstances regarded the acquisition of knowledge as its highest possible goal. Progress, improving one's societal status, was only conceivable through the means of education and examinations. When, however, these goals were realized, and the candidates became government officials, then—either because they wished to polish up their intellects, or in order, as they say, to accumulate merits—they began to create collections of books. In families of more modest means too, for example, the head of the family would begin to collect books in order to assist with the advancement of his descendants.

As Stein has not even the slightest idea—since he only confronts this later, towards the end of his journey—of the significance of there not having been any so-called market in imperial China, he now feels that he is not getting where he wants to with the director. He is interested in the 'reality' of this entire question. Therefore, he tenaciously asks: How did people acquire written works? In what manner were individual volumes purchased? Was there a book trade? Were books exchanged among people? Were they given as gifts? How did the establishment of such a private library take place?

> GONG. In the case of Fan Qin, the creator of this library, it occurred in the following way. When he had achieved the appropriate rank in the imperial exams, his official career began, and so he completed his service in Shangxi and Henan, Guangdong, Guangxi and Yunnan, but he turned up in Fujian and Jiangxi as well, and in all these places he regularly sacrificed time to his passion—book collecting. He dedicated particular attention to local annals, notations of historical events and the documentation of examination papers. But he was also interested in the masterpieces of poetry and prose inscribed in stone. That is how, one step at a time, he brought to life this colossal library. But he was only able to do this because, in China, the printing of books had a very distinguished past. For centuries, hundreds and hundreds of print works had been in operation, where books were printed from wooden blocks. The acquisition of a book within these conditions was a question of money and in what regions the official in question had completed his service in the course of his work. But the essence, I repeat, was money, because a book was very expensive.

Fine, but—Stein interrupts yet again—not everyone could have had so many copper rosaries, or gold, and not everyone could have been of such high rank as Fan Qin. So would intellectuals of his societal status have had enough money to buy books?

GONG. A person without official rank could not really collect books in enough quantity to be able to create a library. But, naturally, every literate person could have a library room where on a little table there would be a few books lined up or a cupboard with five or six shelves of books. This general state of affairs cannot be compared to a library of the significance of Tianyi Ge. Because the owner of the Tianyi Ge was a very particular person. He collected the most valuable books, and his goal was undoubtedly to create a large library of unsurpassable value.

Stein stubbornly persists with his original question and he repeats: Fine, all is well, he understands, but how did the literati acquire the desired volumes? Did they buy them? Or did they get hold of them another way?

GONG. You could say that the veneration of the book in ancient China was general. Every volume was greatly cherished. Very frequently it occurred that if one or other important volume was in the possession of a certain literati, his friends would borrow it. Or they would say to each other: There is a such a work, I have only half of it. I know you have a copy, so please lend it to me for two to three months. I will make a copy of it, or I will have it copied, then give it back to you. And when you need something from my collection, I will lend it to you. The respect in passion for books not only meant that they purchased them in accordance with their abilities but also that they made copies of them at home. Even Fan Qin did so with a few rare volumes.

What was the value of a book?

GONG. Today we say that the most beautiful books are from the Song era. A single page of a book from the Song era is measured in gold. There is a certain kind of calligraphic style, the Song-era calligraphy—well, the value of a calligraphic work such as that can only be measured in gold. As a matter of fact, that is the essential thing—all these books are protected artistic treasures, so it isn't possible to express their value in terms of money, only their notional value which, however, is determined by innumerable factors: the kind of paper, the quality, printing methods, the era the book dates from, the contents, the rarity of the volume and so on.

The visitor does not give up and once again begins to pester the director: In the old days, what determined the worth of a book?

GONG. There used to be printing and cataloguing experts. They were aware of the publication value of a book. These experts worked with the data found in the colophon of books—if the book had a colophon—otherwise they examined where and when the printing blocks were engraved and determined the price on the basis of that. There were cases where the binder, or the person who rebound the book, or the owner could be determined from the seals and marginalia. So a thorough knowledge of seals also pertained to the knowledge of books. For example, if they found the seal of Li Taibai[142] in a book, then they knew that the book was published before the time of Li Taibai. Much is revealed by the so-called system of name taboos. This meant, for example, that during the time of the Kangxi[143] or when Li Shimin[144] founded a dynasty, if a written sign identical to a written sign in the name of the ruler appeared in the book, then, from this data, the experts knew when the book was published, clearly during the rule of a certain emperor or afterward.

Stein perceives by now that his obstinacy is not being crowned with success, and because he naturally does not understand why the director will not speak directly about 'the goods,' 'the book market' and 'the book trade', he tries a different approach, and says that he would like to picture to himself that Chinese literati of old, that Chinese official of old, that erudite literati, and because of that he asks to be excused the naive question: *How* did they read in the old times? And how does a Chinese intellectual read today? Is there a difference in the modes of reading, the reasons, the forms?

The director lowers his voice now, so that no one else will hear, only his guest, and suddenly the proud and official director becomes a somewhat sad, disillusioned director.

GONG. There are things which do not change. Sometimes reading is necessary for work, sometimes it is a requisite of the soul. Sometimes it's a question of mood—yesterday I felt like reading, today I don't. It's like that today, and that's how it was in the old days too. I think the change does not affect reading itself, but the world in which people used to read, and in which we read today. In the world of old, reading—in a memorable fashion—was conditioned upon perfect tranquillity. This tranquillity—this peace in a garden, in a pavilion, as a person takes a book into their hand, sits down in front of the opened doors of the pavilion, and hears from the silence out there the singing of a bird, or the whispering of the wind—this tranquillity is no more, and never again shall it be. Times have changed, the world has changed, and, as you know, nothing can be done.

After his words there is silence. Amid the confusion that has set in, Rong Rong finally recommends: maybe they should go and have a look at what is possible. What is possible?—Stein looks at her. Rong Rong gestures to him that all will be explained, patience.

And they see everything, the Mingzhou pavilion[145] with the Stele Forest, as the museum of steles is called here, the room of Qian Jin[146] with the renowned collection of inscribed bricks from the Jin dynasty;[147] they see the Bai E pavilion,[148] this unusual shrine carved from stone, with scalloped ornamentation, the site of sacrificial ceremonies, transported here from the Zuguan mountains; they also see the Temple of the Ancients of the Qing Family,[149] they see the open-air opera stage, breathtakingly beautiful, gilded in baroque fashion, decorated with baroque profusion; then they see the rooms where the books and the calligraphic works are displayed, the Zhuangyuan pavilion[150] which belonged to the Zhan family, and the Yunzai building which belonged to the Chens, they see the Northern Garden and the Southern Garden, and once again they see the Han-era animal statues in the grass, which they had noticed upon their arrival, and finally they see Tianyi Ge itself, the former, two-storey library building, built in strange proportions, and they learn everything about it that they possibly can, in brief, they see everything and they come to know everything, everything that could possibly be seen and known—it's only the books that they don't see anywhere, and the library that they don't see anywhere, because inside, in Tianyi Ge, there is not a single volume to be found—Where are they? Stein asks, at which point Mr Gong purses his lips, clears his throat and informs them that, oh yes, the books, they aren't here, they were moved from here to over there in the back, he points somewhere into the distance, to some spot where modern concrete buildings stand, well, they're over there, says the skinny director, because over there they can assure the books the greatest possible protection, as you know, he turns confidentially to his guest, the necessary conditions of moisture, the necessary dryness, modern protection against insects, they have been able to keep the books under Western technological conditions—The books? Stein asks in remonstration. So well, the library? So it doesn't actually exist—but it does, Mr Gong contradicts him nervously, here it is, he points at Tianyi Ge which is empty; but Mr Gong, says Stein, that isn't the same thing: a library is where the books are in their places, do you understand, Mr Gong, *in their places*, and Tianyi Ge will be a library when the books, all 13,000 of them that have remained, will be in the bookcases, every last volume in its appointed place, but at this Mr Gong, like a person who has run out of patience, hurries on to discuss the details of the upcoming luncheon with Rong Rong; they go outside, this is goodbye, then Rong Rong, their brand-new dear friend remains behind so Stein can catch up with her, places her hand on his shoulder comfortingly and drags him along to some restaurant next to Yuehu ('Moon Lake')[151]—Stein asks her: Why did they do this, Tianyi Ge, the pride of the nation, the last thing that remained, and they lock it up in a safe?—Rong Rong just nods as the interpreter translates, and squeezes Stein's shoulder even more tightly, they walk in through the doors of a restaurant on the shore of Yuehu where they will be able to bid farewell to all their friends from Ningbo who have gathered to say goodbye, and Rong Rong whispers to Stein: At least it existed—What existed? Stein asks the interpreter, because he doesn't get what she's referring to, well, this Ningbo was here, Rong Rong explains, smiling, and at least once upon a time Tianyi Ge was here with its 70,000 wondrous volumes . . .

The next day they set off early at dawn; a rusty 'soul-loser' takes them across the ocean. Their goal of their journey is Putuoshan,[152] the residence of Guanyin, the renowned, distant Buddhist place of pilgrimage, a true gem, they read in a cheap brochure, the boat is three quarters below the surface of the water but they do not sink, instead, by some miracle, they anchor at the island after more than an hour; on the shore are hotels, strident vendors and taxi drivers with malevolent faces, further inland are luxury hotels and luxury restaurants, and wealthy, elegant tourists, with bored expressions on their faces, amid the luxuriant, wonderful tree-lined alleyways; my God, says Stein to the interpreter, after they find a relatively less-exorbitant hotel, and they set off, this is Yangzhou, this is Beijing, this is Hong Kong, this is the Mallorca of the Shanghai elite, this is the Chinese Riviera, good God, where are they, says Stein at first, then the interpreter repeats it, and they just wander through this tourist paradise named Putuoshan where everything is extraordinarily enchanting, and everything is extraordinarily arranged for maximum comfort: the Jinsha ('Golden Sands'), the Baibusha ('Sands of One Hundred Steps') and the Qianbusha ('Sands of One Thousand Steps'),[153] the beaches and the restaurants in this built-up gem, in the former residence of Guanyin and in her empire which seemed as if it were eternal—and it is good when they find the three large monasteries, it is good that the colossal Puji Chan Si,[154] with its unsurpassed beauty, still exists, it is good that the placid Fayu Chan Si[155] still exists as well as the Huiji Chan Si,[156] built on the peak of the mountain so as to be closer to heaven, and it's good that they can find, although with difficulty, to the west from the Fayu, an unforgettable stele containing Yan Liben's[157] indescribably beautiful depiction of Guanyin, propped against a concealed wall in one of the back shrines of a tiny insignificant temple; it's good, they keep repeating that they will only be here three more days, because in the end they will forget why they are here, and why they came to this island, because at the end, forgetting about their goals, they too are affected by the pleasant marvels and the unspeakable natural beauty of Putuoshan, and they will just let all this torment and classical this and classical that go straight to hell, as well as their search for the true face of the Buddha, just as the whole lot of tote-bag-carrying, feral and aggressive groups of pilgrims are affected as well by the beauty, this suggestion of this agreeable charm, for whatever they step they meet only people on excursions: dressed in the uniform of pilgrimage, or merely elegant gentleman and bored ladies of fashion lying on one of the beaches; it's good, says Stein to his companion on the third day, as they embark onto the speed boat which will stream ahead to Shanghai within four hours, back across the undulating ocean; it's good that they can bear to leave this place, and that later on, no one but absolutely no one will ask them if they saw that Guanyin, the saint of Putuoshan, the Chinese counterpart of Avalokiteshvara, the bodhisattva of compassion, no one will ask if they saw her, because everyone will only ask—and, really, later on it does happen that way—everyone will only ask, enviously and desirously, in Shanghai, in Beijing, in Tokyo, in Budapest, in Berlin and in New York: Oh, how wonderful that they were in Putuoshan!—For, the water there is the most amazing thing in the world, isn't it?

8. The Empty Throne

When they get back to the flat they have rented in Shanghai, they are so exhausted that for the next few days they only sleep and go for walks, and then, because the first so-called walks seemed perhaps too daring, they only sleep—more precisely, they lie in their beds next to Fudan University,[158] in a flat in the housing estate built in the spirit of international socialist realism, comprised of four-storey buildings, cobbled together from concrete panels—in a place which millions and millions of residents of Shanghai regard as home, their days are filled with sleep or with a kind of half-awakened state, days in which there is no light, not even outside, a massive and unmoving cloud cover hovers over this metropolis of inexpressible proportions, and because there is no change, they lie in their beds in vain, the exhaustion in their limbs does not pass, just as the cloud above them does not disperse;

they decide, however, that they will not cancel any of their meetings, so they go to Shanghai Museum, after they have admired the truly dazzling collection of statuary and its careful arrangement, so that Mrs Liu Huali, one of the directors, the chief executive—they read this for the second time, after their meeting in Zurich, from her business card—so that Mrs Liu, who is beautiful and constantly seeking to mask her beauty, can answer their questions: if there are any, she adds coldly, and they descend, taking an elevator, quite a distance below the earth, then, passing through a few corridors, they step into a truly colossal, unexpected space, into an underground grove whose presence could never have been deduced from the modern style of the building; they step into a grove, an air-conditioned garden, one could say; they step into the open air beneath the ground, trees incline over a pleasant tea room, plants bloom resplendent around the tables, birds chirp and, if they look up, they see the bluest sky, a pure heaven above, but to their consternation everything is made of plastic and with the total incomprehensibility of garish Chinese kitsch, so that in the first moments, as a young girl appears with the tea at a silent gesture from Mrs Liu, Stein can't even tell if he is going to ask anything here at all, but with a sip from the fine bowl he gains strength, and begins, with a somewhat bad conscience by now, for he has already begun in this way so many times.

My esteemed Mrs Liu, you know very well, since I spoke to you about this in Zürich where we met, the deep respect I have for classical Chinese culture. I have been engaged in many conversations with many different intellectuals, I have been in many places now and, as before, now too I have committed a huge error: I have continued to believe that China is still that ancient empire, in this respect the very last one. It is also unparalleled in world history because, somehow, it is still guided by the classical spirit despite the factors of modernity—renewal, opening, as you call it—all indisputable and, in its own way, breathtaking. I believed this, in the course of my travels and my conversations I believed this, and continually called this into account, here in this country, but I have paid bitterly for this stance of wanting to call things to account, because, well, this is clearly no longer the case. I am shattered, if you will permit me such a confidential declaration so soon, but I know that I have only myself to thank. For example, I continually asked if there is any chance for that which held China together, if we can put it that way, for millennia—if there is any chance at all for the teachings of Confucius to return, to be revived, and for China, this new empire, once again to order its life in accord with the teachings of this great philosopher, to adapt morality into daily life. You see, Mrs Liu, how foolish I was, but I still am, a little bit, because I now ask you the same question: What is your opinion of the teachings of Confucius? Is there any hope that anything from the original spirit of these teachings can return to the Chinese society and culture of today?

A reply follows which would be absurd to quote. Surging from the woman's words are banalities, the reality of which is so crushing and unctuous that already in the first minutes of the conversation, there in the underground garden, Stein begins to wrack his brains, searching among the requisites of courteous behaviour for the one act that would allow him to close the conversation immediately, as—Stein looks at Mrs Liu's unflinching gaze—it is more than obvious that nothing will come of this. He, however, becomes entangled in another question and, instead of extricating himself from this atmosphere, encloses himself even more within it.

You, Mrs Liu, state that the national culture has entered into a newer and more resplendent age which, however, does not lack difficulties. I understand. Then please permit me to express it this way: if you go out onto the streets, and you look at the people out there, or look at the crowds standing here in line at the ticket desk, with the best intentions in the world you could not say anything else than that these people—for instance—have arrived at a point of perhaps beginning to respect their own ancient culture. But to say that this culture will now be their own, or that it ever could be, is either an error or a lie.

Needless to say, the answer this time does not diverge one whit from the terrible onslaught of banalities launched just a moment ago, so that Stein is silent, Mrs Liu keeps talking, sometimes in English, sometimes in Chinese, he cannot bear to listen, he looks at the interpreter in supplication—can he give him some advice about how to get out of this?—but the interpreter can't, he just struggles to convey in complete sentences the painfully empty train of thought of the fashionably dressed Mrs Liu who conforms in every measure to the image of the wealthy, world-travelled chief executive, so that Stein, even more clumsily, entangles himself in even more questions.

He speaks of how admiring a culture or respecting a culture is not the same as living it, experiencing it and practising it as a part of one's everyday life. The Europeans, as Mrs Liu knows very well, are in a similar position, for they truly respect the ancient cultures of Greece and Rome but they would never imagine for a moment, even in their dreams, that their contemporary culture is, in its 'depths', identical with the Hellenic or the Roman. What is painful in the case of China, however, is that the extinction of this amazing ancient culture has only taken place in the recent past, when a person could still make the mistake—and as for Stein, he still makes this mistake—could still deceive himself, dupe himself, pamper the belief within himself that maybe this dramatic turn of events had not occurred, that nothing had really been decided, that nothing was final, and that in China that which *has been here* for millennia need not completely collapse.

But Mrs Liu is cut from too stern a material to be thrown off her rhythm, and Stein feels as if he were listening to a speaker at a Chinese Communist Party meeting, the platitudes gushing out unimpeded and unswayed; but what is even more dispiriting in this plastic paradise is that Mrs Liu doesn't understand what they're talking about, Mrs Liu cannot comprehend what they want to say to her because, as far as Mrs Liu is concerned, 'change is the natural law of historical development' in which 'the modern and the traditional must coexist in harmony'—well, from this point on Stein makes no effort to try to force things, and it isn't even necessary, because the chief executive of the justifiably renowned Shanghai Museum needs no questions in order to say what she has learnt, and Mrs Liu recites and recites her lesson—when suddenly they notice that a single human trait of this highly placed functionary, this inaccessible official, this being whose beauty and femininity are by necessity concealed in the neutrality of the uniform of a high-ranking civil servant, a single human trait remains undisguised, perhaps because it cannot be disguised; that while speaking, like someone occasionally giving in to a bad habit, Mrs Liu takes a lock from her wondrously glittering, ebony black hair, from where it falls above her shoulder near her tiny, fine ear, she takes one lock, more precisely, the end of a completely fine strand, she pulls it in front of her face and places the end in her mouth, evidently unconsciously, and she recites and recites what she has to recite but all the while sucking for a few seconds at this clearly sweet lock of hair. Then like someone who realizes what she is doing, she quickly throws it back, straightens it, then a few minutes later, as she forgets herself, starts the whole thing again.

Not a single sentence remains, not a single word from the so-called conversation which lasts for about an hour, only this one tiny fault in the Liu mechanism; they cannot remember her beautiful noble face with any precision, they cannot recall the colour of her clothes, already after three or four days it is all mixed up if she had two or three glittering diamonds on her fingers, if she was wearing, for example, a bracelet, no, not even that, almost nothing, they can only recall that movement, as she sneaked that little black lock of hair into her mouth and sucked a little bit on the end, only this remains from the beautiful Mrs Liu, one of the chief curators of the famous Shanghai Museum, everything else is swallowed up by time, and they just lie in bed for a few days at home in the dark apartment, then another farewell approaches, and they begin to try and figure out how to bid farewell to Shanghai, they begin to go walking again, and nothing—they can't find the heart of Shanghai, they wander from Peace Hotel to the former French Quarter, from Shanghai Railway Station to Yu Yuan; when on one of the very last evenings they turn out towards Nanjing Lu[159] from Fuzhou Lu, frequently sought out because of its bookshops, and amid the skyscrapers from the period of the first economic boom, in the illumination of the evening's neon lights, they suddenly notice a peculiar, tall building—in the first minutes it's just a feeling, among the glances cast here and there, that one's glance had come upon something important, they search, again they try to find what it was, and then they see what they had glimpsed a moment ago, they see that high-rise block, due to the other buildings not even its entire mass, only the upper third, but that is precisely enough, because that is what is essential: for them to see the roof against the background of the dark sky.

The building's architects wanted to create something specific on the roof, something memorable, something that would draw the attention of the people to the form, as it were, the symbol of the new Shanghai, and so they decided that the best thing to display on the roof would be a huge, a gigantic, lotus,[160] painted in gold, and illuminated at night, and really, Stein grabs his companion's arm in his excitement, as they stand there in the undulating crowds of Nanjing Lu: on the roof of that building, reaching down so far, there blooms a colossal, gold-coloured lotus, its descending petals illuminated in some secret fashion with the most resplendent of neon lights, and there in the heights, a monumental lotus in the dark evening sky, a lotus throne, says Stein to the interpreter, and they stare and they bid farewell, and both of them are thinking that since this kind of sculpture of a deserted Lotus Throne, perhaps with the exception of Sri Lanka, was never too prevalent even during the aniconic period in Buddhism, so that no memory and no kind of tradition of this sort could have really survived, especially here in China, there is no question of there being some sort of reference here; so then why didn't they think about it, the architects, why didn't they consider that this throne means that there is no one on this throne, and were they at all aware that they were, involuntarily but perfectly, expressing how this city could designate itself: that in the most skilful way possible, they had found the most eloquent symbol of this new Shanghai, this Lotus Throne of phosphorescent gold, a Lotus Throne upon which no one sits any more, thus creating an image of how the Buddha has left the city, how this gigantic Shanghai is left to itself beneath its own gigantic scintillation, how it blindly rushes ahead with its own horrific speed, and all the while the throne is empty.

CONVERSATION ON THE RUINS

1. Today It's Over, but That Didn't Start Just Now

The interpreter gets a day off, and Stein sits in an excellent Sichuan restaurant with the renowned poet Xi Chuan. They haven't begun dinner yet, and Stein tries to summarize, to this worldly, erudite artist, the experiences and impressions with which he has returned from the Great Journey. Xi Chuan listens attentively and, after Stein has finished speaking, he thinks for a long time. Then he points at Stein's bag.

> XI CHUAN. I would like you to take out your tape recorder and turn it on. OK? Are you ready? Is it working? Good. Then listen to

me. You said China has lost its traditions, China has lost its culture, China has lost itself. For me, the problem is a little more complicated than that—namely, the story begins a little earlier. First and foremost: it begins in 1919. This is the year we should designate as the year in which China was destroyed by the Japanese and Western alliances. China was forced to open itself. And what followed—the age of Sun Yat-sen[161] and Chiang Kai-shek[162]—was an era in which China could no longer maintain or organize itself as a society. China disintegrated. China died as a nation—it no longer existed. Accordingly, when Sun Yat-sen and Chiang Kai-shek appeared, their goal was to create order, not freedom. They needed European knowledge in order to acquire weapons against the West. This was the background. Then Mao took power. With that came Marxism. Mao thought that European scientific knowledge wasn't necessary: Marxism was enough, Marxism would be the weapon against the West. Marxism is a product of the West—but why didn't anyone say at the time that China had lost its culture? Why didn't they say it back then, even though Marxism came from the West? Maybe this example is childish, so let me mention another: I know people in the West who collect stamps. They collect stamps from the Mao era with great enthusiasm. And they don't say that those are not Chinese stamps! On the other hand, they don't collect contemporary stamps, because they say those're not 'Chinese' enough. They're happy to collect stamps from the time of the Cultural Revolution . . . They like the red colours, the characteristic forms, the shapes. So, to summarize—the Mao era was, therefore, still Chinese . . .

Then China changed. And we lost our traditional culture. Mainly that's what you say, and that's what other Westerners like you say. It's just that I see it a little differently. I think that we lost our culture a good one hundred years ago. Not today, that's mistaken. The entire past century was about the fact that we lost our culture.

Stein says that he understands, fine, but facts are facts . . .

XI CHUAN. Well, yes, in a word . . . There are intellectuals who just say: Bye bye, China. Then there are others who say that, in order to preserve traditional culture, you need a lot of money. This is really important. I know foreigners who live here, who buy traditional Chinese houses and renovate them . . . And it's only people like that who can do so, because it's incredibly expensive. The average Chinese cannot permit themselves something like that.

But, still, Stein tries to interrupt, the preservation of traditional culture is not . . .

XI CHUAN. There is India. Our problems are similar. Our cultures are old. At the same time we have a common need to somehow escape from poverty, from isolation. The Indians too want to know what happened here in the past few decades. What does development mean? Let's begin with this concept. At the time of the Song dynasty, development was halted. The reason: China had reached maximum prosperity, the ruling class was very wealthy and people simply had no need for development.

So you claim that . . . ?

XI CHUAN. Yes, yes, my claim is that from that age onward, Chinese culture began to founder. That was the time of the Mongolian conquest, the arrival of the Manchurians . . .

This is really surprising, Stein answers. This entire train of thought is really surprising. But, he admits, at first glance it's very persuasive as well. So then the ruin of traditional China is not a question of only a hundred years, but . . . !

XI CHUAN. Yes, this is what I claim! That process that began in the Song era led directly to the collapse of the Qing dynasty. This question needs to be examined critically by the Chinese as well. I wrote an article about this once. About how there are different kinds of moralities. One is the morality of culture. Another is the morality of life. And these are two different things. We all must bear the burden that is life. And so you can't be surprised that, given this burden of life, the people—especially the people of today—want to make their lives easier. In the 1970s, the essence of our crisis was that we needed scientific knowledge in order to change our way of thinking. Today, however, there is another kind of crisis. And one of the signs of this crisis is the attempt to re-introduce Confucianism into Chinese education. There exist, in Beijing, schools in which instruction takes place according to tra-ditional principles. There are professors who say that we really have to return to this: we need to build a new Confucian struc-ture, we need to reject foreign influence. I, on the other hand, think that is difficult.

Many people, Stein says, think the exact same thing, they would agree with these professors, and in his exper—

XI CHUAN. There are dangers. The biggest danger is that there are moral principles deriving from the imperial times. These moral principles were reinforced by means of the heavens. After the rev-olutions, people expunged these moral principles from their lives. Now, once again, we have moral principles but we have no way at all of supporting them. We don't know how to construct them, what to build them on, how to ensure them . . . Today, for example, we essentially accept Christian morality, even if we don't agree with it, but here the danger immediately presents itself that we have morality—but without any assumption of responsibility. We want and we undertake modernity, but we do not want and we do not undertake the burdens of modernity! This is extremely dangerous! Marxism has completely collapsed. It has no influence at all on young people. And they have become really cynical.

And so . . . ?

XI CHUAN. But where is the axis of this morality—that is my question. The pace of change is enormous. All the old things have collapsed. I was in India. They greatly appreciate what has happened in China. They appreciate the development, the enormous speed of development. But the reason for that is: we had Marxism! Marxism, though, is gone now, there is only a new modernity with its own specialized morality not supported by anything. The whole thing is just hanging in the air. All the older moral principles, including Marxism, were based on something. Today, principles exist but there is nothing holding them up. That is really dangerous. The problem is not that there are no principles but that behind these principles there is a void.

Accordingly, there is no ideal towards which society . . . ?

XI CHUAN. It doesn't exist. Nonetheless, we don't want a society which will collapse again. We need something which we can hold onto, something which we can grasp with our hands. But if we open our hands, they are empty. And this is truly dangerous. The solution is horrendously complex. Let's assume, for example, that Confucianism will be revived.

And you consider that to be possible . . . ?

XI CHUAN. No, I'm just saying, let's assume that Confucianism could be revived. The West is very hypocritical when it comes to this. It criticizes China because China is not a democracy. OK, OK, fine . . . it's just that sometimes I feel that this criticism is contradictory. Westerners love traditional Chinese culture, but that was completely dictatorial! They say that dictatorships are bad . . . Well, but dictatorships are also really ancient! So they should love those too, right?

He pauses for breath and sips his tea, and, taking advantage of the brief silence, his interlocutor tells him how he too believes, as many others do in Europe and America, that the organization of society according to functioning democratic principles could not work in China . . . China is too big for that. Anyone who has never been here could never understand that. And so he, says Stein—he, who is the embodiment of these contradictions—he too thinks that without some kind of strictness, without which no decisions could ever be made, everything could conceivably fall apart in the space of a minute . . .

XI CHUAN. Take Montesquieu. He criticizes China because it is based on this horrible dictatorship. At the same time he announces that a country this size can only operate in this way. So, in addition to his praise for our democracy and his condemnation of our dictatorship, he claims that a democratic system could never work here. How is that possible?!

Stein interjects that Montesquieu probably didn't know too much about China—at that time he couldn't have known more than what he knew. Neither could Schopenhauer who, however, loved China . . . One thing is certain: the Europeans have never really understood, and still don't understand, what would be right for China. He, Stein, however knows one thing: what is happening today with Chinese tradition is definitely wrong.

XI CHUAN. The situation is very complicated. And it is really very dangerous.

At that moment, Ouyang Jianghe, another renowned figure of contemporary poetry, appears. Xi Chuan turns to him, encouraging him to express his opinion.

OUYANG. What's going on?

XI CHUAN. What kind of answer can intellectuals give to the crisis that is going on today?

OUYANG. What's with the intellectuals?

XI CHUAN. What kind of influence or strength do they have?

OUYANG. The intellectuals' what?

XI CHUAN. Well, their role . . .

OUYANG. In the New China?

And he comfortably seats himself at the table.

Dinner arrives.

2. Of Course, It's the End

On the plates are exciting and wonderful foods, full of promise, and brought to them in such great quantities; the waiters suddenly start bringing the plates, so for a while there can be no question of paying attention to anything other than the spectacle unfolding before them. They have partaken of many similar meals with the Chinese, so that they know, for now, there can be no conversation, they must wait until the first, then the second and then the third platters are finished; fortunately the hunger at the table is great, so the locals reach a satiated state fairly quickly, and quite soon there is a chance for them to address Ouyang. Accordingly, Stein begins: Mr Ouyang, after a very long journey he, Stein, has an opportunity to talk with him. And the result of his journey is that he has returned to Beijing in deep disappointment. What has occurred is that where in principle there still might be some trace of classical culture, it has been supressed, in the course of reconstruction, to the inferior values of the tourist industry, meaning that he, Stein, has come upon monuments essentially destroyed: instead of something real, he has seen forgeries; instead of truth, he has taken part in deception, not even to delve into the reasons for his disillusionment. What is Mr Ouyang's opinion on this? Was it just the accident of bad luck that cast these things in Stein's path? And if this is not the case—and his experiences have shown him reality in its true light—can anything be done to halt this process? Because it was only in the museums that he, Stein, saw any kind of an attempt at the 'preservation of values'. But there are too few museums, considering what needs to be done or, rather, what should have been done to save all this from the claws of the repugnant figures of the tourist industry . . .

OUYANG. The Chinese intelligentsia of today see this entire process differently than the Europeans, and their relationship to classical Chinese culture is completely different than what you think. In my opinion there are not too few but, rather, a huge number of museums in China. Moreover, I do not see this museum culture in as positive a light as you do—I see it as something foreign to us, something which comes from Europe and European thought. The Europeans believe that their culture can be preserved in a museum—but the Chinese don't think so. Europeans believe that culture is something they can grasp and touch because, for them, culture is comprised of objects, or remnants of objects, and this object, this remnant, conceals within it the essence of the original. For the Chinese, the matter is completely different—for them, the essence of culture can only be preserved in a spiritual form. For example, the Chinese always make their buildings out of wood, and not stone, because the important thing is not how long the building is going to stand. This doesn't mean, however, that the Chinese don't wish to preserve their culture or their past, but that they see the manner of preservation completely differently. The Chinese intelligentsia has always felt that the past merits preservation in writing. Chinese writing is an extraordinary phenomenon: a character in the Chinese language is not, in its essence, merely a word, the written form of a concept, but a vision, an apparition—immaterial in its essence. This is radically different from the European languages, just as there is a huge difference between the Chinese and the Europeans who see, and have always seen, the question of the past and the preservation of its values as possible only through its objective forms. The essence of Chinese culture is not graspable in a material sense because, for the Chinese, no material can divulge the essence of the culture which is entirely spiritual in nature and therefore accessible only through writing . . . In contrast to European tradition, which preserves its cultural values through objects and thus actually does not preserve the essence, the whole, but only evokes its outer forms, thus dismantling into pieces the entirety of that cultural value, its reality, well, in contrast to this the Chinese are able to preserve the entirety of their culture— and the essence of that entirety—in the spiritual, in the immaterial, hence in the most secure place: in writing, where that essence is exclusively transmitted and preserved, and from where it may be revived and evoked.

The friendly atmosphere in the restaurant, as well as the presence of Xi Chuan, encourages Stein to state frankly that perhaps Ouyang is slightly oversimplifying the essence of European culture. It is not simply a culture of objects, he explains to him, nor is it altogether certain that an objective creation—as, for example, the cathedral in Rheims—would not be capable of conveying the same immaterial essence of which he, Ouyang, is speaking . . .

OUYANG. Fine, fine, but the difference is not only perceptible in that: for the Europeans—to take one example—the invention of a new object has always been radically more important than to the Chinese. Here, in China, an invention was always esteemed because of its 'spiritual' value, because of its philosophical content. Our inventions were therefore, first and foremost, spiritual and philosophical inventions—and that is what a Chinese discerns most of all in his own culture. Once again, therefore, I would say that traditional European culture is a culture of objects whereas Chinese culture is a spiritual culture.

Once I was at Princeton University, and there, in the museum, I saw an old Greek coin which in its time was worth maybe 1 yuan. Today, maybe it's worth 1 million yuan. The main thing is that today its value can be expressed in money. This cannot occur with a Chinese spiritual discovery or philosophy—its value, naturally, cannot be expressed in the form of material or money.

Stein tries to call attention to the dangers of the faulty comparison: Does he really think that the philosophy of Kant or Plato could be expressed in euros? Or does he think that Europe never created any values in a so-called immaterial form at all?

OUYANG. Fine, fine, fine, but I see the problem differently. For example, I think the problem is that modern Chinese culture has become ever closer to European culture. Take modern Chinese poetry, where a contemporary poet does not live in his own past but in European culture, which he considers to be world culture. And, in general, the Chinese intelligentsia of today, as well as the masses, want to liberate themselves from their own objectified past—they tear down the old houses because they are inconvenient, they are uncivilized, there are no toilets, no air-conditioning, why should we live in them?—and yet those are the very buildings that a European seeks out and admires, those are the buildings in which he sees the essence of an idealized past. We—to cite the words of Calvino—are living in Time Zero, neither in our past nor yet in our future, a future presumed to be ever wealthier, so that for us the ancient culture can only be beautiful in an idealized sense. In fact, if anything at all has remained from this ancient culture, for the contemporary Chinese it can only be a burden. I have a foreign acquaintance who no longer likes to come to China because in his view the China of today no longer manifests that exquisite spirituality—which you too admire—of the ancient age. For the Chinese of today, he says, only money counts, they're only interested in what things cost. The China of today lives in the market economy where the remains of our ancient culture can only be seen in a museum, in exchange for the price of an entrance ticket . . . And the Chinese don't even go to those museums. Because for them, their ancient culture is already a museum—it is no longer identical with their own ancient culture.

Stein intervenes on two points: One, the Chinese, as Ouyang puts it, really do go to the museums, in huge masses—he himself has experienced and suffered from this hundreds of times . . . Two, with reference to the cited acquaintance, with Ouyang's permission, Stein would disclose that, as of this moment, he has yet another acquaintance who is not very happy to come to the New China for even a short while. He sits here before him . . . But there is yet another dilemma associated with this greater problem, namely, that classical culture no longer exists; the realization that foreigners who take a strong interest in it are increasingly no longer really wanted here, their questions are not welcomed, they are warned, lectured, told not to seek out what they are seeking; they won't find what they're looking for, especially not him, the foreigner—he will find absolutely nothing, nothing at all. For all intents and purposes, he is told to go home. Stein, however, is someone who is feverishly enthusiastic about this ancient culture. Not the culture of today, that is alien to him. What is there to love in New China, what?!

OUYANG. This will probably surprise you but I think it's possible that the China of today is much more beautiful than the China of old. Traditionally, China was always a poor country. But now China is, simply put, a country of enormous potential. The elements of this potential are tangible—such as the immeasurable economic and democratizing political possibilities. These can be numerically quantified and expressed. But there is another aspect of these possibilities which is much harder to grasp, and that is that they lead to a much deeper, more mysterious transformation of reality. It is this aspect of the new possibilities I feel to be the most crucial. Some foreigners say, in response to this, that I'm just fantasizing things into reality. Still I say that this reality exists, atmospherically. And everything in the best of contemporary Chinese literature speaks of this. Two hundred or three hundred years from now, people will be able to tell from these writings what China was like at the turn of the millennium, what the essence of culture was at that time. And so it is so important that you Europeans be acquainted not only with our classical authors but also with the writers and poets of today.

You know—Stein replies—nothing is ever accidental. It is no accident that he, Stein, and others like him come to China in order to admire the culture of imperial times, or its remnants, if its reality and everything else can no longer be admired, because he—Stein points at himself—and others like him are no longer attracted by what he, Ouyang, defines as modern. It is by no means an accident that it has become so crucial for someone like Stein—coming from where he does—to be able to inspect a highly accomplished, highly refined classical culture, because the culture from which he comes—this so-called modernity, directly confronting China and towards which China is rushing—is no place at all for either a highly accomplished individual or a refined one. For him—Stein once again points to himself—and for people like him, the modern appears as a destructive force, annihilating reality, which is itself expressed in an ideal form, mysterious, enchanting, uplifting . . .

OUYANG. Fine, fine, fine, but here I have to say something. So we allow ancient culture to be, we respect it, we highly esteem it, fine, but we are living in a completely different world today—this fact has to be confronted. We have to address our own problems: ancient culture is finished. But if you will permit me, there is a larger problem connected to this, and that is the question of contemporary literature. In the China of today, there are two major generations of contemporary writers. One of them, the older one, to which I belong, and of which I spoke just now, pays attention not only to literary forms but also to its societal and political experiences, and these are evident in their works. We write in many different genres, I, for example, in addition to poetry, write prose and drama. And it may come to pass that the literature of the future will not know what to do with us, because the other, the younger, generation, which looks only to Europe and America, uses literature exclusively for making money and the attainment of success, quick success. It is conceivable that art will completely lose its true content—and this is the essence of the literature of the future, literature going forward into the future . . . So where are we now, in terms of ancient literature? When we ourselves are in danger! And not only in terms of the sense, the meaning, and the content of the ancient but also with regard to every single art form! A new age is beginning, I know.

Stein, in sadness, agrees. Well, that is definitely certain. But he hopes that Ouyang will believe him when he says that something suggests to Stein that Ouyang's relationship, and that of the Chinese, to their own classical culture and the literary-spiritual crisis of his generation are deeply interconnected.

OUYANG. Fine, fine, fine, I get it, I get it, but unfortunately, I have to go.

The last plates are cleared away, he says goodbye and then disappears through the door. And as if this were a sign, almost immediately, clearly thanks to the kindly arrangements of Xi Chuan, another guest arrives: one of the favourites of, and a star among, the contemporary Chinese literati, the amazing, particularly beautiful fashion designer Wang Xiaolin takes a seat at the table. Her face is like that of a sphinx, and her manner is so severe that while she is replying to a question, no one dares speak. Stein, in his entire life, has never met such a hard-edged woman.

3. The End? Oh Yeah, Business

The new guest hardly touches the food. Sometimes she takes a sip of
tea. And after Xi Chuan tells her in Chinese what Stein is up to and
why he's here, she doesn't wait for any questions at all—she does not
wish to converse but to declaim. She waits for the tape recorder to be
turned on, and, casting her unflinching beautiful eyes onto Stein, she
begins.

WANG. In 1993, I came up from Sichuan to Northern China, to Beijing. Well, as for these Chinese clothes . . . hmm . . . Since I didn't
live in the time when they . . . wore traditional clothes, traditional
Chinese dress had already become a thing of the past, it had lost
its meaning. Only a few things remained. For example, we still
wore . . . some kind of miao, and something else, um, the . . . xiao
lingzi,[163] clothes from the 1970s. There was another one, aozhao,[164]

a little coat with cotton lining, and inside there weren't any . . .
of those things. Well, once I saw, at one of those what whatcha-
macallits, a denim shirt, ordered from abroad and prepared for
export, with Chinese traditional buttons on the front, and I was
really amazed, I felt a kind of excitement, because denim is a very
modern fabric, and how could it have that kind of buttoning on
it? I sensed there was no clothing like that at the time, modern
fabric with traditional buttoning . . . And the two together . . .

Then I got hold of a bit of patterned material, something
very modern, and I sewed a few Chinese-style lian[165] with it, the
kind of clothing I had never seen. And I wore one of them, and
many people began to ask me where I'd got it from. So I made a
few more, put them in a shop, and they sold well.

At the time . . . people . . . in China . . . if you're talking about
the 1920s or 30s, people weren't wearing such clothes, at least it
wasn't the usual thing . . . well, after the 30s, people wore traditional clothing less frequently, from that point on you couldn't
see things like that. Then, after the people went through a lot and
survived, a kind of nostalgia crept in, a kind of thinking back to
. . . the past.

The clothes you could get at the markets, before the reforms,
were all very simple, then after the opening and the reforms,
European and Western clothes began to come in, modern clothes.
People began to seek those out, because they compared it with
the clothes from the 1970s and 80s, they began to create connections between the traditional and the modern, and we had never
seen anything like them.

As for my clothes . . . briefly put, in the summer I sewed a ma jia,[166] then it got colder and it needed sleeves, then it got even colder and it needed longer sleeves, then people began to ask if it could have a lining, and so on. So I was forced to start thinking, and I thought that I would create a specialized shop just for that sort of thing. So it was the market that spurred me on . . . Later on, it became a fashion house, specializing in modern and traditional attire. At first I thought that the market for this was . . . small, but then Hong Kong was reannexed, then Macao, then Taiwan—where Chinese culture is taken seriously, the Taiwanese really love traditional clothing—came into the picture . . . many Taiwanese jump onto a plane and come here to buy clothes, and so they began to come here, to Beijing, to me.

At first I thought it would last three or four years, and then people would stop liking my clothes and not buy them any more. I've been doing this since 1996, but even now people are interested in my clothes. I think it's because the Chinese have experienced a continual fading of the brilliance of their homeland, its magnificence, and they feel they have to find their own roots, find their own culture in this modern age. And that they have to develop this culture. In designing traditional clothes, I take the demands of the market into consideration, I observe what's going on from one year to the next: maybe this year blue is fashionable, then next year green . . . I try to satisfy people's requirements for their lives and . . . well, you understand. Now I continually connect tradition with the marketplace and the contemporary era. People find their roots in my clothes. At the same time they're modern. Something like that. I think that is the essence of my clothes.

I want my clothes to become as famous as Peking duck or Wangfujing,[167] or any of those well-known traditional Chinese things, like . . . oh . . . the Peking Opera, so I want my company Muzhenliao to have a special mission within the world of Chinese attire—to present the coexistence of tradition and modernity . . . like something eternally evoking the classical, so that even if we go to Hong Kong or wherever, then tradition and modernity won't be forgotten—it will be eternal, just like Tiananmen.[168]

Culture is something that I'm continuously developing, and then it turns into something new. I read all the time about traditional architecture, instruments, music. I have a dress, in front, below the neck, there's a circular neckline with a Chinese button going over it. Now where did I get that from? There's an old piece of furniture, a large armoire, in the middle of it is a round copper lock. It comes from there.

My clothes are one way of representing Chinese culture. While I'm designing them, I add many original factors. When you look at my clothes, you should not only feel that they are beautiful but you should also see the culture in them. The people who buy my clothes are doing cultural work. You could say that. A lot of French people in particular buy my clothes. There are many foreign embassies here in Beijing, and they come from there to order my clothes. Why? One reason is that these foreigners really like the fabrics in these clothes. For example, you can't get satin like this anywhere in the world, it's really bright, the qipao[169] of the waitress (*she points*) is also made from that. That is something you can find only in China. Another reason is that foreigners don't like it when something is too old, they want something modern in it as well, they're willing to pay to wear some kind of 'culture' (*laughs*) . . .

For me, Chinese tradition—all of these things—because China's history goes back a few thousand years, all of this . . . history, is really weighty, strong. And you can't compare this with a modern culture that has no past behind it. In the olden times, people took traditional culture so very . . . seriously—how should I put it?—they really took it to heart. Not like today, when what you have here is too much of all this and that, all kinds of . . . shit. As I see it, in China, after the acquisition of material wealth, spiritual demands became even more important. We don't need America or Japan, because here, for us . . . here culture, classical culture, is the basis of everything. There are, for example, tall buildings here, it's possible that their upper storeys have been completed by the Americans or the Europeans or the Japanese, but the foundations have been dug by the Chinese. And that is the basis.

China went through many difficulties in its past, but now everything is much better, so that we have to see it like this: China was asleep but has now woken up. In our brains, there is one part in the depths which has not changed, that's the part we think with, that's why we're independent. Just as a person never forgets his parents, the Chinese never forget their classical past. China has gone down many wrong paths: there were many contradictions and misunderstandings between some people and other people, between people and the Party. Anyone who thinks otherwise and who says that today—when we have finally awoken and are returning to our past—anyone who denies this, saying that it's just some chaotic modern culture that we have now, well, that person is lying, is somehow sick, spiritually . . . something like that. And there is nothing to fear in business. The market is the decisive factor. The demand. Yes, the past is really important to me, but in the end? The end is business. That's the bottom line. That's where a person can measure up what he's done. So there is no problem here. Later I'll give you some clothes (*laughs*), come to Muzhenliao, we'll talk about it, it's here on the Wangfujing, you can pick something out and then you'll see. OK? Just don't be afraid of business. (*Her cell phone rings and she answers it*) Wei[170] . . . ah . . . just a bit longer, yes, a bit . . . about 10 minutes or so, and fine, you wait . . . Are you going home? Wait a bit, and then I too will . . . Because I'm still talking . . . One of Mr Yang Lian's friends is here . . . he's also a foreigner . . . what?! . . . Me? Fine. We'll talk about it later. Aha. OK.

Miss Wang stands up, and, as she extends her hand in farewell, Stein is prepared for the grip of a strong handshake, but it isn't that at all: it's gentle, her hand hardly touches Stein's. During her monologue she looked at her watch maybe 10 times, and she laughed twice. Now she is saying goodbye to Xi Chuan, she is smiling, and in this smile you can see how truly exquisite she is, then the two men escort her to the door, they watch, as she gets into a SUV worth many millions and the chauffeur zooms away with her into the Beijing night. Xi Chuan and Stein return, silent, to their table, neither man speaks a word, they both keep looking towards where she has zoomed away to, as if gazing after the exit of a stern spirit—until at last they slowly come back to life, and, no longer speaking of 'serious matters', they eat and drink, their manners are loosened, more dishes arrive, the face of Xi Chuan becomes smooth, at times he leans back, clasps his hands over his pot belly, and laughs, liberated.

4. Mama

When he gets home at about midnight, he finds that Mama is still awake. At first he silently inserts the key into the lock and opens the door so as not to wake her, but then he sees that the light is still on in her room; he softly goes to her door, and calls into the room, Mama, are you still awake?—Of course, she yells out gaily, and says something to the effect that there's nothing to worry about, for if he, Stein, is coming back to the flat, she would never go to sleep.

Stein really loves Mama.

She is so tiny, so frail, so soft-spoken, that it seems a miracle that she has endured until now, and unbelievable that she, working her entire life as a doctor, has been able to withstand these 60-odd years. And she would be working now, were she not confined to her bed due to illness. For weeks she has not been able to get out into the fresh air;

she can't even leave her room, she is enclosed there. Whenever he can, Stein sits next to her and listens. Mama has an upright piano, which Stein used to play for her sometimes; she was always so deeply affected, though, that Stein stopped doing so. Instead he would tell her about his day, then get her to talk about her life. Just like now.

Mama, there's one thing I never asked you: What was life like when you were a small child? What was everyday life like back then?

MAMA. As you know, I was born in 1934, but of course I don't have any memories directly from that period. The first things I can remember are from the time of the Japanese occupation. The Japanese . . . (*she tries to recall the word in English, the language in which they are speaking*) . . . war. The whole thing was more of a decisive impression for me, rather than a memory. I might have been three years old . . . I heard the sound of a huge explosion. It was horrifyingly powerful. We lived in alley, and in my room I was really afraid. I hid underneath the bed (*laughs*). Otherwise . . . I recall nothing from that time.

And thus, so to speak, my life began. With that huge explosion. Later on, when I was a little older, I already knew about some things, I knew that the Japanese had occupied Beijing, and my feelings were . . . they were such that I felt that in my life there was nothing happy . . . nothing cheerful . . . nothing, not a single happy thing. When the Japanese occupied our country, life was not secure. The mere fact of remaining alive was not secure. Nor was my father's work. Because my father was 48 years older than me. He worked at the Shifan University,[171] and he was already considered old. So we were afraid he would be dismissed. And prices were really high! At that time the Japanese just left us one single thing to eat—xiliang, millet grains. We could hardly get any rice. For the most part it was cornmeal or barley. Unfortunately, even the grains that we got from the Japanese were ruined, they had a bad taste and a greenish colour. The Japanese gave us whatever could no longer be eaten. So the only thing we could do was to keep hens at home. They laid a fair amount of eggs. I really liked that. We hardly bought anything, we had no money. So we ate mainly eggs. We didn't eat the grain, but gave it to the hens. That's how it was.

At that time, life at home was not too good. In a material sense. Because my father was the only one who earned any money. There were four of us siblings. My mother stayed at home with us. She took care of the household. My father always worked, my mother was at home, and their life was quite bitter. They were crushed by poverty in every respect. We were never allowed outside, except to go to school. And there was no place anywhere where we could have played.

What about friends? Was it possible to play with them somehow?

MAMA. We had no friends! I'm telling you that they only let us out to go to school, and there we only had lessons—of course there were no games in school, so where could there have been any friends? Later on, even when we were older, we couldn't go to the movies. Because the Japanese soldiers went to the movies for their fun. Not that we could have spent the household money on something like that. We never went to the movies at all. As soon as school was over, they let us out to go home immediately. We couldn't even stay in the courtyard because there were Japanese living next door. And, usually, the Japanese children bullied the Chinese children. They were always out there in the courtyard, and they could play. Not us. If we went out when they were there, they beat us. So we couldn't go into the courtyard unless an adult was with us. Either my mama, or the house supervisor. We were even accompanied on the way to school, I remember that. It is easy to beat a child. Because of that, there was always an adult going with us to school. Once we were inside school, there were no problems.

What were the lessons like?

MAMA. It was just an average school. I have to think a bit . . . (*laughs*) . . . Oh yes . . . There was a huge entrance with a horizontal inscription above it . . . I don't remember anything specifically. What was written there . . . Maybe it was something like 'Li Yi Lian Chi',[172] a quote from Confucius, it was a quote from him, that is certain . . . Then there was the classroom. Well, that was pretty basic. Little tables, little chairs, a blackboard on the wall, the teacher wrote on it in chalk. At the beginning of the lesson, when the teacher came in, the class steward yelled: Stand up! Then: Sit down! During the lessons, we sat with our hands behind our backs.

Were the girls and boys together?

MAMA. Yes, usually they were together.

How many grades were there in primarily school?

MAMA. I went to school for six years from the time I was five, until 1945. Then the Japanese surrendered—15 August. The surrender. Then I began middle school.

Wait, let's not go so fast! Mama, what did you learn in primary school?

MAMA. Poetry recitation, the national language, mathematics, from Grade Three there was also Japanese . . . as for the rest, now . . .

How did a class proceed?

MAMA. . . . And a little later . . . we had history, geography . . .

So how did a class proceed?

MAMA. We were taught from textbooks. The teacher explained. We wrote it down. But when the teacher explained, there was nothing for us to do, we had to pay attention, our hands behind our backs. We weren't allowed to fidget, to whisper, nothing like that . . . (*laughs*) . . .

Mama, I don't understand how it worked . . .

MAMA. Well, in Grade One the teacher wrote something on the blackboard, then we read it aloud, all of us. The teacher wrote, we read aloud. For example: Tian liang le—no, that wasn't it . . . (*concentrates*) . . . For example: Tian ping te yi an tian . . . In the old days, there was a kind of pinyin, it was called zhuyin zimu. We had to somehow write down the pronunciation until we knew Chinese properly, in fact it's the same today . . . (*chants*) bo-po, like that, mo-fo . . . de-te . . . ne-le, it was like that, it's the same as the pinyin everyone uses today, the transcription with English letters for the Chinese characters . . . But we used the zhuyin zimu[173] system. We learnt this first. And after we learnt that, there were lessons and we had to take notes. In Grade One, they called it guoyu.[174] Now they call it yuwen, that is, language and literature. The first lesson was Tian liang le—'The heavens have become radiant.' That was the first lesson in my primary school! Yes— Tian liang le! The first lesson!

The first lesson? The very first one? And who says that Mama doesn't remember anything . . . !

MAMA (*proudly*). Yes. Tian liang le. Then the second lesson: Didi, meimei, kuai qilai—'Younger brother, younger sister, quickly rise!' That was the second lesson! I remember now! And the third lesson: Jie shuo—'Little sister says': Wo ai taiyang hong, wo ai taiyang liang, wo ai zaoshang de taiyang guang—'I love the red sun, I love the sun's brightness, I love the light of the rising sun.' That's how it went from one lesson to the next. Then there was tian as a sound: te-yian: tian—the sky—the teacher read it out, tian, we repeated after him, te-yi-an: tian . . . The entire classroom echoed with our voices. Everywhere you could hear only our voices, we repeated it so much! First, that is, we had to brush up on it, then the next time the teacher would call us to come to the black board and write it down. He called on this or that pupil to come to the board. While they were writing, the others could take notes. But if you weren't writing, you had to keep your hands behind your back. Your hands couldn't be like this (*demonstrates*), only nicely behind your back. That was how you had to behave during classes. Also during maths. After the teacher finished his explanation, writing it down and pronouncing it, we chanted the same thing, like this (*recites, chanting each syllable*) yi jia yi dengyu ji, yi jia yi dengyu er . . . 'One plus one is how much, one plus one is two' . . . And that's how it went until the exams . . . During the exams, they handed out a question sheet and we had to fill it in.

Did they teach you Confucius?

MAMA. I wouldn't say that they taught Confucius but that Confucius was there in all of our lessons. In the yuwen class.

So they didn't have you reading the *Lunyu* right away?

MAMA (*laughing*). Of course they did, how could they not have . . . But the spirit of Confucius permeated the schoolbooks. And as we got older, there were more and more Confucian texts. But as for what Confucius meant in the old order—before the Japanese came—well, that was taught at home. Because at home we learnt the most basic laws of life, based upon the wisdom of Confucius. At home it was said, for example, that we must respect our parents and that we must help our siblings. And it was at home that we learnt how to do what is necessary. *How to be a human being.*

Mama, exactly what was it that they taught you at home?

MAMA. To study hard. To greet people in the proper way. To take care of ourselves. We were very obedient. We were taught to be diligent, so that later on we would be able to work independently for China . . . And not to leave.

But what was there of Confucius in that?

MAMA. Everything. All of it. Actually it wasn't necessary to teach us. Because we observed how the elders conducted themselves. They didn't have to say: do this in this way, do that in that way, because we saw how they did it, and we came to know for ourselves what was right: to respect our elders, to help them . . . There was also a book in my childhood, *Kong Rong Rang Li,*[175] and the hero of that book taught us that we must give everything to the elders and to the little ones, that we must not keep the good things for ourselves. We knew the story of Kong Rong from a very early age, and that story, and others like it, taught us how to be good. For example, if you had four apples, you had to give the two bigger ones to your parents, the smaller one to your sibling, and then keep the smallest one for yourself. Parents also adhered to the principle of giving everything to their children. We did everything as we observed. We knew that we had to respect our parents. And we didn't have to be taught that. We knew by ourselves. *We knew.*

Mama, were your parents religious?

MAMA. No.

And your grandparents?

MAMA. I don't know anything about my paternal grandparents, I never saw them. I don't think they could be called Buddhists, although Buddhism did make some impression on them. Some kind of impression on their lives. It influenced them.

What about Taoism?

MAMA. They didn't believe in that either, neither my parents nor my grandparents. If they believed in something, then it would have been Buddhism. But we couldn't really know what they believed in. All I can say is that the philosophy of Buddhism and Taoism had a certain effect on them. They were also strongly influenced by scientific and Western ways of thinking. They did not, for example, go to pray to the Buddha. They respected the fact that, in Buddhism, one has to be good. One's heart has to be good, and one must not do evil. For evil brings punishment in its wake. Not that someone comes and punishes you, but that *there will be punishment* . . .

Mama, who was considered a bad child?

MAMA. In those days we were afraid of robbery, because there were very many poor people, and there were those among them who had learnt bad ways—the heart of a poor man must remain good, but it happened that some turned into thieves. Every house had a flat roof in those days, and well, one of these bad children climbed up on top of the house, and from there he climbed down into the courtyard, and that is how he stole things. My mother kept chickens at home, and someone stole two yellow chickens! So we were afraid, and at night we had to tightly lock our doors and gates. We were afraid that someone would sneak in. Our teacher told us a story: he had a white shirt which he washed and then hung in the window to dry, but the window only had paper in it, and someone tore the paper and stole his shirt, our very own teacher told us this story. So how could we not have been afraid of thieves?

So, a bad person is someone who steals?

MAMA. Oh yes, and something else, the Japanese soldiers were also bad. We were afraid of them. They wore leather boots, and they always had a sword on their backs. We were afraid of them. Then there were the beggars. There were so many of them, countless children, they lived there, next to the street, and they begged, and even though we felt sorry for them, we knew that among them were many bad children. We were still able to eat, and so we were not counted among the poorest of the poor, and yet I have many memories of how cold we were in the winter . . . We nearly froze to death! The cold came in through the windows and the door!

Were your mother and father strict? Did you love them? Or were you afraid of them?

MAMA. The educational demands placed upon us children were very strict, but not pitiless. My parents were full of love for us. They were loving and protective. Their principles were important: we had to study well and not waste our time, but they loved us very much as well . . .

Mama, aren't you tired? It's already past midnight, past one o'clock . . . !

MAMA. No, not at all! Stay! Let's keep talking! A few hours of sleep is enough for me.

So tell me, then, what it was like in the evenings?

MAMA. We came from school, we made dinner, nothing special.

Did you eat dinner together?

MAMA. Many times we didn't. Because my papa worked a lot, and sometimes we had already gone to bed by the time he came home. My mother always stayed up to let him in. There was no key—the door could only be opened from the inside. I remember, once, in the winter, there was a lot of snow, and the road was very slippery, and I, under the blanket, was really afraid that my father would slip on the way home. At times like that I couldn't fall asleep, and so I waited with my mother for my father to come home.

What did you dream about? What were your greatest desires?

MAMA. We didn't have too many aspirations back then because life itself was very tense. We just hoped that we could always go to school. That we could buy what we needed for school. That there would be enough money for that. I hoped that my parents would remain healthy and happy. And of course they hoped that one day life outside would be secure. In those times you could not dream of anything else . . .

But every child has some kind of dream! A nice red dress?

MAMA. I never fantasized about things like that then. Because I felt it was enough if there was something to eat. And there was no point to daydreaming. We didn't want to burden our parents with dreams like that! We did not want to make their anxieties worse. During the Lunar New Year we always got a new pair of shoes. Our mother would make us new clothes now and then. Once, I remember, we were taken to our one relative in Beijing, a great-aunt, who gave us all some money. That was the happiest day of my childhood. Each of us got our money in a red envelope. And I never spent mine. I kept adding to it, watching over it, never touching it, until liberation. And then came liberation, and, from one day to the next, my money suddenly was worthless.

How many years did you keep it?

MAMA. Many, many years. As a matter of fact I was a little sad, because I had been saving it for my parents, to give it to them one day. All my siblings would have liked to buy something, but not me. I loved only my parents. But I'd saved it up for them in vain.

Mama, I'm beginning to get sleepy now. But something just came to my mind. How did children sense the love their parents had for them? Did the parents show it?

MAMA. Yes, and very much so! But we had to study hard.

And if someone did something bad, what was the punishment?

MAMA. We were never bad.

Stein looks up at the wall clock above her head, it is really very late now. He sees that Mama's eyelids are also beginning to close. Stein finally bids her goodnight, and goes to lie down.

We were never bad.

Stein adjusts the pillow beneath his head, and then pulls the sheet onto himself.

We were never bad.

Mama, why can't you live for ever?

5. The Last Mandarin

Right before his trip to China, Stein meets with Yang Lian in Munich. Yang, aware of his Hungarian friend's experiences in China in 1998, as well as Stein's opinion—based upon his experiences—of the situation 'at home', does not share Stein's view at all: in his formulation, the spirit of China is not dead, the spirit of China is still essentially alive in the 'depths', and when he finishes this pronunciation in response to Stein's question, he is silent for a moment, then he looks at Stein with an impish glance, as it were reinforcing his words, and then adds: Wait a minute, just go see my father in Tianjin, do not fail to do so, and then you will see that Chinese classical culture is certainly still alive, you will see classical culture in its fullest dimension, because he, my dear father in Tianjin, is the embodiment of classical culture.

And so now Stein sits with this dignified, marvellous, grey-haired, elderly man in a destitute, tiny flat on one of Tianjin's housing estates, which reminds Stein of the one he rented in Shanghai in the vicinity of Fudan University; there he sits across from Yang Qinghua, and he immediately begins by repeating what his son has said about him. At this, the elderly gentleman laughs greatly, but does not express his opinion in any other way. Then he becomes serious, he thinks for a while and finally he says:

YANG. I am interested in Chinese classical culture.

Then, in order to get to the heart of the matter, Stein asks about Yang's opinion as to the role—or potential role—of classical culture in contemporary Chinese life.

Mr Yang thinks for a bit, then takes a deep breath. From this it is clear that what is to follow will be a performance. For it quickly emerges that every verbal communication of Lian's father is a pronouncement. Stein realizes, however, that the articulation of his thoughts demands precisely this mode of expression. There is a structure to everything he says, a kind of noble rhetoric, a very ancient rhetoric, unknown today and emerging from a great distance, the vastness of which Mr Yang himself may not be fully aware. Or of which he prefers not to be aware.

YANG. It is my view that the influence of classical culture on modern life, upon us . . . upon all of us . . . has an effect. We are the most illustrious of ancient civilizations. Unparalleled in the world. For our culture, in the annals of history, is truly singular. Every other ancient civilization, Egyptian, Roman and so on, all came to an end, they disappeared. Ours is the only one which is still living, and that is why our traditions have such an extraordinarily singular character. Our history is a written history, and by that you should understand that this is a culture built upon the unconditional primacy of writing. Chinese history developed under the influence of the written language. Writing was always of the most crucial importance for the Chinese nation. And here I must speak of Confucius. I personally do not like the philosophical system of Confucius, and that is because he over-emphasized the role of authority in society. If you exist in this society, then you are determined by means of authority. You are subjected to the authority of the father, to the authority of the emperor. I do not like authority. I like freedom. Freedom of the spirit. There is a counterweight to Confucius in Chinese tradition: Laozi and Zhuangzi. In my view, it is them and their philosophy that form the highest order in China. They are also the ones who have exercised the greatest influence on us.

But as I pronounced these words in judgement of Confucius just now, I must immediately adjust them somewhat. Of course Confucius is present in my thoughts and in who I am. I am familiar with his works and many of his teachings, especially those dealing with his views on the world: those works have influenced me deeply. The Confucian school of thought does not influence theory but everyday life. If I had a friend who came from a distant land to visit me, that would make me happy. How could it not? And this is Confucius—clearly you know what well-known passage and sentence I am referring to.[176] So, to summarize: we have all lived, and continue to live, in the shadow of Confucius.

Nonetheless, when I was 21 years old or so, when I began to be acquainted with the Western intellectual world, I came across, for example, the notion of democracy. There is nothing like it in Chinese culture. Of course, I understood that this was a very good thing. Equality, freedom, democracy. I thought that all these were very positive, appropriate concepts. And at once these concepts began to be incorporated into my own Chinese culture. And since the basis, the starting point, and the roots of my thinking all originate from Chinese culture, the information and influences I acquired from abroad never really drew me away from my own culture. There came to be a kind of balance within me, and that was possible only because I based my own culture upon that of Laozi and Zhuangzi, both of whom taught us that if your inner world is free, then you too are free. So we can state that whether it be a question of Confucius or Laozi, everyone here is somehow influenced by the Chinese culture of ancient times.

But if you go deeper, then you have to speak about the intelligentsia. In our tradition, the intelligentsia has always been comprised of the best, the noblest part of society. They are the people who protect tradition. Without them, there is no progress and no culture. So they are the most important: they are the brains that think. As for the workers—manual labourers, peasants—thinking is not their strong point. They are under the influence of the wider public. Their thoughts are ordinary thoughts. What they think about is ordinary, and what they do is ordinary. Nevertheless, they live their lives under the influence of our ancient civilization. While they are unchanging and perpetual, the intelligentsia, and only the intelligentsia is rejuvenated again and again in its own spirit: they, the literati, are the ones who turn to the spirit until they begin to perceive the true meaning of life.

Then I would say that I . . . I will speak a little about myself. I have children: there is Lian, there is my daughter, there is my younger son, I have three children. Their opinion of me is very good. They love me very much. And I can say that there are no generational conflicts between us. Because I am an intellectual, I have never had and still do not have any great desire to pressure them. I have always spoken to them freely and I continue to do so, not just to them but to anyone with whom I may have had the opportunity to speak. I believe that if one speaks freely and openly, there can be no faults in his speech. And if I am not right, you should interrupt me. My daughter says that I am the best person in the world. She says you can't find anyone like me anywhere. Someone who lets her speak. Who lets her say what she really wants to say. There are some truths that I say, and some truths that she says: if she is right, I accept it. If she is right, I adjust my opinion. I can even accept that part of your opinion which isn't right. I never say: I will not permit this . . . Do what you like. I know, of course, what isn't right. There is my younger son. When he was a soldier, around the age of 20, what happened? There is a very bad tradition in the Chinese army—everyone smokes cigarettes. They smoke dreadfully! It is bad for one's health. But I never said to my son: Stop smoking! He stopped by himself. The correct thing, therefore, is to let a person decide freely for himself.

Maybe that's why my children love me. They tell me their worries, and I tell them what I think about them. But I do not force my opinions on them. It's possible that my opinion is not always correct. They must decide. They must think over whether it is correct or not.

Well, now, getting back to the intelligentsia: they are the people who bear the glory of a better world. This is very important for our tradition. That this quality of humanity exists: the quality of the intelligentsia in Chinese culture. This is a huge difference between the Western and Eastern systems. From early times, European states strived to be forceful military powers. A European state always devoted serious attention to the military side of things. The most outstanding people were always those who could kill the most enemies. At the same time, here in China, Confucius tells us: 'I do not think much of those people who are brave in reaching the eastern sea while carrying mountains on their shoulders . . . I do not value such people very much. I like people who think.' So: those who think, those who teach are important. Well, that is our tradition.

And this tradition is very closely linked to language. Our language is comprised of characters contained in squares—every single character can fit, with perfect proportions, into a square frame. There is great meaning to this. And every cultivated intellectual was and is aware of the significance of this.

The guest interrupts, saying that he, Stein, has a different view of Confucianism, but that he does not live, nor has he ever lived, in China. And that he has as much esteem for Confucius as for Laozi and Zhuangzi. Because, he goes on to explain, for him Confucianism is the only social philosophy which introduces the concept of morality into everyday life. Christianity was not able to do this. And when he has spoken of that here, every one of his interlocutors nodded, telling him he was right and saying that without Confucianism there would be no China. They also told him that although they sensed how much danger there was in the development of contemporary society, they denied that Confucianism had disappeared from the societal order. This, said Stein, was really shocking, because his experience has been precisely the opposite.

YANG. I agree with you. The Confucian school of thought had a good effect on people. It always placed morality above success. You can be successful, you can be a successful official, but from the viewpoint of morality this means nothing. Confucius said: Place morality above success. This Confucian influence was without a doubt good. I agree. And in that sense as well, Confucianism had a greater influence here than either Buddhism or Christianity. The Christian and Buddhist religions are both very good. As far as I can see—and I attended a Methodist school, so I know about it—Christianity is a very positive religion, first and foremost, because it devotes special attention to love. It says that you must love other people. This is much more important to me than Confucian morality. Because here in China we never paid enough attention to personal love. There are two kinds of people who are difficult to deal with: children and women, as both are led by their emotions. Confucius never spoke about the love between a man and a woman. He never engaged with the question of love. In Christianity, by contrast, love is at the very centre of things, and this has deeply touched me. In my life, this always meant: love your children. More precisely: show your love to your children. This is more important than anything else. This is what has caused, and still causes, so many problems for us. Everyone tortures their children, saying, study, study, but *there is no love*! Everyone will say to you: But I love my children! Then my answer would be: So then love them, really! Show them that you love them! The greatest mistakes, the greatest misapprehensions and the greatest lack of understanding all stem from this. So, to summarize, I truly respect Christianity because it emphasizes the importance of love.

Buddhism speaks of emptiness, the emptiness of all that exists, that is, the end of everything is emptiness. I believe that this is perfectly, immaculately true. Everything has a beginning, everyone and everything must live and then must die, everything and everyone must come to an end; the universe too will come to an end. We don't know what the beginning of time was, nor do we know what the end will be. We know that there are boundaries, but we also know that, in reality, everything is boundless. It is never possible to come to the end of anything. We have knowledge neither of the small nor of the large: neither of the small nor of the large epochs, neither of the small nor of the large domains. And then Buddhism comes along and says that everything is empty, everything becomes empty. And this is irrevocably true. This is the whole truth. I believe we must learn from this. I do not believe that we need to devote too much attention to fate, to the world, because all this will become empty. Our own lives will also become empty. Nothing. This is what Buddhism teaches, and that is why I hold Buddhism in great esteem.

But for us in China, Laozi is the most important. Laozi was a very wise person. If someone reads his books, then he will have the most profound knowledge. Because how did the whole thing begin? The truth cannot be pronounced. We cannot say what is true. Neither can we say what is not true. Truth is something of which you cannot speak.

You cannot get to the end of things.

And now we are speaking of the modern world.

And I am very worried.

I am worried about the future of humanity. Not just about the future of China. But of the entire world. I am really worried.

The twentieth century witnessed as much progress as perhaps all the twenty previous centuries put together. We can be certain that the twentieth century represents the greatest development in all of history. On the other hand: all things now develop with horrific speed, and I don't know who is going to stop this. In vain will we stand in the ruins, by then it will be too late. I am really worried.

I do not care for the modern world. I do not like speed of things. The spirit is not happy in this world. You have too many things. You have a television, you have a computer. Take, for example, the computer: no one knows what it actually is. Or what we can do with it. Computers bother me. Why? I know that computers are very interesting. I like to play. I can spend hours in front of the computer. But I have no energy for it. It will be the death of me. Well, just wait! Wait, wait a few years, and I'll catch up with you. But my life won't be enough for that, and I can't spend so much time in . . . play! I am worried, really worried about this speed, this frightening speed. Worried for all of mankind. Who will stop it? You can't stop it. What is just a fantasy today becomes—in the space of a few days—reality. And then you'll be able to connect your brain to the computer. Then you'll be able to learn everything. All knowledge will be in your personal computer. I don't know Hungarian but it will be in my computer.

This is truly terrifying. All the cultures of the world will disappear, including the classical imperial culture of China, which

I love so much! It will become nothing. Take young people. They are not interested in classical culture in the slightest. They have no time to study. You need to read books in order to know what is what, but you have no time. I want to play computer games, I want to relax, I want to listen to easy music and dance in the evenings. They are not interested in the ancient era, they're not interested in culture. They have no relationship to it.

And you can't stop this either. Progress is horrific. When a change like this has taken place, you cannot follow it with your feelings. Nor can you do anything to make it stop.

He expresses himself simply and precisely, and, behind the simplicity and precision of his words, one senses the deep prudence of a harmonious worldview. In more confidential tones, Stein tells him that he seeks a metaphysical force in the background of this process which he too feels to be unstoppable. So he thinks that *if* evil does appear, no one will be able to do anything against it. Only a new metaphysics can be of help. But such a metaphysics cannot be built on any kind of dichotomy, it cannot be built on contradictions, on duality, on some new kind of enigmatic designation, it cannot be built on expression with its redemptive strength. He does not believe—László Stein propounds at the Tianjin housing estate—that words can have any role in it. Nor, he believes, can concepts. That is enough for now. He is, however, much more curious about Mr Yang's sincere opinion: Is there any chance at all for the creation of a new metaphysics?

YANG. This is a very difficult question. No one can solve a problem like this in a Communist regime. The government can't do anything. The teachers, the writers, the intellectuals don't even think about it. They do not sense that there is a problem. Nothing seems problematic to them. They only sense that there is progress, that everything is better than it was 10 years ago: they are happy now. They sense no danger. But, in my opinion, we are at a turning point—and now I am thinking of all of humanity. We have reached the end of one era, and now we don't know what is all around us. Because we're already in a new era, and it is very different from the old one. Science and the world of technology are both changing everything so quickly, even our bodies. So the original ancient culture was present here, but to no avail, at this point in history it has come to a stop. It still has some effect, some kind of continuity, but it cannot analyse and reformulate things, it cannot impact things with absolute strength. The age to follow will be full of dangers. It will be full of difficulties. In all likelihood, it will not be a good future for mankind. It is even possible that this new era will mean the end of mankind.

But no one can stop this.

And so what can I do? I try through my own influence to help the lives of those whom I love, the lives of those around me. Many people listen to me. They hear what I say. They love the kind of spirit which is mine. I can have an effect on them. Maybe even a good effect, so that they will try to do good in their lives. Of course I am most interested in my children. The future of my children. What can they think about the world? What can they do for the world?

What? I believe it is necessary to help them so that they can live happy lives. So that they may live happily. This is the most important thing. They must live a happy life. If they are successful, if they earn a lot of money, if they become famous, all of this may occur but it isn't important. You can be successful, you can be unsuccessful, but you can be happy too. And that is what I do. Many people live in big houses—I live in this little housing-estate apartment. I have nothing. It doesn't matter. Many of my class-mates went on to become successful people, many of them are very powerful. But of all my classmates, I am the only happy one. My strategy is to be happy.

I am not interested in being famous, I am lazy, I don't like to write. In order to write you need to get your brain together, and I don't like doing that. My children want me to write something, but I refuse to do so. Even that doesn't interest me, nor does wealth. Only happiness does. My grandfather was a mandarin, and he was very wealthy but he was never happy. I would not like to be like him. He treated poor people very ruthlessly, and so everyone was his enemy. You must know exactly what is impor-tant and what isn't. Fame is not important, that does not bring happiness. Nor does power. I have friends who became powerful. They have power now: I am a nobody, and I bow down to them. But one day they'll be tired, and they won't have any more power, and suddenly no one will be bowing down to them. Is it worth it? Are they happy? They believe themselves to be important, but it's just a dream, a spectacle, an apparition that will disappear—it will come to an end and that will be that.

What you can do is to tell people what happiness is, and how they can become happy. I have lived my entire life in happiness. Because I have been free.

Something comes to mind—Stein now speaks again—and it always comes to mind when he hears someone speaking about personal happiness. For years now, he's been wandering around the world, now he's here in Tianjin, tomorrow he'll be in Beijing, then in Suzhou, then somewhere in the West, and before this he was in Berlin, then in Zurich and London and Paris and Sarajevo and in the eighth district in Budapest, and before that he was in New York and Barcelona and Kyoto and Tokyo, but it doesn't matter where he is, he walks along the street and he sees misery, he sees unhappiness, he senses the horrors, there is always evil in front of him and evil behind him, and if he thinks of this then he really doesn't know what to make of his, Mr Yang's words, he is confused, because how can he follow his advice, how can he aspire to personal happiness—when he is amid the unhappy, in misery and in the consciousness of the horrors and the presence of perpetual evil?

YANG. For me, this is an easy question. You love others, you must love other people. You must represent love and friendship. You must express compassion with those who suffer. That is enough. You must do what you can. You must help everyone you can with the best part of your being. Show compassion for them, and that is enough. There is a horrific amount of suffering in the world, you must try to help those who suffer, but *you cannot do everything.*

But he, Stein, is not able to feel compassion for the depraved and the hardened.

YANG. Of course. You must hate them. You must love those who suffer, but you must hate those who are evil. I too hate certain people, but I cannot do anything against them. They could easily kill me. But I couldn't kill them. I have no power for that. And I don't even want it.

Mr Yang is quiet. Stein suddenly realizes how tired he is and he realizes that if he is tired, how exhausted this old man, almost 70 years old, must be. He has to leave, and he thinks for a long time about what Mr Yang said. After a long silence, he finally speaks again.

Mr Yang, he says, never has he found it so difficult to end a conversation. But he has looked at the clock, and he has looked at the face of Mr Yang, and he sees that he is tired. Surely now he would like to go to sleep, and Stein is detaining him. It is night-time already. Please don't be angry, Stein says, that he has stayed for so long, and has not let him rest.

YANG. Nonsense! I never sleep at night. Only in the morning, before noon. I sleep seven times a week, but always just a little bit. But not at night. Never.

I never sleep at night: the words of Mr Yang echo in Stein's mind, and he cannot move, he does not get up, he does not start off, it is, however, already time, and maybe even necessary that he get up to catch the last train back to Beijing, and it could already be night-time—it's just that he is incapable of movement, unable to get up and set off, because he just keeps listening to Yang Qinghua who begins to speak again, he just listens as he speaks, he just looks at his grey hair, his noble features, he just marvels at this mandarin on the housing estate in Tianjin, as he just keeps speaking, in his own extraordinarily precise English he just keeps pronouncing and pronouncing his sentences, the most simple sentences in the world, and outside, it is already late at night—very late at night.

A DREAM IN THE COURTYARD OF THE GUANGJI SI[177]

By now he is really tired and he has nowhere to go. He no longer wants to see any temples, any museums, or any exhibits. He wanders like a lost man around Beijing. He can't stay home, nor can he sit forever next to Mama's bed. So every day he comes out of the house, and he walks along the same streets, and he ends up in the same place:

in the Guangji Si, a forgotten, abandoned Buddhist monastery situated amid a few remaining buildings—because no one is ever there, not a soul, just as there was no one here yesterday, neither monk, nor pilgrim, really, no one comes here. He finds his place, the place where he was yesterday, the day before yesterday as well, he goes to one of the inner courtyards at the back of the little temple, and there he sits down on the same step of the ruined pavilion, and he doesn't do anything, he doesn't think—nothing.

It's afternoon, or twilight is already beginning to descend, the weak sunlight falls flatly. It warms him a little, and in that warmth he falls into a deep sleep.

Then suddenly he wakes up. Tang Xiaodu is sitting next to him. Stein is really surprised; he doesn't understand how he could have ended up here. How could he have known that he comes here? For while he does not speak, he lights a cigarette, then slowly blows out the smoke. He doesn't look sad but tired, like Stein. Before he could ask how he was able to find him, Stein begins to describe his situation. That he is no longer curious, he doesn't want to see anything, he doesn't want to talk to anyone, and that he was always comes here, into this protection; and then he confesses that he is in despair because he cannot find what he was searching for, and it now seems to him that he never will find it because it no longer exists, or nothing remains of it; and that, moreover, he believes he has only himself to thank for all this despair, because no one ever forced him to believe that what he was looking for was still here, anyone whose word he might have trusted never made any such claim; so that in all likelihood the whole thing was his concoction: he made up the idea that it still existed somewhere, and it was he who began to search, and of course he didn't find anything at all, just a few sad people and a few sad places, and already this stream of words is beginning to gush forth; Xiaodu listens, he nods silently, and Stein just keeps on talking: he was here in 1998 as well, when he came in search of the entirety of classical China, and although he kept telling people that his quest was for Li Taibai, well, of course then too it was the idea of Chinese classical culture that was in his head, and you know, Stein tells him, that journey was still a happy one, he didn't find anything back then either; still, in the end, there was something, and he formulated it like this: that the sky that clouded above him was the same sky that clouded above Li Taibai and all of Chinese classical poetry, and all of Chinese tradition, and this filled him with happiness just to know that it was the same sky; only now he feels so uncertain, so that he will place his trust in in his dear friend Xiaodu, may he be the one to tell Stein now: Are the heavens here above them still the same?

Tang Xiaodu does not reply for a long time.

No, these are not the same heavens, he answers very softly, all the while not looking at Stein. Here below, on the earth, everything has changed. There is no more Buddhism, no more Taoism, there are no monasteries, no painting and no music, no poetry and no tradition— everything here below has changed, so how could the heavens above us be the same?

He rises, takes a few steps back and forth, then walks around the entire courtyard, stopping here and there where there are still patches of sunlight; he stands, warming himself in the sun's rays, and Stein watches him, and he feels that in a moment he will fall asleep in this peaceful silence, here in the innermost courtyard of the Guangji Si.

But he doesn't.

He wakes up.

And there is no one beside him.

The sun has set.

The air is chilly now.

The courtyard is empty.

IN SUZHOU, NOT AT ALL IN SUZHOU

The Road That Leads There, 1

Go to Suzhou, Tang Xiaodu says one day, and this is so surprising from him, as he always helps with everything but never directly intervenes in Stein's plans, he just supports him, and with his solicitude creates the opportunity for what he, Stein, wants, to come about as optimally as possible within the given circumstances, but for Tang Xiaodu to call upon him to do something specific is so unlike him that Stein asks, very cautiously, if he has understood correctly? He should go to Suzhou? To the queen of gardens? To the city of the most

beautiful gardens in the world? Yes, Tang Xiaodu nods seriously—
there, where the Zhouzheng Yuan,[178] the Shizi Lin,[179] the Liu Yuan,[180]
the Yi Yuan,[181] the Canglang Ting[182] and, above all, the Wangshi
Yuan[183] are?—Yes, there, says Tang Xiaodu—but, asks Stein, he
should go to this world-famous location, this tourist paradise to the
south of the Yangtze? He should go to the very citadel of the Chinese
tourist industry? Yes, his gentle friend from Beijing answers, as seriously as he can, and this is so unexpected, and he provides no explanation as to why Stein should go to Suzhou when he has already
travelled around that region fairly thoroughly—so that from this point
on Stein asks him no more questions, he just packs his bags, and
already he is sitting on the train, and already he has arrived one
morning at around ten o'clock, and of course he is walking with the
interpreter out from the station and towards Suzhou, and since it is
not just at any old place that they have arrived, they almost don't need
a map, there are signposts almost everywhere, at least for the most
famous sites, so that at first they don't use anything to help guide them
along but follow their noses, follow the tourist signs: the first one is
next to the Beisi Ta,[184] the monumental structure of the pagoda of
the Northern Temple, and immediately they are at the most famous
site, the Zhuozheng Garden, and the crowd is horrific, horrific with
its unrestrained groups of tourists, the live loudspeakers, ignominious
to the enormity of Japanese tradition so relevant to this place, horrific
to keep bumping into the so-called tour guides, so that they just
remark as much as they can—walking along the winding, labyrinth-
like paths situated among the enchantingly airy pavilions and courtyards—that the Zhuozheng Yuan is *truly astounding*—they are already
going across into the nearby Shizi Lin, into the Lion Garden, where
fate determines that they can wedge themselves into the breach

between two attacking crowds of tourists, and so they are able to give themselves fully over to wonder, because, despite the difficult circumstances, the largest garden in Suzhou nearly strikes them dumb: they are, this time, in one of the authentic places of the art of the Chinese garden, and here—if they perceive anything at all—in the Lion Garden they are forced to state that the beauty with which the weave of its fabric has been spun is simply amazing, despite the extreme quantity of the extreme rocks of the Tai Lake, because these gardens, in their eyes, seem too crammed full of all these innumerable stone structures, in accordance with the unique use of stone in Chinese gardens, the masses of huge unique stone formations here or there— pock-marked, morbid, really extreme in form—in Zhuozheng as well, but this, the Lion Garden, is enchantingly beautiful—so that afterward, going directly by bus to the southern part of the city, and ending up in the famously hard-to-find Wangshi Yuan, the tiny garden of the Master of the Nets, they give themselves over once and for all because, following the given directions, it is very hard to find—they have to stumble along alleyways promising nothing, and simply believe that, amid the scaffolding and mortar trowels of witheringly banal, ugly little houses, unfriendly gazes and old, crumbling plaster walls, they are on the right path; they are, however, on the right path, and they do find it, and what they find sweeps away their doubts as to whether something original can remain in an area flooded by tourists; much more has happened by the time they have arrived, namely, that they perceive that the Suzhou Garden exists, and that the classical beauties of this stratum have remained, in their essence, undisturbed—if someone steps into the spaces of the Zhuozheng, the Shizi Lin or the Wangshi Yuan, then he has stepped into the lost traditions of China; Stein does not understand how this can be possible, but this is how it is, clearly the tourism experts have been here as well, huge crowds of them, they too have been here, they have set up the ticket offices, they have created the routes for the luxury buses, they have built parking lots for the buses, in a word, they have put the Suzhou gardens on the list in order to let in endless series of tourists, but . . . nothing has been ruined here, it seems almost impossible but that's how it is, the gardens are intact, and they are so surprised by this, and so enthralled, that it is only now, towards the end of the day, that they notice that they haven't spoken a word to each other, they travel along the Renmin Lu, from then on it is their Main Street, going back towards the north, so that they may conclude the day in the Yi Yuan, a day in which the sun has been scorching them, and now is beginning to lose some of its strength, by the time they reach the Yi Yuan it only illuminates and warms, they pay the entrance fee, it is already late, almost closing time, someone at the ticket window tells them, but they interpret it like this: that the Yi Yuan seems almost desolate, and in the obliquely following light, in the pleasant elderly warmth, they stroll into undoubtedly the most affecting of the gardens they have seen in Suzhou on this amazing and mysterious day, they stroll along the silent paths into another immortal creation, into this tiny paradise where, although it is almost closing time, as they were told at the ticket window, it is as if someone had made time stop here, because they still somehow have enough time to stroll slowly around the pavilions, they can in a leisurely manner inspect the steles built into the walls, at the end they can even sit down by the lake in the garden, in front of a pavilion, and give themselves over to the tranquillity gathering over the garden, the beauty inexpressible in words, and, without even looking at their watches, they are able to contemplate the mystery of why they have been sent here and what exactly must be waiting for them now.

Because from this point on, what occupies their minds, most unconditionally Stein's mind, is the question: Why did Tang Xiaodu send them here to Suzhou? No matter what he sees, no matter where he goes, no matter who he meets, he is unable to give himself over to what he sees, where he goes and to whom he speaks; because he continually looks and listens in such a way that he must always decipher what must be deciphered, so that he will not fail to notice, if it happens to come before him, that garden, that street, that person, because of which Tang Xiaodu—or happenstance, or the inscrutable workings of fate—has led him here, in the form of the quiet but determined recommendation of Tang Xiaodu.

The next day, one of Tang Xiaodu's friends is waiting for them, the kind of middle-aged man of whom one could think many things, just not that he is a poet—which however, he is—Tang Xiaodu prepared them for this; a poet, moreover, of Suzhou, one with great influence on contemporary Chinese literature, Xiao Hai, awaits them in a clumsily elegant modern conference centre, part of the world of New China; he is able to make some time for a conversation with Stein during a break in a literary historical conference taking place there. He creates the impression of a tense, very busy person, continually stealing a glance at his watch, someone who always unfortunately has to be rushing off, but he does not seem like a poet with great influence on his contemporaries; he seems instead a functionary, moreover a petty functionary, whose contemporaries have great influence over him, and, as it emerges during the introductions, it really is that way, he has taken up an official post, and because of that, even with the best of intentions, he could be designated a so-called functionary-poet, clearly he got into this so that he could earn a living somehow, but it's as if the entire thing doesn't sit well with him, there is within him some sense of misfortune, something ungainly—instead of an inner tranquillity of the poet, there is the inner nervousness of the official—still, they listen to him attentively in the huge conference centre, somewhere in a hotel room on the first floor, where they sit on the bed, and after hearing from the interpreter why László Stein is here, he embarks on a monologue, and leaves no doubts that he has neither desire nor time for a dialogue, nor is he of that disposition, he is a person of long explanations, presenting his train of thought thoroughly; serious, and deliberate, for as long as he sits there on the edge of the bed in this hotel room, he chooses his words carefully, the air trembles from his nervousness and impatience, clearly he has to get back, back to the conference room from where he sneaked out for their sake, so that perhaps it also bothers him that he may not express himself with complete thoroughness but only very succinctly, clearly he is forced to formulate his thoughts with much, too much succinctness. He does not look at Stein while he speaks. He creates something of the impression of a person who always feels that a great crowd is listening to his words—even if he is sitting on the edge of the bed in a hotel room, trying into summarize in a mere half hour, in answer to the questions of a foreigner, what he thinks of the current position of classical culture.

XIAO HAI. Since the 1990s, the Chinese have had to turn back to their own cultural past more and more. In the 1880s and 90s, when Chinese artists confronted European art and the European world for the first time, it had a huge effect on them: they took a lot from that world, and they began to imitate it—but I have to say that, looking at it from here, it was more on a formal level, not on a spiritual level. In more than one instance this encounter took place amid great disaccord, namely, that there, on one side, was an extraordinarily significant, modern and, for us, radically new artistic point of view—the European—whereas here, on the other side, we had our culture, and many felt that to abandon it, to allow it to perish, was not permissible. My viewpoint is as follows: I know and respect European culture, but I consider the study of the classical Chinese texts to be more important. Because the fundamental question is not what we will do with European influence, how we will amalgamate it with our own traditional culture—as the issue is formulated today, on the level of banalities—no, that is not the essential thing at all. The essential thing is that I, the poet who has been hopelessly wandering around in this conflict for who knows how long, should be able to find my own path.

There are an extraordinary number of explanations as to what is classical, traditional Chinese culture, that of which we are now speaking, but none of them are interesting. Now, for example, for almost a week, I've been sitting at this conference where the discussion is about the unification of modern and classical literature and the crisis regarding this, but I am bored, bored to death, because it's actually very simple, no conference is needed, it is completely obvious that classical culture is nothing but the personal path which leads to it. Culture, then, only truly becomes culture when it is embodied in someone.

These days, many scholars are engaged in the task, completely superfluously, of comparing Eastern and Western culture. We, too, are doing the same thing, here in this building. But this can only lead to a formal result, and in the meantime the essence is lost.

Because culture is a living thing, something that appears within me, within a person. It's just that tradition, which becomes a living tradition within someone, is not the same thing as that which corresponds to the so-called formal criteria of this tradition.

He sits slightly hunched on the bed, then becomes tired in this posture as well, so he puts his two hands behind him and, leaning on them, stretches out a little.

XIAO HAI. The teachings of Confucius (*he continues his monologue*) was a profound assembly of the general stipulations relating to personal moral behaviour. It has lost its validity in the China of today. The China of today is not built upon moral principles. For example, the most fundamental Confucian command, that the rulers and the leaders must demonstrate their virtuousness by example, is not at all characteristic of the political life of today, and so no one understands any more what it means when Confucius says that the rulers and the leaders do not lead the country with their decisions, neither with their will, nor with their intentions, but with morality. The principles of the *Lunyu* are dead today. And this is the most significant collection of moral principles. I mention this because in the *Lunyu*, and what came afterwards, the Confucian tradition understands something completely different by the term 'morality'. Today, morality represses something in people: crime, mistakes, sins. But this is not at all what is meant by morality in Confucianism. In Confucianism, morality serves personal human fulfilment.

I see the position of modern art as tragic, because I see the position of the modern artist as tragic in contemporary society. The modern artist no longer bears within himself that hidden or manifest goal—clearly originating from an ancient mandate—of demonstrating, in his life and in his work, how a person can become, through the means of morality, humane: how he can become ren.[185] It is important to know that, in the Confucian tradition, morality was an aesthetic criterion: for Confucius, a work was beautiful that taught one the good. In contrast, contemporary art is floundering in various muddied formal objectives, and, as far as I can judge, in Europe the situation is the same. As if it were possible to elevate, among the most fundamental factors of these works, one of them—the aesthetic—and simply renounce the others, the most essential: the criterion of morality. In my opinion, this is partially the reason for the general trend by which the readership of high literature has radically dropped. And this is also the reason for poetry having lost its leading role.

So that, well, now I would simply finish what I have to say by repeating, and emphasizing, that the work of the artist is to find his own relation to his own culture. The artists of today should be the same as they were in the days of old: in order to bring forth their works, they must withdraw from the world, they must keep a great distance from it and they must create a completely individual way of life. An artist cannot be identical with a member of society. His role, his significance is extraordinary—if he loses it, nothing will come in its place.

Altogether that is what he says, he remains for a moment on the bed, leaning back on his hands, as if he were thinking over his words and if they corresponded to what he unconditionally wanted to say; then suddenly he excuses himself, he has no more time, he nervously says goodbye in the doorway and already he has disappeared into the colossal building.

They never see him again, and later on when Stein makes some attempts to find him—in vain—he cannot explain the event in any way other than to think that Xiao Hai is an envoy, an emissary, a messenger of what is to come; and yet the envoy, the emissary, the messenger is quick, he gets to the point, transmitting what has been entrusted to him, and already he is gone, he runs on further.

The Road That Leads There, 2

They lose all trace of Xiao Hai, but his being is still there somewhere in the background because, thanks to his hidden manoeuvres, they end up the next day back in the Zhuozheng Yuan which, in terms of its meaning, can only be translated stupidly, and they do translate it stupidly, because it sounds something like 'The Garden of the Politics of the Common Man'—obviously a quotation, namely, from Pan Yue,[186] as well as the fact that this brilliant designation of this artful garden, existing as it does amid the rules of the Chinese language and spirit, is, however, completely untranslatable, or only in this clumsy and misleading form, so that Stein does not even try to interrogate the garden's dignified director as to its name when, at exactly eleven o'clock in the morning, he appears at the crowded entrance to the garden to receive him, and leads Stein across a tangled confusion of passageways and side gardens, through an area closed to the public, into a large, magnificent pavilion, the receiving hall of the Zhuozheng Yuan, offering Stein a seat in one of two wondrous Ming-era armchairs placed in the middle of the hall.

After the formulaic introductory courtesies, Stein requests the director's forbearance, as he, in a manner uncommon here in China, tends to get straight to the point of the questions that concern him, so if the director will excuse him—he nods towards him once again, asking for his leniency—he, Stein will once again proceed in this manner. He will burden the director with such questions that he has certainly heard and answered thousands and thousands of times: Would he be so kind, Stein smiles at him, to answer these questions this time as well? First and foremost, he is curious as to the origins, in other words, what led to the creation of the Chinese garden? How did it happen that the garden—came to be?

FANG PIEHE. The oldest foundations are represented by the culture of the Wu State.[187] The Wu State designates the region to the south of the Yangtze. The intellectuals and literati of the Wu discovered that, in expressing their feelings through man-made lakes, mountains, plants, pavilions and furnishings, they could create a kind of reality in which their emotions would be manifested. The gardens of Suzhou, however, originate directly from Chinese landscape painting. For example, the garden connected to the receiving room in which we now sit was planned 500 years ago by the owner of the garden, a reclusive censor by the name of Wang Xianchen,[188] on the basis of his own conceptions as well as those of traditional landscape painting. In his garden, it is not nature as such that is depicted but, rather, nature as it appears in Chinese landscape painting.

So then, as a matter of fact, the Chinese garden should be viewed as fine art, to be completely precise, as an artistic creation? One that would have nothing to do with the reality of nature?

FANG. Everything that you see in this or any other garden in Suzhou is, down to the last detail, man-made. Every tree and every plant has been placed there by a person, every strip of vegetation running along a wall has been planned by a human being. Even how it should run along that wall has been planned. At the same time, the Chinese gardens in Zhuozheng—and this applies to ours here as well—gather together differing spiritual strands: the original Taoist conception of immortality, the eternal desire of a Chinese person to be free of the burdens of life, to immerse himself in nature, in the solitary worlds of the mountain and the waters,[189] just as there is present the desire of the old Chinese world to express what it knows of the universe, and to wonder at this, and there is joy as well, joy which can be savoured in a garden planned for tranquillity, peace and unclouded freedom. The garden was always a source of joy, and it has remained so.

It is clear that it is not an official sitting across from Stein but a scholar. Stein asks: What, more specifically, was the goal of the original owner of the gardens? What kind of person was he? What kind of feelings was he trying to express here?

FANG. The most important thing is that the garden of Suzhou was always a garden of joy, namely, of the enjoyment of the natural world. That is—and this is important—these gardens were built for reasons of delight. And the attainment of that delight, that joy, that happiness was the real goal of the owner as well as the builder of any other garden. Regarding the philosophical content of *this* garden, that would be difficult to determine. He did not build it—and this is the important thing—as a direct statement of a philosophical thought or picture. It would be a mistake to think that. It was because of joy. Because of delight. It is altogether another question of how this intention—this intention of delight—immanently contained a philosophical thought in every instance.

Did the owners live in these gardens? Was this also their residence? Or did they come here from where they lived to delight in the densely manmade reality of the life of nature?

FANG. In Suzhou, the owners lived in the gardens as well. I think this was the norm. In every case, these structures are comprised of two large parts: in the front are the living quarters, in Chinese, zhaiyuan; and in the back is the garden: houyuan, both of which build upon the principle of feng shui:[190] 'The house must be in front, the garden must be at the back.' Feng shui determined every essential matter in terms of the construction.

The conversation then continues, with the guest attempting to explain why the Chinese garden fascinates him so much. He could say—he leans in closer to the director—that in addition to its elegant design, it is possible that it is because he merely finds the origin of the garden—whatever it may be—to be simply captivating. He is certain that the director has heard such words from his guests while sitting in these beautiful chairs. He, however—Stein motions towards him somewhat confidentially—is fascinated by all this due to something else, the knowledge of which the director himself will possess. And Stein relates that he is fundamentally concerned with the essence of classical culture—and given that this traditional culture, for the most part, has over the past hundred years been destroyed—he wonders if there might be a genre of this traditional culture which, due to some practical, some kind of simple, some kind of palpable reason, might not have disappeared. Which can in a material sense be annihilated but in its essence never, and because of that may be brought back to life again and again. And he thinks that one of these indestructible forms could be the Chinese garden. Because here, the Chinese garden, as an articulation of the classical spirit in an exquisite form, in a given garden, or a neighbouring garden, can nonetheless be destroyed, but the Garden in its own spirit remains—since neither can all the plants be expunged from the earth, nor the stones be made to vanish for all time, nor the plans of the pavilions and their depictions, nor all the books that describe the rules of their construction, those can't be burnt or pulped or otherwise made unreadable— so that, if today, someone faithfully follows the prescriptions of tradition, then in every case the original may be rebuilt, namely— Stein continues his train of thought—there still remains something, the Chinese garden: itself destroyed, and what was in it destroyed, and yet it can be resurrected! He has visited many gardens, Stein says, now adapting the most intimate of tones, but, to put it briefly, he did not come across many validations of his original theory. And yet now, on his current trip, thanks to happenstance, happenstance which led him to the gardens of Suzhou . . .

FANG. Yes, I understand what you're saying. If, before building, there were plans made on paper . . .

No, not exactly, Stein shakes his head . . .

FANG. . . . . Many of the plans of the Suzhou gardens have been lost, but here, in Zhuozheng, fortunately they have remained. We know that the planner was someone named Wen Zhengming.[191] He was one of the four most significant artists of the end of the Ming era. There were four of them, and among them Wen was the representative of the highest level of culture of the Wu State.

It's possible that the director misunderstood him but he, Stein, thinks that this line of thought may also prove fruitful. So they will speak of these four. Who were they? Litcrati? Painters? Poets? Gardeners?

FANG. Among these four who were the most famous, there were painters and poets, and such, for example, was Wen Zhingming himself, who also painted and wrote poetry.

There was something Stein should have said, some formulaic courtesy; he has ruined something, or hasn't done something, or isn't doing something that he should, because he can sense that the conversation is beginning to run along a different track. So once again he applies himself, and returns the topic of conversation to the starting point, saying that, yes, as long as the plans are still extant, the garden can be newly created at any point, in that sense it is indestructible . . . This is what he thought, and he was disappointed, he looks openly at the director, but now, here in Suzhou, to his greatest astonishment, he has come upon something that has been preserved, something undamaged, something that is not an imitation, not a falsification, but that has remained in the spirit of tradition, that has been resurrected or that has been carefully maintained. And because of that he would like to repeat, he continues, his glittering eyes fixed upon the director, what he has related just now of his initial train of thought: that everything can be destroyed, can be falsified, it can happen to a building, a temple, a ritual statue, a painting, even, if you will, a manuscript, and this is what is happening day after day, and all of these irreplaceable and irretrievable things are being falsified—but it now seems to him, here in these Suzhou gardens, bathed in their wondrous original state, that in the case of the Chinese garden there is hope. Because, he repeats, it can be repeated: all the vegetation, the chrysanthemum, the hydrangea, the wisteria, the lotus, the bamboo, and the plum trees, the paulownia, the pine and the apricot trees, all were essential elements in these gardens, and they still exist, they can be planted here; the stones which were necessary can also be quarried here, the principles, the plans, the vision of the essence of the whole contained in the plan, it all exists—so that, well there is still something from which we may obtain a definite picture of the traditions that have been lost. Do you agree?

The director is beaming.

FANG. I agree, if we take into consideration the fact that the Chinese garden was an art that was constantly undergoing change, as anything else in the classical tradition. The concept of the garden, the style of the garden, the concrete goal of the construction of the garden always changed slightly according to the era, and everyone added something personal to the essence. So that when today we restore the garden, we still go back to the original, we still work with a view to the original plans, but we must consider these changes, as well as the personal contributions and features that occurred in the various eras. Moreover, we must not think that everything has remained unchanged as it was built here, or placed here. For example, there was a painting here on the wall, the creation of Wen Zhingming. We know from the original plans that it was here, and yet it is impossible to imagine that this picture could remain undamaged for 500 years, if it could even survive at all. So what, accordingly, should we do? We and our forebears have continually had to replace that which continually fell into ruin due to natural reasons: only that this substitution, this completion, had to be subordinated to extraordinarily strict rules. For example, if at one time a painting by Wen Zhingming was placed here, then we should place another painting by Wen Zhingming here, or something from the same era and which in the essence of its theme, its proportions, moreover in its atmosphere is essentially the same. We must always insist that here, in this place, another picture may not hang, only one such as I have described—we could never place a painting here created in a northern or Hong Kong style! This is the correct procedure, if we wish to remain within the same style.

But, Stein asks, how does he know? How does he know what the style is? The style within which he has to remain? Was this also preserved in the plans? In the descriptions?

FANG. It is necessary for there to be an aesthetic sensibility in those who work with these traditions, these gardens . . .

Fine, but where do these aesthetic sensibilities come from?

FANG. This garden is 500 years old. If someone takes care of a garden like this for years, after a while, he will naturally possess these sensibilities . . . Anyone who takes care of, who builds, who repairs a garden such as ours will be strongly affected by it. And I can indeed state with some pride that this process and mutual influence does bring results: the Zhouzheng Yuan is flourishing today. This garden has never been as beautiful as it is now. We have sacrificed a great deal, and we continue to sacrifice a great deal for this garden. And while we could never claim that it is perfect, as concerns my previous statements, I greatly trust that you shall not find them to be exaggerated. For this self-regarding praise does not at all mean that the Zhuozheng Yuan is perfect now. There is no perfect garden. Every garden has its faults. Just like a human being. One can only be en route to perfection.

May Stein enquire about his, the director's, opinion as to the relationship between painting and the garden?

FANG. In imperial times, painting and the garden were expected to fulfil the same functions. The highest order of magnitude in life was considered to be fulfilled when a painting or garden created within a person the feeling that he was returning to nature. The same delight was experienced in the melody of birdsong if it was seen in a painting or heard in a garden. Both were removed from reality. Both were art. Both were the location of the loftiness of the spirit.

It could have been the most amazing thing—Stein tries to lift the mood in the breathtakingly beautiful room—if in a garden, listening to birdsong, one could examine a painting in which just then a bird was singing amid the mountains . . .

The director laughs. This is the first time he has laughed during their conversation.

FANG. Well, yes. There are differing degrees of delight . . .

The more serene atmosphere is not just a momentary matter; it is clear that now Stein has won the director's confidence. Who is the soul of this garden? A person is necessary, who will truly keep it well in hand. Because, Stein says, he sees gardeners here, workers, people entrusted with certain tasks, but for this garden to remain in its splendid magnificence, someone who really understands it is necessary, someone who knows what must be done, for the miracle to remain a miracle . . . Who is this person?

FANG. Of course there is a chief director of the Zhuozheng Yuan, a chief manager, and that is myself. But you know, it hardly works in the way that you just imagined. The division of work is based upon a very strict order: there are groups of workers who watch over the plants, there are other groups who take care of the rocks, there is a particular group which deals with the bonsai trees, and there is yet another that builds the mountains. These workgroups are called ji gong, and within one ji gong we distinguish four levels. These four levels create a hierarchy which means that whoever is at the highest level is considered, due to his experience and knowledge, to be a fully competent, fully responsible expert in his field. And since most of our workers have been here for decades, everyone is extremely experienced, so it is not necessary to manage them in the sense in which you are thinking, because they already know what is correct, what has to be done in a given instance. I, however, their director, am not an expert in these questions. There is, for example, a special case here. We in this garden, located south of the Yangtze, must endure the so-called mildew rain during the rainy season. This mildew rain brings countless termites which ruin the wooden buildings, so the fight against them is of vital importance. We have certain groups trained only in this, and this is their only task—and I have no idea what they do. The important thing is that they protect the buildings from the termites. My role is just organizational, to keep the whole thing going smoothly.

It is clear that, with this, the director has concluded his remarks concerning his role, so Stein now returns to an earlier theme in their conversation, and asks the director what he considers the focal point of the garden to be? What is its centre of gravity? Does the Chinese garden express a cosmological picture of the universe for a Chinese person? Or are these words too big? Or is it nothing like that at all? It's just beautiful? And they, the Chinese, have they sensed this across the centuries? And do they delight in it?

>FANG. It would be very hard for me to express in words the essence, the focal point, the centre of gravity of the garden, as you have phrased it in your question. This question is too big for me. But the garden, including this one here in Zhuozheng, has a focal point, a centre of gravity, so that I would say that the proportions are somehow in harmony. Does this garden, our garden, itself express the universe? It does not. Instead, I believe this: the Zhuozheng Yuan is itself the universe.

It will soon be time to bring the conversation to an end. Stein smiles at him: please permit me one final question, he says. Clearly, the director must remain here alone, after closing time. Is there some place in the garden where he goes at such times, and sits down, and stays there, listening to the splashing of the brook, or the murmurings of the wind, or the trembling of the leaves, immersed in the beauties of this or that plant, when he does not remain here because of work, when he is not thinking of the tasks to be completed, but he can simply give himself over and so therefore he does give himself over to the enchantment of the garden?

>FANG. There are such times. And there is such a place in the Zhuozheng. And at moments like that I do feel something that

connects me to the people of ancient times. There is a pavilion, it is called Yu shui tong zuo xuan ('With whom may I sit') . . . well, I acknowledge that if the occasion arises, I am in the habit of sitting there.

And what do you do then?

He answers so quietly that Stein can hardly hear him: 'Oh, nothing. I just am. *I think so.*'

Their farewell is warm, Mr Fang accompanies them to the pavilion door, and, before they disappear into the garden to marvel in it again, he waves, smiling, to them.

And Stein looks at the garden, but he does not see it. He tries to think about why Tang Xiaodu sent him here. He thinks of Xiao Hai, he thinks of the gardens he has seen, and he thinks of the words of Mr Fang. He goes over everything in his mind, searching for the reason why he is here.

But he has no idea. He knows nothing, and he understands nothing.

There is a name in his notebook. A Shanghai publisher, Chen Xianfa had him write it down earlier: if he happened to be passing through Suzhou, he could call upon this person, a resident here, for practical assistance. Otherwise, said Mr Chen, he's a writer but not a particularly interesting one. Just if Stein needs something taken care of, he explained.

And only then.

They look for a telephone booth.

They decipher the name: Ji Yinjian.

The phone rings.

The Road That Leads There, 3

The Canglang Ting, the oldest garden in Suzhou, is also in the southernmost part of Suzhou. They have arranged to meet with Ji at one of its entrances—Ji, recommended by their Shanghai friend as a good person for help with practical issues—which would seem to render this meeting completely superfluous, as Stein doesn't have any kind of practical issues right now that need to be solved—his problem is that he doesn't know what to expect, and he doesn't understand what he should be waiting for. Master Ji, as they soon come to call him because of his clownish disposition, turns out to be a very particular individual, following in the spirit of the designation of the painters who entered Chinese pictorial history as the renowned 'Eight Eccentrics of Yangzhou',[192] they should in fact designate Master Ji as the 'Ninth Eccentric of Suzhou', so droll is he, so morbid, continually play-acting, he says something, indeed, he speaks continuously and then suddenly he leaps up, and he enacts what he was just speaking of, he has no regard for anything or anyone, he doesn't care where he is or if anyone heard what he just said, and he seems to decidedly take delight if one or two visitors notice his thundering tirades now and then, he takes delight in his own voice, he takes delight in the fact that he can perform for the two Europeans, that they are not looking for anything here, because this Canglang Ting is no longer identical with the Canglang Ting of the past, because the whole thing here is nothing more than a paltry forgery—he leads them around the garden—nothing here is how it should be, he points to a place on the ground and they look at the flagstones, do you see these square concrete slabs: these square slabs should never have been placed here, only ceramic tiles of much smaller dimensions should have been placed here, and crosswise, diagonally, in a word, the whole thing as it is now, he shrieks in rage, is a miserable desecration of tradition, but what can we expect, he bellows—and suddenly the pavilion falls silent—where are we exactly, and just what can we expect from an era like that of today, in which the garden of Canglang—where, he says, I kissed a woman for the very first time, at its entrance gate, and which is the oldest garden in all of Suzhou—has been utterly deprived of its meaning—its meaning, Master Ji yells in anger, not only at them but at everyone: for they have taken away its river, because why do you think its name is Canglang Ting? Well, why do you think? He looks around with a frightening and yet somehow amusing expression, asking: Who knows, now?!—no one—he purses his lips, they have not been taught this in the schools, he says sarcastically, no, not this, so then what have they been taught, and suddenly he will be severe again, with no trace of amusement, ah, let's forget it, he says, and, leaving the frightened little group standing there in the room, he leads his two guests out of the pavilion, and they walk beside him like two faithful disciples beside a wild Taoist come down from the mountains, and it is not possible to know if Master Ji has gone mad or what has happened, they proceed beside him, they occasionally try to put a question to him but he doesn't understand the words of the interpreter properly, he doesn't even care if he finishes his sentences, so that if he seems to reply to the questions now and then, he does not reply directly but, rather, always in a single block of speech, moreover replying at times when a question is not even put to him, but Stein does want to ask him something, as for example when they enter into another room where a high wall on one side is covered with innumerable portraits; these are the Five Hundred Literati, says Ji very seriously, look at them—he now takes up a more intimate tone—here is everyone who meant something back then, and who trod with hallowed feet in Suzhou: here is Wu Zixu, here is Tong Wengshu, here is Bai Juyi, and here is Fang Chouyan, here is Su Dongpo, here is Li Bai, here is Xun Cunei, here is Han Shizhong, here is Weng Cengming, here above is Wen Tianxiang, there is Liu Zifu,[193] here they are all, Master Ji points round the huge wall, and before Stein can ask what, if they were to come to Suzhou now, these great masters would say about the world of today, Ji's face distorts in hilarity, then into a bitter expression, finally as if he were shuddering, and as if anticipating the question, he says: brrr, well, what would they do here today? he asks; it's possible they would change their clothes, they would admire and enjoy all the modern things, like a washing machine, Su Dongpo would do that; I think Li Bai would weep, but the others would watch TV, wash their clothes in a washing machine, Su Dongpo would do that, he'd use a washing machine, of this I am almost completely certain, but not Li Bai, he wouldn't be able to, he would drink, get drunk, fall asleep and curse—and you, he turns to the interpreter, why are you using a camera, why are you using this tape recorder around your neck, do you need it? he shakes his head; well, fine, Master Ji nods; the poets here, he continues and points at the wall, they didn't have any need for anything else, only impressions and inspiration, and that was all—that was all! Ji cries out, and once again the people in the room seem frightened, in particular, the two women at the souvenir kiosk at the end of the room regard them with some alarm, but no one dares utter a word, there is no way to make Master Ji stop, he has caught his stride, and it is clear there is no one who can keep him back now, and as they leave the room, and continue their walk through Canglang Ting, he loses his self-control more and more, he curses the age in which they live, he curses those who have disgraced Suzhou, who replaced the ceramic slabs, who stuck windows in the wall that don't belong there, he points at one spot, but there's nothing anyone can do about it, this is what the age is like, this is what China has become, these people couldn't care less about tradition, these people aren't interested in anything because they don't even know anything, they don't even realize that here—he points around himself at a pavilion furnished with Qing-era furniture—they should have put not these pieces but Ming-era furniture, because *that's what was here*, they're all just uneducated boors here, yclls Master Ji, bursting into laughter, in what is meant to be a frightening but is nonetheless an amusingly strident voice, they just keep walking beside him, so many boors, he repeats, they listen like people who have been struck on the head, they have no words, nor can they have any, because they must comprehend that no, Master Ji is not the master of practical problems, no, he is much more than that, but then what—and this is hard to unravel from the circus with which he is amusing his guests, because he is amusing them, it is clear that he understands hospitality to mean that he must entertain these two Europeans—the close friends of Mr Chen, the famous publisher of Shanghai, and of Yang Lian, the renowned poet—it's a little tiring as well, and it makes one think, and Stein is tired too, and he tries to think, how did this happen, how did Master Ji get into the picture? and who is he, and what does he want to say?—but as for time, there is none for thinking, because he must keep observing Master Ji, who is smoking his cigarettes, one after the other, just like Xiaodu, and he relates and he speaks and he yells, and, leaning closer, he whispers something into Stein's ear, he's a clown, whispers Stein to the interpreter, but it never occurs to him that he should get away from Master Ji, or that now, having passed two hours with him in Canglang, he should go somewhere—no, not at all, it never occurs to him, on the contrary, he tries to ponder how he can extend their time together; all the same, he does not understand Master Ji: what is this combination of buffoonery and invective, if he is angry, is he genuinely angry, or is this some kind of stage production, a jolly and yet acrimonious performance for their sake, a performance about something that is overwhelming and ghastly— well, this is precisely what is going through Stein's mind when Master Ji says that, of course, to see Canglang is really not to see everything, there are still a few things in Suzhou that are worth having a look at; Master Ji, Stein says, he is speaking in all sincerity when he says that he has never felt so good as now, when he is with Master Ji, and he could never have any intention at all of doing anything in Suzhou without Master Ji, at which point Master Ji purses his lips, as it were, signifying that he too is wondering how this could work, asking: What exactly did you have in mind?—well, says Stein, that they should meet again, at which point Master Ji asks why, does Stein need anything—

no, not at all, says Stein, he doesn't need anything at all in the whole world . . . but perhaps . . . it would be good if someone could join their future conversations, an expert on the gardens of Suzhou; well, he knows one, answers Master Ji very seriously, is tomorrow good? he asks in his own fulminating conversational style, tomorrow is good, answers Stein, they will cancel everything that Stein had wanted to do, because now only this interests him, and so they part, with the words tomorrow and telephone and see you soon, and then—the interpreter just shakes his head: Has Stein gone mad? Maybe he's lost his mind?! he looks at him dumbfounded when Master Ji dashes away, what could he possibly want from this halfwit, to which Stein can only reply that it's only this halfwit that he wants: he, Master Ji, is the only one who feels exactly as he does in China, so why shouldn't he spend all his time with him, the interpreter is silent, he is not completely convinced, he was amused too, and he even liked Master Ji, but to subordinate all their subsequent plans in Suzhou to him is clearly going too far and he considers it to be a hasty decision, nonetheless, Stein informs him, from this point on in Suzhou, they are giving themselves over to Master Ji, from this point on nothing else will interest them, only that which is in connection with Master Ji—the interpreter is silent, and Stein wonders again, as they trudge back to the hotel: Why is he even saying things like this? Who is this Master Ji? And why is he so important?

But he knows what he is saying, and he understands who Master Ji is; he senses he is on the right track, and it's no accident that he found him today; he knows, in brief, that he is the one, that it's because of him that he is here in Suzhou, even if he doesn't know what it is that he knows, and, mainly, why he feels so certain in all this, more certain than death. He's the one, he's the one!— Stein tries to whip up some enthusiasm in the interpreter in the hotel room, who, however, just once again collapses dead tired onto the bed, and falls asleep with the phrase repeating in his head, this 'He's the one, he's the one'—even if, of course, at that point, he can't have any idea at all if he really is the one; but he can only lead somewhere, not to his self, but he will lead: and in that there can be no mistake.

THE SPIRIT OF CHINA

The next day, at three o'clock in the afternoon, of course, there is Master Ji in front of the entrance gate of the Garden of the Master of the Nets, with a beautiful woman of noble gaze, about the same age as Master Ji; a marvellously handsome man, a little younger than Stein yet seeming somewhat ageless, with long grey hair reaching down to his shoulders; and a younger woman standing beside him, arm in arm, clearly his wife. After the introductions, Master Ji leads them through the tourist groups—only sporadically destructive at this moment—to the end of the garden, to a hidden nook where, under the greatest protection that could possibly exist in such a place, they take a seat in an empty teahouse. All the doors in the teahouse are open, and the back wall of the inner courtyard, grown over with woodbine and overlooking their table, is flooded with the afternoon sunshine.

Master Ji introduces the unknown couple as Wu Xianweng and his wife. They are from Suzhou, but now they have come from Wuxi in order to spend the day with them. And this, he gestures towards the beautiful woman next to him, who blushes a little, is his own wife. Master Ji orders only some bottles of boiling water, then he takes from his pocket a large bag of tea, and tells them that this is Longjing tea, and that this is what they will be drinking, because this is the best. He places the leaves in everyone's cups and then pours the boiling water over them; for a while there is silence, a little self-consciousness, while from outside, from the courtyard, the twittering of birds can be heard, and the staff withdraws behind a distant counter.

Stein is the first one to speak but it's as if he wouldn't have to begin, as if they were in conversation already: he does not introduce himself, which perhaps would have been proper, but begins to speak about what connects him so closely to the arts of China. He speaks in short sentences so that it will be easier to translate: he feels that it doesn't matter what kind of art one draws close to in China, it doesn't matter whether one starts out from poetry, music, philosophy, painting, architecture, theatre, calligraphy or the art of gardening, because one always ends up in the same place, as if every form of artistic expression were striving for one and the same conceptualization or depiction.

Or as if it were obliged to do so. Because somehow, says László Stein, it is the same with these arts as with our flowers at home, which we really love—we believe that we choose them and we love them. But it is they who choose us, they, who with their enchanting beauty, oblige us to love them and take care of them. Each flower is uniformly beautiful. Together, they share in beauty. What is entrusted to us is to decide the one of which we shall speak. And, he says to Wu, he would now like to speak of the art of gardening, and he would like to know his opinion: What does he, Mr Wu, coming now from Wuxi, see as the essence of the Chinese garden? Is it possible to say that a person can take refuge in a garden of Suzhou, if he wants to be immersed in thought, if he wants to be immersed in a beauty which everywhere else has been lost?

Wu does not answer for a while. He is silent for so long that everyone at the table becomes embarrassed. Embarrassed, but not because they don't understand his silence but perhaps because they presume that it will be difficult for Stein to understand it. Stein, however, waits patiently, because he thinks that Wu is thinking about his answer. And so he is.

WU. The art of gardening in Suzhou is a product of imperial China. It was created by those who thought they could find their freedom only here, amid the stones, the flowers, the trees and the silence of the pavilions. The Chinese garden is at once the location and the emblem of withdrawal from society. For each individual, the garden was his own world, as it were, the expansion of who he was.

He is a lean man of average height. Up close, now that he is sitting beside Stein at the table, it is particularly striking how beautiful his face is, how immobile. His voice, in contrast to his slender, frail stature, is deep and decisive, full of strength, even if it is barely audible. Stein is sitting the closest, but Wu speaks so softly that he can hardly hear him, and the interpreter—who tries to wedge himself in closer between them—can also hardly hear him. As if he were extremely, endlessly weary. Again he is silent for a long time, but before Stein can speak again, he continues.

WU. The garden, however, is an artificial creation. As for myself, if I try to think of a location suitable for withdrawal, I would never seek out a garden. There are many times when I wish to be somewhere in silence. And at such times I do leave. Then with my wife or my friends I go somewhere away from the city. But it never occurs to us to go to a garden. Only to the mountains, the streams, out into nature.

Stein relates in a few sentences how deeply and radically his own relation to nature has changed over the past 10 or 15 years. He tells Wu about that place, that remote valley high up in the mountains, where he lives. And how his garden is a part of that nature which surrounds him.

WU. That is a fortunate situation. A bountiful life, a life worthy of the human being. I am filled with great joy that you are able to live in this way.

Stein replies by describing how that place where he lives has changed so much in terms of its relationship to poetry. In terms of its relationship to language. That he continually feels as much too crude and harsh that which must be continually, but continually, alleviated—alleviated to the point of infinity.

WU. Art is the means by which one can go from the complex to the simple, but we cannot miss a single intermediary step on the way. Its mission is to penetrate to the essence of something. And that is simple.

Who is this person?! Master Ji sees the effect his friend is having on Stein, and he takes this in with a fairly satisfied and slightly ironic gaiety, like someone who has been equal to the task entrusted to him. After every sentence, Wu is silent for a long time. He sits there, unmoving, his head does not stir, nor his gaze which somehow . . . is looking at nothing in particular. He looks a bit at Stein, then away, at the table, at the steaming tea cups, and then again up at him, and then again to one side. Due to his unusually soft speech, Stein feels that an exceptional silence is looming over the teahouse itself in which furthest and the tiniest sound can be heard. The noise, as one of the staff suddenly clinks one teacup against another behind the counter, seems unbearable. There is an unbelievably deep silence.

WU. And in this, as in so many other things, Chan is the most radical. Chan is not interested in what is written down. It doesn't need any words.

Stein replies that the viewpoint has emerged in Europe as well that the conscientious artist is the one who leaves no works behind.

WU. This is the opinion of the Buddhists. The master never writes down anything, he only teaches. The teachings can never be written. If you are conversing with the heavens, you are never in need of words.

At the same time, Stein says, he could never imagine life without words. Frankly speaking, he continues, unwillingly adapting himself to Wu, as if from this point on this would be the normal course of their conversation—speaking, accordingly, barely audibly—he could never exist without words. Because in order to depict how the eternal emerges from a landscape, some kind of material is necessary. A material which may circumscribe that beauty which cannot be transmitted in words.

WU. The essence rests on the surface of emptiness. It leaves room for thought. Classical Chinese poetry and painting worked with few words and with a small amount of ink. Li Bai, when writing, always used just a few strokes, just a few words, because he knew that what he didn't describe was what gave monumental strength to meaning. It is very hard for someone who comes from the West to understand the meaning of empty space. Your conception of a 'thing' radically differs from what we understand by that. And so, for you, the extraordinarily rich meanings of emptiness do not exist as they do for us. They do not exist, therefore they cannot be compared with anything else. There is no place in you where you could understand what emptiness is. And the essence of Chinese art is this emptiness.

Master Ji interrupts. And he is hardly recognizable now, it is clear that until now he has been listening with rapt attention, he has been watching Stein, who only now realizes that Master Ji hasn't taken his eyes off him all this time.

MASTER JI. Do you meditate?

Stein says yes, he does, in his own way.

WU. That's good. You can go deeper.

MASTER JI. Yes, the strength of the heart is multiplied.

WU. The strength of the heart is boundless.

My God, where is he? This is written on Stein's face. It is also obvious that the interpreter has no idea of where they are: he is gripping the arm of the chair in fright. The atmosphere is completely different than what they could have expected. Serious, lofty, severe. Stein feels he has ended up in a great narrative. The sun is now shining close to their table. He can feel it warming his back. In his mouth is the taste of the Longjing tea. At times the twittering of the birds in the courtyard grow louder. Then it dies away again.

WU. Classical culture is the repository of great merits. These values do not disappear. And while there are few to whom this will be important, there will always be some, so that these values will never disappear completely.

Is it the sunlight that is warming his back? Then perhaps twilight is already falling. But how is this possible? Didn't they just sit down? He looks at his watch: it's impossible. It will be evening in a moment. How could this have happened? The company livens up, the two women begin gaily to speak about something, Master Ji too from time to time tosses a remark to them, then turns back towards the guests, looking at Stein, and it can be seen that he is glad, he is happy, he is satisfied. A lively conversation ensues, and does not cease. And what is curious is that, in the meantime Wu, who is listening attentively to what is being spoken, now, without the instigation of Stein, motions to the interpreter to draw closer and transmits a few sentences to Stein.

WU. It is not always necessary to search for the cause behind every-thing, because every cause is unfounded. A cause only looks like a cause from a certain viewpoint.

And he stops there. He turns back towards the others, and he listens to them talk. Sometimes he even interrupts, corrects someone, and if the company happens at that point to be recompensing the humour of Master Ji, glittering again and again, with ringing laughter, he too takes part in the general gaiety. But Stein is on tenterhooks. He knows that he is going to say something to him again in a minute. And so he does.

WU. We must never allow ourselves to come under the influence of others. And we must never intervene in the lives of others. We must find our own paths. One's own path is the most important thing. At the same time we must not renounce helping others.

Again, such simple words. Stein is confused. Wu is as resolute as a cliff. What is going on here?

WU. The true artist must listen to the voice of the heavens. This voice cannot be heard, only felt. I can see from your gaze that you are capable of this. I hope that what you do will be like a mountain brook.

Stein concentrates on every one of Wu's words, on the tiniest of his movements. The interpreter sits beside him, tense. He doesn't understand Wu, he doesn't understand the strained attentiveness of his companion. Stein reassures him that everything is fine, and asks him to translate this: for 48 years now, he has been observing the world with keen attention, and first he was only beset by questions for which he could find no answers, then later on he could not even find questions but, rather, a kind of current, an impersonal, enigmatic, natural velocity, although he has no idea from where it springs. At the same time, Shakyamuni Buddha has become ever more important for him. That is to say, today, exactly today, and today it is exactly Wednesday, his questions have all run out—now that there are no questions left, and with them dying away he begins to sense that where the questions have ceased to be, something else is beginning, something which perhaps could be designated as perfect immediacy.

In some inexplicable manner he feels a deep confidence about Wu, so that his words begin to sound like a confession—and Stein can sense that Wu understands this. For a long time he says nothing, so that after a while Stein thinks that the conversation is over. In the meantime the atmosphere around the table has been overtaken by the highest of spirits, as if the company were a little drunk, everyone is so vivid and good-humoured, the two wives happily laughing, Master Ji is scintillating, and even Wu laughing heartily after each successful punch line. The staff has disappeared, when Stein looks over to the counter he sees that no one is there; the interpreter explains that he probably wasn't paying attention but that the tea-house owner has left to enjoy themselves in peace, the employees have gone home but they have left the key with Ji's wife, and told her which back exit they should use to leave, and what to do with the key.

They are all by themselves in the Wangshi Yuan?

Yes, the interpreter says smiling, and there is no longer any trace in him of his previous nervousness, the previous tension; yes he says, the whole thing is like a dream. Or it is a dream, he finally laughs again, turning towards the company.

Master Ji fills the tea cups once again, and holds forth with a long oration on the unsurpassable qualities of Longjing tea, and then begins to pronounce toasts to everyone seated at the table. He toasts his wife, Wu's wife, Wu—who he now designates as an artist, without going into the details—then the interpreter, and finally Stein. Nothing can stop Master Ji now. The interpreter is unable to interpret. After every toast, the company doubles over in laughter, cheering, applause, Master Ji is beaming, and he goes on. Words stream out of him inexhaustibly.

At one point Wu motions, with one of his gentle movements, to the interpreter to draw closer.

WU. The aesthetic is not of utmost importance. Neither is morality.

Stein asks: So what is? And is there even any sense to that question? And Wu reaches down into his bag, rummages a bit, then pulls out a

blank sheet of paper and a pen. He nods: the question makes sense.
He motions for the interpreter to come sit beside him, and writes
down some Chinese characters on the piece of paper. He motions to
the interpreter to try and translate what he has written. It's something
like—the interpreter says, excusing himself, because he gestures that
the text exceeds his capabilities—something like 'ethics, ablaze in the
most perfected, the most accomplished beauty, must be humanity's
ultimate manifestation' . . . Wu pushes the piece of paper aside and
looks at Stein questioningly, to see if he has understood. Stein nods,
but he hasn't understood. Wu breaks into a smile, pulls the paper to
himself again, and writes something on it. Now this—he points out
the individual characters to the interpreter—who shakes his head,
puzzled, he spreads his hands apart helplessly and finally says that
he doesn't understand it at all. No problem, says Stein, don't worry
about what the whole thing means, just translate the individual characters. And then, the interpreter, poking at each character, slowly
begins to enumerate:

'Our human nature		message, concealed
Scientific technique		incapable
Heidegger:	conduct	art
Spiritual matters:	human life	meaning
Viewpoint of physiological capabilities:		Olympus spirit
Things	quickly	clarify not possible . . .
Victorious in all		undefeated
Buddhism	not at all	pessimistic
Confronted with	dying	every person vanquished
Ancient person did not see Moon of today		
		Moon of today saw people of old'

And at the bottom of the page, the interpreter shows, is written the following: 'Zither, chess, calligraphy, the art of painting.'

Wu pulls out another piece of paper, but for a long time doesn't write anything down.

At the table, the mood is evermore high-spirited.

Wu begins to write again.

He shows the interpreter the individual characters, where he has written: 'If you ponder the limits of decay, then the uncertainty of human life, its impermanence, shall weigh upon your soul.'

Wu pushes the two papers on the table over to Stein, smiling with a gesture that they are now his. Stein does not reach for them. Master Ji is warming up for a new performance, but this time it is not another punch line but an anecdote he is performing: in the strict sense of the word, he is enacting the various roles, representing the scene and the time when it all took place, the two women utter shrill cries of laughter. Wu pulls out a third piece of paper from his bag. He writes for a long time, his long grey hair falling into his face as he leans forward.

The interpreter shakes his head. Impossible. It's impossible to translate. It makes no sense at all, he speaks in undertones, as if Wu could understand any of what he whispers to Stein in Hungarian. No problem—Stein motions to him—just translate.

This here, he points to the paper, is a quote from Laozi: 'From non-existence is born existence; in existence is born non-existence.'

But after that, he says, there are just various characters.

No problem, says Stein—what do they mean?

This here, the interpreter points at the next line, that means . . .
wait a sec—then he reads them out continuously, as Wu wrote them
down, in their entirety.

'Things next to one another   unspeakable   density

                            uncontrollability

Rare   inconceivable

Suzhou   gardens   groves

Literati   very many   infinite   silence   tranquillity

Life   very difficult pursuit   interest   tendency

When young   go across the mountains   swim in water

                                      infinite grace

Time

Poetry   recite   painting

We grow old   We die.'

Wu gathers up the papers on the table, puts them in order, and
pushes them over to Stein. Again he nods, and gestures for Stein to
go ahead and take the papers. He will study them, Stein replies, and
then asks the interpreter to not translate what he is about to say. He
leans over to Wu, and following a gay outburst, says right into his ear
in Hungarian: He doesn't know how to explain how this is possible,
but he has understood, and he understands, every single word. A
friend of his recently told him to go to Suzhou. At that time he didn't
understand why. He will never forget this afternoon and this evening,
he will never forget the Garden of the Masters of the Nets, this pavilion, the sunlight pouring down onto the vine-covered wall in the
courtyard, he won't forget the chirping of the birds, he won't forget

the people sitting around this table, he will never forget the aroma and taste of the Longjing tea, and he will never forget Wu, his words, the characters he has written down, his voice and his poetry.

It's getting late—he then says to the others—he and the interpreter have to catch the last bus.

The interpreter looks at him in surprise.

The face of Master Ji grows serious for a moment, then he starts a final, very lengthy monologue in which he speaks of the immortal origin of Stein's extraordinary name, and the extraordinary qualities of Stein who has come into their very midst. By the end, the others are clapping and bursting into laughter after each sentence. Master Ji makes his final utterance, gets up from his seat, steps over to Stein and embraces him.

Then everyone else embraces Stein.

They go out in the dark through a back entrance into the narrow alleyway.

Stein and the interpreter are accompanied to the Renmin Lu, where after another heartfelt farewell the two guests get into a taxi and head for the bus station.

You really think there's going to be a bus leaving at midnight?

It is plain to see that the interpreter is mortally exhausted.

Stein pats him on the shoulder.

Of course there is, he says to reassure him. Of course there is.

There is always a way out of Suzhou.

And they step into the desolate building of the bus station plunged into darkness.

WHAT REMAINS: THE END

In the bus headed towards Jiuhuashan, there is no change. The woman at the back still sits motionlessly in her seat. Above their heads, the rain beats down on the roof of the bus mercilessly. Now even the passengers in the front are loudly grumbling about why that shabby-looking woman won't close that bloody window. Everyone is freezing, and they are shivering in the draft coming in through the window. It really should be closed. The bus driver and the conductor, all the way in front, do not notice anything amiss. The woman takes no notice of the general dissatisfaction either, her eyes closed, she seems to be almost holding her face up to the ice-cold air streaming in.

The interpreter gets up from his seat, and speaks to her very courteously, asking her to please be so kind as to close the window, because here in the back, where they are sitting, the draft is very strong.

The woman doesn't move, it's as if no one had even spoken to her. She doesn't even open her eyes.

Then in front, another passenger, a middle-aged man, seeing the half-hearted attempts of the foreigners clearly doomed to failure, makes up his mind, walks back towards the woman, pokes at her shoulder for her to wake up, and open her eyes, and says to her: Why are you doing this?

What? She asks, confused.

Why don't you close the window? The draft is coming in.

At this the woman pulls the window in but just by a centimetre or two.

The passenger pokes her in the shoulder again.

I'm asking you again, why are you doing this? Why are you letting in the wind?

The woman turns red.

Because I like it.

What do you like?

The wind.

The man leans forward and speaks to the other passengers: She's crazy. She has a screw loose somewhere.

With a loud grumbling they reply, fine, maybe so, but that bloody window still has to be closed.

The man grabs the handle on the window and closes it fully.

The woman says nothing. It is clear she is frightened. She's afraid of the man.

And he doesn't leave things there, he doesn't go back to his seat, but remains facing her, then leans in very close, right into her face, until he catches her gaze.

So then tell me: Why do you like the wind so much?

It is clear that the woman is afraid that the man will strike her.

The wind? she repeats the question. She is really afraid. She tries to muster up some reply. No one sees the wind.

Fine, but why do you like it?

Well . . . because it blows.

The man guffaws, then, as is customary with a crazy person who understands nothing at all, gestures at the woman, giving everyone to understand that she will certainly not dare to touch the window again or there will be the devil to pay, then he sits down in his seat. The passengers on the bus calm down, the bus driver pulls his bag over and takes out a snack wrapped in a plastic bag. He is a large, fat, sluggish person; he eats slowly, at his leisure. The windshield wipers squeak across the front windows of the bus. He drives with one hand, biting and chewing his food, and sometimes he leans forward, so difficult is it to see the road in the rain pouring down.

And before them, in the thick fog, supposedly there is somewhere: Jiuhuashan.

Concerning the title of the book, 'beneath the Heavens, that which is beneath the Heavens' (in Hungarian: Ég alatt, Égalatti; in Chinese: Tianxia), namely, 'All that is beneath the Heavens' was the name of the ancient Chinese for the world, which in their eyes was identical with China itself.

1   Jiuhuashan ('The Mountain of Nine Flowers'): One of the four sacred mountains of Chinese Buddhism. Its name is derived from a line from a poem by Li Taibai, and once upon a time it was home to between 200 and 300 monasteries.

2   Huang Shen (1687–1768): A famous painter of the early Qing era. One of the 'Eight Eccentrics of Yangzhou', he is particularly well known for his portraiture.

3   Ying Yujian (twelfth–thirteenth century): A Chan Buddhist monk-painter, his works are characterized by the free-brush technique.

4   Shakyamuni Buddha ('Sage of the Royal Shakya Nation'): The historical Buddha (563 BCE–483 BCE).

5   Lotus Sutra (Saddharmapundarika Sutra; literally, Sutra on the White Lotus of the Sublime Dharma): One of the most popular of the sacred Mahayana scriptures. The most widely diffused translation from Sanskrit was created in 406 CE by Kumarajiva. According to this sutra, the Buddha teaches sentient beings variously, according to their abilities, but the goal always remains the same—to reach Buddhahood.

6   Amida Sutra: The sutras of Amitabha the Buddha of the Western Paradise. The most important sacred texts of the Pure Land School, according

to which the ultimate goal is not to become a Buddha but, through meditation and prayer, to be reborn in the Pure Land.

7   Guanyin (Avalokiteshvara): In Chinese Buddhism, Avalokiteshvara, originally a male bodhisattva, became the goddess of children and of compassion.

8   Sándor Petőfi (1823–49): One of the greatest Hungarian poets and a revolutionary who symbolized the Hungarian desire for freedom.

9   Lu Xun (1881–1936): One of the most significant writers and thinkers of the first half of the twentieth century, and considered the father of modern Chinese literature.

10 bodhisattva: The ideal of Mahayana Buddhism—a being who reaches enlightenment but does not enter nirvana so that he may remain in the world and help others reach enlightenment.

11 Baisui Gong ('The Hundred Years Temple'): A monastery at Jiuhuashan, and named after a monk who lived for 120 years. The statue in the temple is supposedly his mummified body.

12 Huacheng Si ('The Monastery Surrounded by Walls'): Built in 781 in Jiuhuashan, its current buildings date from the Qing era.

13 Taiping Uprising (1851–64): The peasant uprising that occurred over a great part of South and Central China, the goal of which was the creation of a society based on equality. Nanjing was the centre of the revolt.

14 Beiji Tower: An astrological observation tower built in 1385 in Nanjing.

15 Jiming ('Crowing of the Cock'): A Buddhist monastery built in 1387 in Nanjing. Now, the location of one of the very few nunneries in China.

16 Mochou ('Do Not Worry' Lake): The most famous lake in Nanjing whose name derives from a beautiful woman who was forced against her will to marry a potentate.

17 Song dynasty (960–1279): The dynasty named after the ruling Song family, characterized by enormous technical, economic and cultural development, yet relatively weaker military strength.

18 Ming dynasty (1368–1644): Chinese dynasty that provided an interval of native Chinese rule between eras of Mongol and Manchu dominance as well as a period of cultural flowering.

19 Zhu Yuanchang (1328–98): The founder of the Ming dynasty, a man of humble origins. He made Nanjing the capital of his empire.

20 blood-thirsty Japanese: In December 1937, the Japanese occupied Nanjing and subsequently massacred hundreds of thousands of residents.

21 Linggu Si ('The Monastery of the Valley of Souls'): Founded in 514. At the time of the construction of Zhu Yuanzhang's mausoleum, it was relocated to its present location, near Zijin Shan ('The Purple-Gold Mountain') in Nanjing. During the Taiping Uprising it was destroyed in a fire.

22 Wuliang Dian ('The Hall of the Immeasurable Buddha'): A fourteenth-century building in the Linggu Si in Nanjing, built from stone and brick, which is unusual in China. For that reason it is also referred to as 'The Beamless Hall'.

23 Grand Canal: The world's lengthiest man-made waterway, constructed in the seventh century and connecting the lower courses of the Yangtze with northern China.

24 Sui dynasty (581–618): After a long period of disunity, the short-lived Sui dynasty ushered in a period of unification.

25 Tang dynasty (618–907): One of the most resplendent periods in Chinese history, and the Golden Age of Chinese culture.

26 Yangzhou pinghua: A genre of storytelling that flourished in Yangzhou in the first half of the Qing dynasty.

27 Ouyang Xiu (1007–72): A renowned politician, writer and poet of the Song era.

28 Su Dongpo (1037–1101): A politician and one of the most important writers of the Song era.

29 Jianzhen (688–763): A Buddhist monk from Yangzhou who, after many unsuccessful attempts, finally reached Japan in 753 and went on to become a crucial figure in the spread of Buddhism in that country.

30 Wenfeng Ta ('The Pagoda of the Summit of Erudition'): An octagonal building of seven storeys, this is the first building a traveller to Zhenjiang sees from the vantage point of the Grand Canal.

31 Shigong Si ('The Memorial Temple of Master Shi'): A temple in Yangzhou, built in 1772 in memory of Shi Kefa.

32 Shi Kefa (1602–45): A government official and calligrapher who, during the Manchurian invasion of 1645, was responsible for the defence of Yangzhou. He was eventually executed by the Manchurians.

33 He Yuan, Ge Yuan, Xi Yuan: Qing-era parks in Yangzhou.

34 Daming Si ('The Temple of Great Illumination'): A Buddhist temple built in the fifth century in Yangzhou. It is here that Jianzhen studied the sutras and initiated people into monkhood before he left for Japan.

35 Han dynasty (206 BCE–CE 220): The second great Chinese imperial dynasty which thoroughly established what was thereafter considered Chinese culture.

36 Shou Xihu ('The Slender Western Lake'): A lake in Yangzhou, whose name refers to its longish shape as well as to the fact that it is a 'more slender' imitation of the famous West Lake in Hangzhou.

37 Ouyang Memorial temple: Originally built by an admirer of Ouyang Xiu in Yangzhou, the contemporary structure is from 1934.

38 Bai Ta ('White Stupa'): Standing on the banks of Yangzhou's West Lake, this Buddhist reliquary is a copy of the structure of the same name in Beijing.

39 Wenchang Street: Named after one of the renowned Ming-era sights of Yangzhou, the Wenchang Ge ('Revival of Flourishing Erudition') tower.

40 mao: Also known as the jiao, this is the currency sub-unit of the yuan; 1 yuan equals 10 mao.

41 Wang Anshi (1021–86): A famous political reformer, poet and writer.

42 Mi Fei (1051–1107): Also known as Mi Fu. A renowned painter, calligrapher and collector of artworks.

43 Wenzong Ge: The pavilion in Zhenjiang destroyed during the Taiping Uprising.

44 Siku Quanshu ('Complete Library in Four Sections'): An imperial collection of books transcribed by hand since the 1770s, containing approximately 3,500 works and 2.3 million pages in 1,500 volumes. Altogether 7 copies were preserved in separate buildings in 7 different locations in the empire.

45 Beigu Mountain: In reality, just a hill in Zhenjiang on the banks of the Yangtze, but famous because the wife of a third-century ruler threw herself into the river at this spot. The Ganlu Si ('The Sweet Dew' monastery), located on the side of the hill and dating from the third century, was largely destroyed during the Second World War.

46 Jinshan ('Gold Mountain'): Originally an island, now a peninsula in the Yangtze at Zhenjiang. Formerly, it was renowned for its countless temples (according to the proverb: 'In Jiaoshan the mountain covers the monasteries, in Jinshan the monasteries cover the mountain'). During the Cultural Revolution, many of the buildings were heavily damaged.

47 Jiangtian monastery: A monastery that at one time covered all of Jinshan. Originally built during the Jin dynasty (265–420), its present form dates from the Qing era, and its justly renowned buildings have served as models for countless structures in China.

48 Zhongleng quan ('The First Spring under Heaven'): Also known as 'The Centre-Cold Spring', it had its source in earlier times in the Yangtze. It is supposedly still the best water for brewing tea.

49 luohan: In Hinayana Buddhism, a saint who has reached the highest level of enlightenment.

50 Fahai: An evil monk from a popular Chinese fable. He tries to separate a happily married couple; the wife, however, who is none other than the White Snake in human form, battles with the monk to regain her stolen husband.

51 Jiaoshan: An island in the Yangtze near Zhenjiang, upon which can be found many beautiful monuments. The name of the island is derived from a hermit who refused a government position despite it being repeatedly offered to him by the emperor.

52 Beilin ('The Forest of Steles'): A general name for collections of inscribed steles. The Beilin of Zhenjiang is located in the Dinghui temple.

53 moon gate: A circular gate in a wall, a frequent element in Chinese parks and gardens.

54 Orchid Pavilion: Originally the residence in Shaoxing of Wang Xizhi, the renowned calligrapher. A work of the same title immortalizes a meeting

of literati which took place here in 353; its (now lost) afterword by Wang is the greatest Chinese calligraphic work of all time.

55 Zhao Mengfu (1254–1322): The most well-known Yuan-era court painter and calligrapher.

56 Su Shi (also known as Su Dongpo): Politician and writer, and one of the most important poet of the Song era.

57 the stele . . . of Yi He Ming ('Sacrificial Inscription for a Crane'): Dating from 514 and located in Zhenjiang, this inscription is the work of an unknown author, lamenting the death of a crane raised at home.

58 Yu Yuan ('The Garden of Joys'): A private garden in Shanghai, built at the end of the sixteenth century by a solitary government official and based on the imperial parks in Beijing.

59 Bund: The city-centre riverbank in Shanghai. A famous promenade, where most of the nineteenth- and twentieth-century Western-style buildings are located.

60 Huangpu: A tributary of the Yangtze that flows through Shanghai.

61 Pudong: Since 1990, the ultramodern trade and financial district on the banks of the Huangpu, across the Shanghai city centre.

62 'Middle Kingdom': Also known as Zhongguo, the designation for China. According to tradition, this name refers to the Chinese view of their country as the centre of the world.

63 kunqu: One of the styles of Chinese opera among the many (up to 300) which still exist. It flourished most extensively between the sixteenth and nineteenth centuries. Based on the merging of the northern and southern operatic styles, it is characterized by extraordinary restraint and refinement in its music, its texts and its theatrical performances.

64 Yifu Theatre: Originally known as Tianchan Theatre, it is currently named after one of its sponsors. It is the oldest and most well-known theatre in Shanghai which still hosts performances of Chinese traditional opera. It particularly flourished between the two world wars.

65 Cultural Revolution (1966–76): The most extreme period of the power struggles that raged among the ranks of the Chinese Communist Party leaders, in the course of which Chairman Mao Zedong also involved the

youth of the country in his drive to liquidate his enemies. This period in Chinese history was characterized by chaotic interpersonal relations, the crippling of the intelligentsia, the annihilation of cultural values and wildly extreme personality cults.

66 Confucianism: An ancient philosophical school and the defining ideology in the Chinese empire in the second century BCE.

67 Taihu ('Lake Tai'): A lake on the border between Jiangsu and Zhejiang. China's fourth largest freshwater lake, it is a popular tourist destination. Many unusual stone formations can be found in the surrounding areas and are often used as garden ornaments.

68 Qing dynasty (1644–1911): The last period of imperial dynastic rule in China. The first half was an age of consolidation, conquest and economic growth as well as one of greater societal rigidity, whereas the second half was characterized by Western influence, uprisings and the hastening collapse of the old order.

69 Southern Song dynasty (1127–1279): The second half of the Song dynasty. Due to Jurchen invasions from Manchuria, the dynasty was forced to retreat to southern China. However, the cultural development during this period makes it one of the most exceptional eras in Chinese history.

70 Xihu ('West Lake'): West Lake is surrounded by Hangzhou. Since ancient times, it has been one of China's most famous sights.

71 Gushan ('Solitary Hill Island'): An island in the West Lake of Hangzhou. In the eighteenth century, the location of an imperial summer palace.

72 dams of Bai Juyi: Dams in the Xihu at Hangzhou, the construction of which, according to tradition, was ordered by the great poet Bai Juyi during his time as governor of the area (824–26).

73 Chan Buddhism (better known by its Japanese designation, Zen): A school of Chinese Buddhism according to which monks can gain nirvana. The more influential branches taught that individuals who are prepared for that goal can attain enlightenment without conscious striving.

74 Jinci temple: A temple located in Hangzhou, approximately a thousand years old. Seriously damaged during the Taiping Uprising, it was reconstructed in 1949.

75 Feilai Feng ('The Peak That Flew Hither'): A low-lying mountain near Hangzhou, it acquired its name from an Indian monk who lived in the third century and according to whom the mountain is a part of an Indian holy mountain that flew to Hangzhou. On the mountain's slopes and in its system of caves are approximately 300 carved statues dating between the tenth and fourteenth centuries.

76 Yuhuangshan ('Jade Emperor Hill'): A famous mountain lookout next to the Xihu in Huangzhou, it derives its name from a Taoist temple built 400 years ago but now converted into a teahouse. The Jade Emperor was a legendary ruler of ancient times and one of the deities of Taoism.

77 Leifeng Ta ('Storm Peak Pagoda'): A famous tower on one of the peninsulas of the Xihu in Hangzhou, which collapsed in 1924, approximately a thousand years after its construction.

78 Yuquan ('Jade Spring'): A famous spring in Hangzhou. Also called 'Clapping Lake' because, according to legend, 1,500 years ago, it burst out of the ground at the sound of clapping.

79 Hupaquan ('Running Tiger Spring'): According to the Chinese, this spring in the excursion zone of Hangzhou is ranked third in the world with regard to water quality. It received its name from a legend about a benevolent spirit that sent a distant spring from Hengshan mountain to a monk who had settled here.

80 Longjing (Dragon Well): A karst well in the outer precincts of Hangzhou. China's most famous tea, named after the well, is produced in the vicinity. True connoisseurs prepare it with water from the Hupaquan.

81 Lingyin Si ('The Temple of the Soul's Retreat'): A monastery founded in 326 at the foot of the Feilai Feng, in a river valley in Hangzhou. It is renowned for its approximately 20-metre tall Buddha statue. The present structure dates from the seventeenth century.

82 Longmen: A renowned group of temple caves in the province of Henan, near Luoyang.

83 Datong: A city renowned for its temple caves in the province of Shanxi.

84 Louwailou pavilions ('The Palace of Palaces'): A famous restaurant on Gushan island, known for its Hangzhou specialties.

85 Wei Liangfu: A musician of Kunshan who lived in the sixteenth century and who, mixing earlier operatic modes, created the Chinese operatic genre known as kunqu.

86 *Mudan Ting* ('The Peony Arbour'; also known as 'The Peony Pavilion'): Tang Xianzu's most famous play about the power of love's passion, it tells of a complicated amorous relationship in which love at first kills, then resurrects a young girl who may finally marry her lover.

87 Tang Xianzu (1550–1617): The most famous Ming-era playwright.

88 *Chang Sheng Dian* ('The Palace of Eternal Life'): The most well-known theatrical piece of Hong Sheng, it immortalizes the famous but tragic love affair between the Tang-era emperor Xuanzong and his concubine.

89 Hong Sheng (1645–1704): A significant Qing-era playwright and writer. Due to the supposedly immoral content of his play *Chang Sheng Dian*, he was expelled from the Imperial Academy and thus spent the greater part of his life in poverty near the Xihu in Hangzhou.

90 *Feng Zheng Wu* ('The Kite's Mistake'): A romantic play by Li Yu in which the lovers write their thoughts as poems on kites and then let them touch each other in the sky.

91 Li Yu (1611–80): An author well known for his novels, short stories, plays and critical works; he was also a theatre director.

92 *Shiwu Guan* ('Fifteen Strings of Coins'): A famous piece of kunqu theatre in which two innocents, sentenced to death for the savage murder and plundering of a butcher, are saved by a high-ranking and just official and the true murderer is seized instead.

93 Zhou Enlai (1898–1976): A Communist politician, he was the prime minister of the People's Republic of China from 1949 to 1976.

94 *Renmin Ribao* ('The People's Daily'): The official paper of the Communist Party of China.

95 jingju (the Peking opera): A form of traditional Chinese theatre which combines music, vocal performance, mime, dance and acrobatics. It arose in the late eighteenth century and became fully developed and recognized by the mid-nineteenth century. In contrast to kunqu, it has a

relatively free form and grants the actor much more independence and scope for improvisation.

96 gongchi: A traditional Chinese musical score in which vocal duration and tones are indicated next to the text in Chinese characters.

97 Emperor Gaozong: The first ruler of the Southern Song dynasty (r.1127–62), he was able to stop the invasion of the nomadic Jurchens from the north and thus establish his empire.

98 Dashan ('Great Mercy Pagoda'): A Song-era brick tower, 40 metres high. Earlier, it formed a part of a temple of the same name.

99 Xu Wei (1521–93): A renowned Ming-era painter.

100 Wang Xizhi (321–79): A great Chinese calligrapher, he was the first to develop the running script. His residence was the Orchid Pavilion which also served as a meeting place for the literati.

101 Yue Kingdom: One of the many warring state formations in the first millennium BCE.

102 King Yu (c.2200–2100 BCE): Also known as Yu the Great. In Chinese mythology, the 'Tamer of the Flood', a saviour-hero and reputed founder of China's oldest dynasty, the Xia.

103 Yingtian pagoda: A seven-storey tower, 30 metres in height, built on the top of a hill in the centre of Shaoxing. Originally built during the Jin dynasty (265–420), it was rebuilt during the Song dynasty.

104 Kuaiji mountain ('The Discussion Mountain'): A peak near Shaoxing, it derives its name from the legend according to which King Yu, at this spot, discussed the water-regulation systems with his advisors.

105 poetry competition: A meeting held in the residence of Wang Xizhi in 353, attended by 44 well-known literary figures.

106 Tiantai mountain: A mountain range to the south of Ningbo, and a famous place of worship. One of the most important schools of Buddhism derived its name from this mountain.

107 Guoqing Si: A monastery and the centre of the Tiantai school, founded over 1,500 years ago, at the foot of the Tiantai Mountain. Most of the extant buildings date from the eighteenth century.

108 Zhiyi (538–98): A famous Buddhist monk and founder of the Tiantai school. He built his hermit's abode here in 575; later, it became the centre of the school. According to his teachings, based upon the Lotus Sutra, the world is undifferentiated and yet all is transient, and the Buddha is present in every speck of dust.

109 Hinayana ('The Small Vehicle'): The earlier, more 'orthodox' version of Buddhism. Its doctrine of salvation is concerned only with the liberation of the individual.

110 Mahayana ('The Great Vehicle'): A version of Buddhism which emerged in the first century BCE and which promises the universal salvation and liberation from suffering for all living beings. This form of Buddhism spread to China.

111 Saicho (767–822): The renowned Japanese monk and founder of the Tendai school.

112 Tendai: The Japanese school of Tiantai.

113 Daban Niepan Jing (Mahaparinirvana Sutra; also known as the Nirvana Sutra): An important scripture of the Mahayana school. According to tradition, it conveys the sutra spoken by the Buddha immediately before he entered nirvana and thus contains his 'most perfect' teachings. This work describes nirvana—characterized by a state of eternal happiness—for the first time.

114 Dazhidu Lun: Attributed to Nagarjuna (c.150–c.250), this treatise of a hundred chapters concerning the theory and practice of Mahayana Buddhism was rendered into Chinese by the great translator Kumarajiva.

115 Zhongguan Lun (Madhyamaka Sastra; also known as 'A Treatise of The Middle Way'): Written by Nagarjuna, one of the most fundamental texts of the Madhyamaka school of thought which avows the emptiness of all phenomena.

116 chan ding: 'Contemplation and reflection', that is, the practice of Buddhism.

117 zhi hui: 'Knowledge and wisdom', that is, the theory of Buddhism.

118 ding hui: 'Concentration and wisdom', that is, the conjoining of Buddhist theory and practice.

119 wuji bajiao: The Five Periods and the Eight Teachings. Tiantai classified the Buddha's teachings into five periods during which he delivered different teachings, aimed at different audiences with different levels of understanding; and eight teachings, consisting of the Four Doctrines and the Fourfold Methods.

120 shoujie ('made a vow'): An individual who takes part of the precepts. A kind of novice.

121 biqui: A monk who has completed the final induction into the order.

122 biquini: A Buddhist nun.

123 Yulan fenghui: Something like a Buddhist 'All Soul's Day' and falling on the fifteenth day of the seventh lunar month.

124 *Lunyu* (The Analects [Conversations and Sayings]): The ancient work of Confucius, containing his brief aphorisms and teachings.

125 *Yijing* (The Book of Changes, I Ching): An ancient Chinese work. Originally a divination book, it was later attributed with philosophical intent and ranked as one of the canonical works of Confucianism.

126 *Zhuangzi*: An ancient Taoist philosopher as well as the book attributed to him. Much more voluminous than the *Laozi*, it is the most important summary of the philosophy of Taoism.

127 Mengzi (Mencius, *c*.371–289 BCE): An ancient philosopher in the tradition of Confucianism, one of whose most famous teachings is that humans are inherently endowed with a good nature.

128 *Laozi*: The legendary ancient philosopher and the most important representative of Taoism; the philosophical verses attributed to him are known under the titles *Laozi* as well as *Daodejing* ('The Book of the Path and Virtue').

129 *Tripitaka* ('The Three Baskets'): The collection of Buddhist scriptures.

130 Ananda: The cousin and disciple of the Buddha who accompanied him for more than 30 years, and thus was witness to most of his teachings. After the Buddha's death, Ananda took part in the First Council and

played an important role in deciding what should be considered as the teachings of the Buddha.

131 buddha: In Mahayana Buddhism, an individual who has attained perfect enlightenment and gained liberation from the cycle of being. There are many buddhas, one of them being the historical Buddha.

132 Agama Sutras: A collection from the Sanskrit Buddhist canonical scriptures, consisting of four parts.

133 Mahaprajnaparamita Sutra (Da Zhidu Jing; also known as 'The Great Treatise on the Perfection of Wisdom'): A fundamental Mahayana text which expresses the ultimate emptiness of all things.

134 A Yu Wang Si ('The Temple of Prince A Yu'): A temple near Ningbo dedicated to the memory of A Yu or King Ashoka, the Indian ruler who was responsible for the spread Buddhism in the third century BCE.

135 Tiantong Chan Si ('The Monastery of Heaven's Child'): One of China's largest Chan Buddhist monasteries near Ningbo, founded approximately 1,500 years ago.

136 Taipei Mountain: A mountain 30 kilometres away from Ningbo.

137 Jiajing: The period of the Ming dynasty, between 1522 and 1566.

138 jinshi ('presented scholar'): A title awarded upon passing the highest rank of the three civil service examinations, held once every three years.

139 Qianlong: The emperor of the Qing dynastic family (r.1735–99). During his reign, the Chinese Empire, then experiencing enormous prosperity and cultural efflorescence, gained most of its territory.

140 liang: One ounce, the weight of silver used as a means of payment.

141 Yuan dynasty: The period of Mongolian rule in China (1271–1368).

142 Li Taibai (also known as Li Tai-po, 701–62): One of the greatest poets of the Tang era.

143 Kangxi: An emperor of the Qing dynastic family (r.1661–1722), his long reign was characterized by the consolidation of the Manchurian dynasty, economic stabilization and territorial expansion.

144 Li Shimin (598–649): Under the name of Taizong (r.626–49), he was the second emperor of the Tang dynasty.

145 Mingzhou pavilion: The building in the Grove of Steles (Beilin) which contains the collection of 173 inscribed stone tablets in the Tianyi Ge in Ningbo.

146 the room of Qian Jin: A clerk who lived in the early days of the republic and donated several thousand inscribed bricks from the Jin Dynasty to the Tianyi-Ge. Hence the collection's name: One Thousand (Qian) Jin.

147 Jin dynasty (265–420): A period of Chinese history characterized by weak central power, invasions by nomadic groups and internal division.

148 Bai E pavilion: A stone structure from the Ming era. Originally it stood by a grave in the Zuguan Mountains but in 1959 it was moved to the Tianyi Ge in Ningbo.

149 The Temple of the Ancients of the Qing Family: Constructed between 1923 and 1925, it was used for offerings.

150 Zhuangyuan pavilion ('Principal Graduate' pavilion): One of the buildings in Tianyi Ge in Ningbo which houses the picture and calligraphy collections.

151 Yuehu ('Moon Lake'): A picturesque lake in the centre of Ningbo. In times past, the famous poet-official He Zhizhang sought seclusion here.

152 Putuoshan: A small ocean island near Ningbo, it is one of the four most significant Buddhist places of pilgrimage and the centre of the cult of Guanyin. At one time it was home to 300 temples.

153 Jinsha ('Golden Sands'), Baibusha ('Sands of One Hundred Steps'), Qianbusha ('Sands of One Thousand Steps'): Sections of beach on the southern shore of the Putuoshan.

154 Puji Chan Si ('Temple of Universal Salvation'): Founded in 1080, the largest temple in Putuoshan, once home to a thousand monks.

155 Fayu Chan Si ('The Temple of the Rain of Dharma'): A temple on Putuoshan, founded in 1590. In one of its halls is a throne room, built for the Ming rulers and brought here by a Qing emperor.

156 Huiji Chan Si ('The Temple of Wise Help'): The third-largest temple on Putuoshan in whose interior is a renowned stone pagoda. Traditionally, pilgrims perform prostrations every three steps on road leading up to the temple.

157 Yan Liben (600–73): A Tang-era court official and painter. His (now lost) painting of Guanyin formed the basis for a stone carving in 1608 and which can be seen even today.

158 Fudan University: The most renowned university in China.

159 Nanjing Lu: The most famous shopping street in Shanghai.

160 lotus: In Buddhism, a symbol of the Buddha, infinity and beatitude.

161 Sun Yat-sen (1866–1925): Chinese Kuomintang statesman, and president of China from 1919 to 1925.

162 Chiang Kai-shek (1887–1975): President of China from 1928 to 1931 and 1943 to 1949; president of Taiwan from 1950 till his death.

163 xiao lingzi: A high-collared shirt.

164 aozhou: A lined overcoat, frequently worn in north-eastern China.

165 lian: A one-piece woman's garment.

166 ma jia: A kind of waistcoat worn by those of high rank during the Qing era. There were styles for both men and women.

167 Wangfujing: The most famous shopping street in Beijing.

168 Tiananmen ('The Gate of Heavenly Peace'): A fortified gate in the centre of Beijing, as well as the square named after it. In imperial days, it served as the entrance to the palace.

169 qipao: A traditional long, one-piece, high-collared garment for women.

170 Wei: Hello.

171 Shifan University: The Faculty of Education in the Beijing Normal University.

172 Li Yi Lian Chi: Ceremoniousness, awareness of responsibility, honour and sense of shame— the four significant virtues of Confucianism which are important in education.

173 zhuyin zimu: A system of transcription for Chinese used in the time of the republic, and later in Taiwan, which conveys the tones for each syllable.

174 guoyu ('national language'): The designation for Standard Chinese, used in the time of the Kuomintang and based upon a northern Chinese dialect.

175 *Kong Rong Rang Li* ('Kong Rong Lets Go of His Pear'): A story about Kong Rong, a descendent of Confucius in the time of the Han dynasty, according to which the four-year-old Kong took the smallest pear from a basket so that the older relatives could have the bigger ones.

176 'well-known passage and sentence': A reference to the *Lunyu* in the first section of which Confucius says: 'When someone comes to a friend from a faraway land, should he not rejoice?'

177 Guangji Si ('The Temple of Universal Assistance'): A Buddhist temple in Beijing, the foundations of which date back to the thirteenth century. Currently the home of the Chinese Buddhist Association.

178 Zhuozheng Yuan ('The Garden of the Politics of the Common Man'; also known as 'The Humble Administrator's Garden'): The largest garden in Suzhou. Created in 1509, it represents the style of garden common in the Ming era. Its name is derived from a line by Pan Yue: 'The creation of gardens, in order to serve one's daily needs, is the politics of the common man.'

179 Shizi Lin ('Lion Garden'): A garden in Suzhou built in 1350 in the memory of a Buddhist master, embodying the style of gardens common during the Yuan era.

180 Liu Yuan ('The Garden That Remained'): Originally a Ming-era garden, today it is a private garden in the Qing-era style. One of China's four nationally protected parks.

181 Yi Yuan ('The Garden of Joys'): A private garden for government officials in Suzhou, built in the second half of the nineteenth century.

182 Canglang Ting ('The Pavilion of Meandering Waves'): A true masterpiece of the art of gardening dating from the Song era. It is located in Suzhou and was created in the tenth century. Its name is derived from a poem by the great poet Qu Yuan. The present form dates from 1873, and one of its buildings houses 500 portraits of the renowned figures of Suzhou.

183 Wangshi Yuan ('The Garden of the Master of the Nets'): The smallest garden in Suzhou, it was built by a government official in 1140. Considered one of the most beautiful Chinese gardens, part of it has been rebuilt in the Metropolitan Museum of Art in New York.

184 Beisi Ta ('The Pagoda of the North Temple'): A nine-storey, wooden-framed building in Suzhou. Its present form dates from 1673, and it is considered one of the most beautiful pagodas in southern China.

185 ren ('humanness'): One of the most important values of Confucianism.

186 Pan Yue (247–300): A poet known for his melancholic verses on the themes of beauty and talent. The name of Zhuozheng Yuan derives from his poem entitled 'Xianji fu' ('Verse Describing a Careless Life').

187 Wu State: A Chinese kingdom that existed between the eleventh century BCE and 473 BCE in the area of today's Zhejiang.

188 Wang Xianchen: A censor during the Ming era. After he lost favour in the court, he built the Zhuozheng Yuan in Suzhou. Later, his son was to gamble away his entire inheritance—including this garden—in one single evening.

189 the mountain and the waters (shanshui): The two indispensable elements of Chinese gardens, parks and landscapes which always must be present, at least in symbolic form (for example, as rocks and basins). Because of this, shanshui also means 'landscape'.

190 feng shui ('wind–water'): The science of geomancy in China, based upon the belief that the forces that determine individual places influence the fate of those who come into contact with them. For that reason, all kinds of human dwelling, for the living and the dead, must be chosen in accordance with the principles of feng shui.

191 Wen Zhengming (1470–1559): A renowned Ming-era poet and artist.

192 'Eight Eccentrics of Yangzhou' (Yangzhou ba guai): Jin Nong (1687–1764), Huang Shen (1687–1768), Zheng Xie, also known as Zheng Banqiao (1693–1765), Li Shan (1686-1762), Li Fangying (1695–1755), Wang Shisen (1685–1759), Gao Xiang (1688–1753) and Luo Pin (1733–99)—artists active in Yangzhou, reformers of the Chinese art of painting.

193 Wu Zixu, Tong Wengshu [. . .] Fang Chouyan, Su Dongpo [. . .] Xun Cunei, Han Shizhong, Weng Cengming, Wen Tianxiang, Liu Zifu: Renowned personalities whose lives were somehow connected to Suzhou.

ACKNOWLEDGEMENTS

This book could have never come about without the unforgettable and irreplaceable assistance of Dr Surányi György and Dr. Joachim Sartorius; as well as that of Marguerite and Cäsar Menz, Dr Jörg Henle and Ginka Tscholakowa, Dr Barbara and Wolfgang Sietz, Dr Eva and Frederic Haldimann, Doris and Franklin Chow, Christine Hürlimann, Marika Heller, Frank Berberich, the Zuger Kulturstiftung, Dr Hanna Widrig and Dr Heinz A. Hertach; and Yang Lian, Tang Xiaodu, Xie Zhimin, Zeng Laide, Ouyang Jianghe, Xi Chuan, Wang Xiaolin, Yang Qinghua, Tang Hu, Varga Mariann, Chen Xianfa, Xiao Hai, Lai Guoliang, Liu Huali, Fang Peihe, Ji Yinjian, Yao Luren, Jiang Yuqing, Rong Rong, Wu Xianwen, Gong Liefei and Abbot Pinghui.

The author particularly wishes to express his thanks for the truly invaluable suggestions and advice as well as the interpretation of extraordinarily difficult texts, of Professor Barnabás Csongor and Mária Ferenczy, as well as—for their heroic translations of the Chinese texts—Yu Zemin, Évá Kalman and Dorka Kopcsányi, just as he thanks them gratefully for their editorial work; in addition, to Gergely Salát for the preparation of the notes; and, last but not least, Zoltán Hafner, the editor of the original Hungarian edition of this volume, whose support for the creation of this work went far beyond the usual editorial tasks.